The Lost Tribe

A Search through

the Jungles of

Papua New Guinea

THE LOST
TRIBE

A Search through
the Jungles of
Papua New Guinea

Edward Marriott

PICADOR

First published 1996 by Picador

an imprint of Macmillan General Books
25 Eccleston Place, London SW1W 9NF
and Basingstoke

Associated companies throughout the world

ISBN 0 330 33619 3

9 8 7 6 5 4 3 2 1

A CIP catalogue record for this book is available from
the British Library

Typeset by CentraCet Limited, Cambridge
Printed and bound in Great Britain by
Mackays of Chatham plc, Chatham, Kent

For Milla

And this gospel of the kingdom shall
be preached in all corners of the
world for a witness unto all nations;
and then shall the end come.
Matthew 24:14

Be a good boy now. If you are
naughty, look out . . . for the white
man will get you.
Mothers' warning, Papua New Guinea

The lost tribes until the last tribe.
Slogan, New Tribes Mission

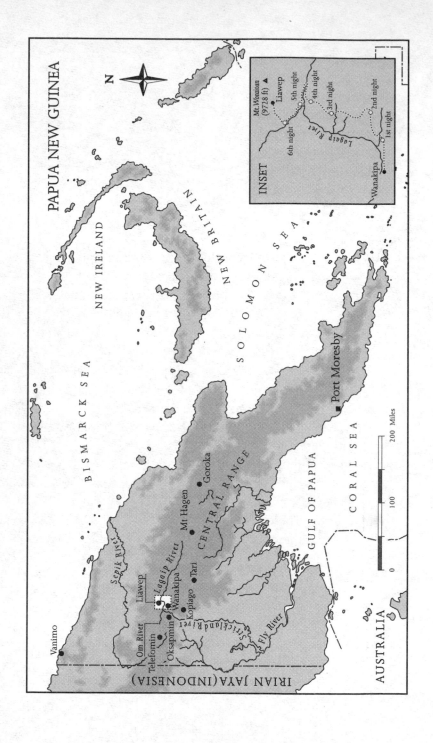

PAPUA NEW GUINEA

N

INSET

Mt. Wonaian
(9778 ft) ▲
Liawep
5th night
4th night
3rd night
2nd night
1st night
6th night
Lagaip River
Wanakipa

NEW IRELAND

BISMARCK SEA

NEW BRITAIN

SOLOMON SEA

Sepik River

Vanimo

Om River
Telefomin
Oksapmin
Liawep
Lagaip River
Wanakipa
Kopiago
Tari
Strickland River
Fly River

Mt Hagen

Goroka

CENTRAL RANGE

IRIAN JAYA (INDONESIA)

GULF OF PAPUA

Port Moresby

CORAL SEA

AUSTRALIA

0   100   200 Miles

Prologue

Two years before this story begins, the Liawep were a lost tribe. There were seventy-nine of them, living in deep jungle in far northwest Papua New Guinea. They worshipped a mountain and dressed in leaves. They hid when planes flew overhead, believing them to be evil sanguma birds. There was no record of the Liawep in census books; as far as the outside world was concerned, they did not exist.

Once they had been the fiercest and most feared warriors in the jungle. But, as they began to learn about the modern world, they grew more timid. Coastal men who had begun to trade with them, who took weeks to carry their parcels of beads and salt from the heat of the coast into the dark jungle, warned them that the penalty for tribal fighting was now jail.

But they also learned of hospitals and it was this information that started all this, everything that follows.

One of the Liawep elders was dying and his grandson, Kohi, decided to find help. The traders had said the nearest hospital was at Oksapmin, a government station six days away. No Liawep had ever walked this far.

It was a hard journey, across mountains that rose sheer out of boiling brown rivers, up through mist, then down again through the cathedral-canopied jungle of giant buttressed garamut trees, the tentacle roots of strangler figs and stilt-rooted pandanus pines. Kohi passed through tribes speaking languages he had never heard before. By Oksapmin, exhausted, he understood nothing.

The government officer, Peter Yasaro, was astonished to see this elf staggering in from the forest, grinning and dumb. He renamed him Jack and, over a period of six months, taught him pidgin English. He gave him a pair of shiny nylon football shorts to replace the leaves he had worn when he arrived. He drove him up and down the airstrip in a jeep and flew him to the coast in a Twin Otter. He showed Jack the church and explained that God lived there.

Bombarded by novelty, Jack forgot all about his grand-father. As he picked up pidgin, he told Yasaro about his people: that they had used stone axes until the men from the coast, two years before, introduced steel; that they cowered from planes; that they hunted wild pigs with bows and arrows.

Yasaro began to get excited. He knew his history. He had read of the glory patrol officers in the 1930s and 1940s showered on returning from their epic, ground-breaking expeditions with news of unknown populations. Jack's story confirmed his belief that the jungle still held lost tribes. Six months later, when Jack returned to Liawep, Yasaro set about organizing a patrol. The Liawep would be his discovery.

Peter Yasaro returned from his three-week expedition in October 1993 and boasted of his discovery in a radio interview. Papua New Guinea's two national newspapers followed the story the next day, describing the Liawep as nomadic Stone Age tribesmen who had been rounded up and would now be 'prevented from living their nomadic life'.

The combination of 'Papua New Guinea' and 'lost tribe' induced the usual slavering in journalists all over the world. The following day the *Sydney Morning Herald* splashed the story – Baptist missionaries, it added imaginatively, were building a church – and at the weekend Britain's *Daily Telegraph* compounded the fiction by publishing a gloriously inaccurate map.

It was hard to believe tribes were still being discovered, even in dense Papua New Guinean jungle. Wasn't every corner of the earth mapped? And, if lost, what would happen to them now they had been found?

Only weeks from the start of Papua New Guinea's wet season, I wrote to Peter Yasaro. I'd read about his heroic patrol. Was he planning another? I begged to be included. He replied a month later. I had to seek permission from his boss, Ignatius Litiki, who was based in the provincial capital, Vanimo. If I did not, I would not be allowed to visit the Liawep.

Litiki never replied. Friends who lived in Port Moresby said I should stay at home. If I came on a tourist visa, they warned, I would surely be deported.

I ignored their advice and flew to Papua New Guinea. My plan was simple: to find Litiki and persuade him to let me go. Surely it could not be that hard.

Chapter 1

Ignatius Litiki, the committee chairman, wore square steel-rimmed spectacles, a Hawaiian print shirt and a permanent sneer. His skin was very black. 'Well, gentlemen,' he sniffed, 'come in.'

There were three of us: myself and two well-briefed anthropologists, armed with box files, who had been photographing ancient carvings down the coast. They were here to explain their findings, and adjusted their ties confidently – they had booked this appointment weeks ago. I, on the other hand, had arrived unannounced and underdressed.

The three of us had spent the last hour together in the town's only hotel, a collection of mould-skirted wooden buildings near the beach. My nerves had made me hungry, and I'd gone there to eat. They were alone in the restaurant when I arrived, at a small table with a red plastic ketchup-tomato and white easywipe tablecloth, reading their menus in silence.

They were booked to see the research committee half an hour before me. Both wore jackets and ties; their faces were shiny with sweat. The white man was an American: 'Dr Robert Scott, pleased to make your acquaintance.' He was fortyish, bald, with a soft sandy moustache, bee-stung pink lips and splayed teeth, over which he drew his top lip when he spoke.

He introduced the Papua New Guinean beside him as 'Wilfred, my colleague'. Wilfred looked at the tomato. He wore a brown wool tie on an orange plaid shirt. When he ordered, he loosened the tie and wiped his brow on a paper napkin.

I told them that I, too, was due to meet the committee. I suggested we go together, hoping that some of their purposeful formality might rub off on me.

Scott looked at me. 'Surely. You an anthropologist too?'

'No, a writer. I want to visit the Liawep. The lost tribe.'

Scott raised an eyebrow. 'The so-called lost tribe. It's all a load of bullshit, cooked up by some patrol officer to get more funds for his district.' He stroked his moustache. 'And even if they are lost, how do you know you'll get there? It's the hardest walking you'll ever find. When I was younger I walked a lot and even when you're in peak fitness it's like you're going to die. The mountains go straight up and straight down. This is the wet season, remember, so the rivers will be flooded and half the tracks washed away. If you twist your ankle or break your leg, no one's going to help you. It's tough, buddy, and excuse me for saying so but you don't look too tough to me.'

We sat in silence. After a while the waiter pushed backwards through the saloon-bar half-doors from the kitchen with three plates balanced down one arm. I picked desultorily at the fish, extracting the bones, peeling away the skin, pushing the flesh around with my fork.

The sight of food stirred Scott to speech again. 'So why exactly are you seeing the research committee?' He funnelled salt over his steak until it was as thick as icing sugar.

'For permission to visit the tribe.'

'Well, good luck, my boy. You'll need it.'

I fancied that, as well as condescension, he might have useful advice to offer, so attempted flattery. 'You're the expert. You tell me how it's done.'

'There's not much you can do. They've likely made up their minds already. Isn't that so, Wilfred?' Wilfred was chewing.

'And if they haven't?'

'Tell them how good your book will be for the province. How it will help tourism. That's all they care about.'

I asked whether I should mention money. I imagined the committee as provincial simpletons whose decisions might be immeasurably eased by a well-placed bribe.

Scott sniffed. 'They'd expect big bucks − Landcruisers or choppers. Tell them money's not the point. You're doing it because you love the country. Lay it on thick. They love all that shit.'

The time of the meeting was fast approaching. I paid my bill and stood up to leave. 'Get our check, would you, Wilfred?' Scott ordered. Wilfred coughed into his hand and loped after the waiter.

I now had a list of points that I hoped would sway the committee. I had no idea which would work, and often they contradicted each other. Halfway down the list I'd written 'Not making any money from it − good thing' and, two lines below that, 'I might sell a lot of copies − good thing for tourism'. I felt duplicitous.

We walked in silence. When we reached the offices, Scott said, 'We're going round the front. It looks better.' We climbed to the first floor. Below us, on a gravel sweep, ten yellow Land-cruisers were parked, noses in line.

The government offices were ugly buildings, in peeling ply-board, in the middle of Vanimo, a nondescript sandblown town with torn mosquito mesh in the bungalow windows and a single rotting fishing boat moored to a skeletal quay. I'd flown across the country from Port Moresby to reach this lonely peninsula on the far northwest coast. Here there were bureaucrats who were deciding the fate of the Liawep, deep in jungle to the south.

We were shown into a large room with a long table. I shuffled in last. It was hot and dusty despite the air condition-ers. Litiki, the chairman, sat at the head, near the green blackboard. His shirt was tight round his belly and when he spoke I smelled stale tobacco smoke. The ten committee members – farmers in too-tight jackets, bureaucrats in shorts and T-shirts, a mechanic in a boilersuit – ranged themselves in descending order of importance. There was a slight scuffle for seats; the mechanic gave way.

Scott and Wilfred sat near Litiki, placing their files purpose-fully in front of them. I sat opposite and opened my notebook on the table. It looked rather small.

'Dr Robert Scott,' Litiki read slowly from a typed sheet, his accent heavy and lisped, 'and Dr Wilfred Pania. We'd like to hear from you first.'

Scott smoothed his pink freckled pate and stood up. Wilfred looked down at his hands. 'Thank you, sir,' Scott murmured, casting a terrifying smile round the room.

He walked to the blackboard and ran his finger along the gutter. He turned round, pinching a piece of chalk between manicured fingers, and spread his arms wide. 'Thank you all for asking us here,' he began, looking at each face in turn. 'And thank you', he added, moistening his lips, 'for making our research possible.'

He turned to the blackboard. 'My name's Dr Robert Scott,' he said, writing it in large capital letters across the top. He worked for the Field Museum of Natural History in Chicago, and for the last six months he and his Papua New Guinean colleague, Dr Wilfred Pania – he paused, scratching the name below his – had lived just down the coast. 'I can report that we have had a very meaningful relationship with the people and we have, I believe, made some important discoveries.' Litiki turned his chair to see the blackboard. The rest took notes.

Scott was proud to refute the popular view that, until white men came, coastal people had been kept in their villages by a state of constant war. On the contrary, he announced excitedly, they had always roamed free. 'We knew that,' muttered the mechanic, inspecting the oil underneath his fingernails. 'It's only white men who thought different.'

Scott ignored him. He babbled on for fifteen minutes, about how the two universities had enjoyed 'a story of collaboration and co-operation'. While he spoke, Wilfred sat back in his chair, picking at his ear and watching the fan spinning on the ceiling.

After fielding a few questions, Scott sat down. Litiki turned to me. The light caught on the edge of his glasses. Everybody stared at me.

I stood up so fast my chair toppled on to the floor behind me. Someone laughed. Blushing furiously, I righted it and sat down again. My words came tumbling out. I was a writer, I said, planning a book on Papua New Guinea. I'd come to ask permission to visit the 'lost tribe', the Liawep. I tried to play down the importance of permission. Naturally, I was also writing about their province, and hoped the book would foster 'a wider knowledge and love of this beautiful place'. I looked round the table. All looked solemnly at me.

My argument began to unravel. 'I've written to Peter Yasaro,' I burbled, 'the patrol officer who discovered the Liawep. He was happy for me to go on the second patrol, but said I had to come here first.' Litiki looked severe.

'I hope my book will increase interest in this province,' I added, repeating myself. 'I'd like to help in some way with the cost of Mr Yasaro's next patrol but I couldn't pay very much.' I looked frantically at Scott, realizing my mistake too late. He raised his eyebrows. I tunnelled on. No one spoke.

Naturally, I added, I wrote as requested, but when no one replied, judged it best to drop by in person. I was planning to move on to Oksapmin soon to meet Peter Yasaro. Would it be possible to gain permission by Monday?

Litiki looked grim. 'I'm afraid, Mr Edward,' he said, looking round the table, 'that your trip has been wasted. No foreigners are allowed to visit the Liawep. It is possible you will be dangerous to them. Or they to you.'

I reminded him there was a missionary there. 'You let him go in.' My voice was rising.

'When you've been here a little longer,' he said, 'you will see you cannot stop missionaries. Even we cannot stop them.'

It seemed hopelessly final. Might they reverse their decision? Was it worth my writing again?

'Yes, you may write again. Try in July.'

Six months away.

Chapter 2

I stalked out of the room on to the balcony, angry and humbled. Behind me, someone pushed the door shut.

I had made a poor start. Conscious of the distrust the government reserved for foreign journalists, I'd come well briefed. In the weeks since my arrival I'd met anthropologists and missionaries and had hoped to impress Litiki and his committee with my diligence and understanding of the country's history. I had failed.

At least, I reflected gloomily, it was a beautiful day. The government offices were the highest buildings in Vanimo and from here, in the middle of the peninsula which swelled bulbous from the jungle, there was sea on all sides. It was early and the sun was high. On the beach, twenty yards away, nut-brown children splashed about in the inner tubes of tractor tyres. I climbed down the steps and headed over.

The sand was fine and very white, sloping into a cobalt sea. Tiny porcelain crabs, gathering themselves, scuttled away sideways. From here, on the coast, it was hard to imagine the interior, the endless jungled mountains and impassable rivers. Only the flight from Port Moresby, across endless green, high over the mountains' spines, had given any impression of the country's vast unknown. But when I looked up, inland, the mountains were all around, rising darkly from the sea.

It had been a struggle, and I was still so far from my goal. Already I had encountered wildly differing views – the Liawep were the blackest cannibals, the most trodden-down innocents, and every shade in between.

I had begun my journey two weeks earlier, in Port Moresby, at the tail-end of the dry season, the city baking hot, roadside flowers bent over with dust. In the anthropology department of the university, the senior lecturer had goaded me, unable to believe I had flown across the world in search of a lost tribe. He saw me as a pitiable amateur; when I used the word 'lost' his lips pursed in disgust. No one was lost any more, he believed; even the remotest tribes would, by now, have heard of the outside world, not that they necessarily welcomed it. 'Make sure you take a lot of people with you. I have a nasty suspicion these guys like a bit of flesh for dinner. I once interviewed an old man who had a bone tool with him. "Oh yes," he said. "We killed him and ate him and this is his leg."' The lecturer had an alarming laugh, keyboards of betel-pitted teeth.

Yet it seemed that the real flesh-eaters were the missionaries, of which Papua New Guinea boasted more per head than anywhere else – one for every 2,000 people. When I moved on from Port Moresby I had met them in the highlands, planning their advance. What I saw convinced me that the race for the Liawep soul had begun in earnest.

Deep within their razor-wired compound, dismissed by the locals as 'Little Americans', one such mission worked day and night at its grand plan: to translate the Bible into each of the country's 800 languages. So far, they had managed only five, but persevered, dogged, buoyed by Jesus' words in Matthew 24:14: 'And this gospel of the kingdom shall be preached in all corners of the world for a witness unto all nations; and then shall the end come.'

I found the Summer Institute of Linguistics a bizarre, displaced suburbia, arranged along Vietnam Street and Philippines Street, isolated above a lonely valley, with tennis courts, junior and high schools. Newspaper cuttings about the discovery of the Liawep were blown up and pinned to noticeboards. They were planning to despatch volunteers within the next two months.

When I had flown onwards, heading north to Vanimo and my appointment with the committee, I had picked out the compound as the plane circled upwards, this brave new world of neat bungalows standing in striped lawns, huddled on the mountainside, barricaded from the jungle. Then it was just the endless green, broken by snaking rivers and half-vanished clouds.

And now I was here by the edge of the sea in the sun, watching children, sand ridged inside my shoes, the tide advancing. I felt stymied, fogged and undecided. In the heat the colours began to blur and I slipped, unthinking, into a delicious fantasy. All would come right if only I could track down Peter Yasaro, the patrol officer who had discovered the Liawep, and to whom I had written before leaving England. He was an adventurer, he would understand. He would overlook my failure to secure permission, perhaps even wave me on with some of his men. But reaching him would not be simple. Oksapmin, his home, was so remote that supply planes dropped in only once a week. In high winds or low cloud, there was be no plane at all.

Yet if I reached him, I had a blind confidence I could sway him. Earlier, a missionary obsessed with the Liawep had given me a copy of the report Yasaro had filed on completing his patrol, and which I now leafed through again. If I was to record the story, the missionary had said, pressing it on me, I must know the facts. First, it was a Lutheran, not a Baptist, who was now living with the Liawep. Ever since the Revd James Chalmers had cruised the south coast at the end of the nineteenth century, gleefully setting to work among a people not yet exposed to commerce, the lure of the innocent and untouched had brought missionaries in their thousands. Now, sanctioned by the freedom of religion granted by Australia in 1921, there were hundreds of churches, with new ones born every day, all of them spurred on by the thought of uncontacted tribesmen who could be swiftly brought to their knees. The Lutheran would be just the start – soon, if history was any guide, Mormons, Assembly of God, Christian Revival Crusade, Summer Institute of Linguistics would all be greedily squabbling over the Liawep. Their techniques were similar to that of the fiery, bearded Chalmers, a man likened by Robert Louis Stevenson to a volcano ('as restless and as subject to eruptions') – rule by fear; reading matter restricted to the Bible; baptism alone averting damnation. The twentieth century may have seen man walk on the moon and split the atom but, in Papua New Guinea, evangelists still lived in the 1880s.

The tide was advancing and spray flecked the pages of the report. I stood and walked up the beach, into the shade of a tree, brushing sand from the soaked paper. The report was eight stapled pages, the type faded and blurred by the end. I read it again, searching for clues to my next move. It was resolutely official, filled with facts. The tribe had settled at Liawep in the late 1970s. Yasaro had their future mapped out: 'They are nomads and, I believe, if forced to move will do so.'

Yet, through the cramped prose and official posturings, Yasaro came alive. His moans at the harshness of the journey only made him seem more human and approachable: 'Six full days to Liawep and another six days to return was very hard and tiring. We climbed very high mountains, crossed big rivers, followed long ridges, were hit by natural disasters such as walking in heavy rain and swimming across flooded rivers.' All I had to do now was find him.

Nearby I heard footsteps, the crunch of boot on gravel. I sat up from the tree and turned. Twenty yards down the beach road a man was striding towards me. He wore khaki trousers and high-laced army boots and trod purposefully, as if he was a soldier off-duty, marching home to base. Only a baseball cap, tipped back on his head, softened him.

I turned to the sea again. It had become oily calm. Nearby, a rusted container ship was mooring, edging closer to the pier. Trucks lined up alongside, sagging on to their springs with the weight of newly axed tree trunks, still weeping sap. Others, empty, tailed away into the jungle, up rutted tracks.

I was about to lean back against the tree when a voice called out. I looked round. The soldier had stepped off the road and was moving across the grass towards me. He had a face like a prune, with oddly mean, inset features.

'Are you the white man?' I stared at him. As far as I knew, I was the only white man in Vanimo.

He walked the last three steps with his hand outstretched.

We shook. He smiled aggressively, his eyes cold. He had followed me from the government offices, he said, lowering his cap to keep the sun out of his eyes.

'The Liawep. You are interested in the Liawep?'

'Yes. And you?'

'I am Peter Yasaro.'

He talked. I was too astonished by the coincidence to offer much. He was down in Vanimo on a routine visit, updating his boss, Litiki. He needed little prompting to tell the story of the patrol: the obstacles his men had overcome to reach the tribe; the clothes he had insisted the Liawep wore. He spoke with a mechanical deliberateness, staring out to sea, ignoring my questions. Between sentences he worked his jaw muscles.

I had misjudged him completely. I had thought that, as a black man in charge of his own people, he would be more confident, gentler and more flexible than the white Australians who had patrolled the jungles before Independence. I had hoped for a man who would soften to my will. He was none of these things. He was proud, and stood apart. When I explained that I wanted to visit the Liawep, he eyed me coolly, with intelligence, saying nothing. I did not push it.

He stood up, finally, and gestured for me to do likewise. He had something to show me, he said, something I would find interesting. I asked what it was, but he had already turned. I scuttled after him.

We walked in a silence he did not seem to find awkward. He led the way along a pitted dirt track, past an overgrown football field with milk cartons and sweet wrappers banked up in one corner of the goal. Eventually we came to a peeling bungalow, raised on stilts, with a hole punched through the door where once the lock had been. He made me wait on the grass while he climbed the steps. Inside I heard a woman's voice, raised and exasperated. I sat on a log in the shade of a banana tree. When he came out he was carrying a black plastic photograph album.

These were his shots of the Liawep, he said, sitting down beside me. I reached out for the album, expecting him to pass it, but he clutched it jealously, laying it squarely on his knees; to see it I had to strain round his shoulder. In many shots he had tilted the camera through forty-five degrees, giving each scene a lilting, drunken feel. He evidently considered himself something of a photographer.

I was drawn by one photograph in particular. Like the other Liawep, this man wore leaves and a bark loincloth. Yasaro was lifting something over his neck. It looked like a medallion – a silver coin on a string. The man looked straight ahead, attempting a smile.

This was Jack, whose story had covered two pages of Yasaro's report. It was his journey to Oksapmin, to find help for his dying grandfather, that had first alerted Yasaro to the lost Liawep. A year on, when the patrol reached Liawep, Yasaro had given Jack a medallion. Yasaro tapped the picture. 'I'm making Jack the luluai. Like a sheriff. He is their leader now.' Breezily, he had created a new order.

I felt uneasy sitting there with Yasaro, and was still struggling with the randomness of this meeting, my sheer good fortune. I wanted him to like me and hoped he would help me on my way, but he kept a professional distance, content to indulge my interest in the Liawep, to open his album and reminisce, but no more. When I suggested that I, too, wanted to make the journey, he fell silent. He rubbed his eyes hard and asked if I had a visa. I changed the subject.

Another photograph, taken by someone else and therefore roughly horizontal, showed Yasaro about to shoot a pig, the barrel at its temple. On the ground three Liawep women crouched away in fright. It could have come from the album of one of Papua New Guinea's first explorers, the gold prospector Mick Leahy, who passed through the highlands sixty years earlier, demonstrating the power of his Mauser by blowing a pig's head away.

'Yes, Masta Mick.' Yasaro smiled dreamily. He'd grown up in the coastal town where Leahy had lived out his dotage. But it was Jack Hides, another white man, who occupied pole position in his pantheon of heroes. Born in Papua, Hides spoke Motu, the Port Moresby language, before English. Aged five, he had run away to a native village for a few days. He loved the wilderness and the people. He looked a little like Errol Flynn – a hero's looks, dark and tall – but lacked the actor's strength. When the two once fought in the hotel at Port Moresby, Hides had to be peeled off the floor. In 1935 he became the first white man to explore the central and southern highlands, a bloody, fraught journey. It was the opening-up of unknown areas, standing on a mountain ridge and seeing a whole new undiscovered people, that drove him. When he travelled, he believed himself to be constantly on the edge of some great discovery.

Yasaro saw Hides as a 'great man'. He'd read his book, *Papuan Wonderland*, and did not believe the excesses, did not credit Hides as the murderer he was later proved to be. He admired him because he was 'Number One'.

'Like you?'

'Me and Liawep, yes.'

One of Yasaro's sons, a bumptious five-year-old, had scampered down the steps and now was nosing up close to us, trying to look at the photographs. Yasaro stretched out his boot towards the boy, who looked up and backed away.

Yet Yasaro, for all his claims, was not the first to have discovered the Liawep. He admitted this warily. When he'd arrived in the village at the end of the sixth day's walking, he found a Lutheran pastor who had already built a church and, with Jack's help, was learning the tribe's language. While Yasaro was disappointed, the resolve of the three missionaries who had accompanied the patrol – a Baptist, a Seventh Day Adventist and one from the Evangelical Church of Papua – was strengthened. They scouted round the village and decided to return. Yasaro backed them; it did not matter that there were only seventy-nine of the Liawep, he said. 'Choice is good.'

His plans for the Liawep were bald: they had to be moved. How else could they benefit from medicine or Christianity or an airstrip? He had seduced them, leading them on by giving them rice and tinned mackerel. If they moved, he told them, they could eat like this. The women began to chivvy their men.

Yasaro was a man of contradictions. He was straight and honest with me and would, I imagined, have made a strong patrol leader, yet his urge to change the Liawep's life betrayed him as officious and illiberal. This gulf made me uneasy. I did not trust it, yet respected his strength and position. Besides, I had not yet asked the vital question.

The back page of the album had just one photo. I almost missed it. It showed Yasaro, Jack and another Papua New Guinean, hands clasped down, arms forming a deep V. The third man looked cankered, crabbed in black thoughts, glowering at the ground. The contrast with the others' levity propelled him off the page. His rage was palpable.

'That's Mr Herod,' Yasaro said, seeing me stop. 'He's the Lutheran pastor. He was not expecting to see us. We gave him clothes.'

He spelled it out. 'King Herod.' He laughed, stopping anxiously when his wife came down the steps of the house towards us. She walked past, eyed me, raised her eyebrows at Yasaro and walked on. Yasaro let her drop out of earshot. To begin with, he explained, Herod had been cool and unhelpful. Only on their second day, when Yasaro said they would be leaving the next, did Herod offer his house for Yasaro's men to sleep in.

So this was the modern missionary – the more efficient, so it was argued, because indigenous. While those who ran the churches were still white – mostly Australians, Americans and Germans – their footsoldiers were now black. The formula worked with brutal efficiency. The locals knew the country, spoke the local languages. They were quicker than the whites in building relationships with the people and as ruthless in destroying their traditional beliefs.

It was different in the 1930s, when the first missionaries followed Leahy and Hides's tracks into unmapped jungle in their quest for untapped congregations. Then there were the likes of Father William Ross, a Catholic priest who arrived in New Guinea from Illinois and measured a modest five foot two in his wedge-heeled walking boots. He wore a black frock coat and squared-off beard and always travelled prepared. Once, he noticed that a visiting priest, whenever he passed spear-waving tribesmen, held out his crucifix as protection. Ross mocked him. From the folds of his habit he pulled a .38 revolver. 'In these parts,' he said, 'we show 'em this.'

I looked at the photograph again. Herod was slight, almost boyish, yet the fury in his face made him seem dangerous and volatile. It was hard to see him as one who preached love and forgiveness.

I wondered whether Herod, like Ross, carried a revolver as protection. It seemed quite possible his will alone would suffice. I gazed at the photograph, looking for clues. I sat staring for such a long time that Yasaro, fidgeting, snapped the album shut. I stood up too, knowing this was my moment.

'Your next patrol,' I said. 'Can I come too? I want to meet the Liawep.'

He held the album to his chest, looking over my head to the house. He seemed bored now, distracted. 'Did you ask for permission?'

'Yes.'

'And what happened? They said no, isn't that right?' He tilted his head sideways, as if speaking to a child. All the warmth with which he'd talked earlier had gone. He seemed now an engine of bureaucracy, no more. He put forward his hand for me to shake. 'You cannot go if you do not have permission. There is no way. Sorry.' He allowed himself a thin smile.

There had been many frontiersmen before Yasaro; the jungle was busy with their shadows. The first patrol officers and explorers had been white men, mostly Australians. But it was Mick Leahy whom I admired in particular – the bog-Irish opportunist who, hearing of the quick fortunes to be made in gold, took ship from Brisbane in 1929. Prospecting took him into the highlands, where no white man had ever been. Until then, the colonial powers had thought the interior was one vast jungled mountain range, incapable of supporting life. Leahy, the cold-faced gold digger, was the first to discover that the mountains enclosed huge valleys, and that the people who lived there – warriors and gardeners who used stone tools and dressed in leaves – knew nothing of the outside world.

Until the 1930s, the highlanders of New Guinea thought they were the only living people. They had never travelled and knew nothing of the outside world. They had never seen the coast, its vanishing vastness under a sinking sky. They believed in an afterlife of a sort. When a person died, his skin turned white and he passed over to the place of the dead. They thought the strangers with white skin, Leahy and his deputy, Jim O'Malley, were their own dead returning to them.

Leahy's discoveries confirmed what the rest of the world had long believed — that New Guinea really was the last frontier, holding undreamed-of mysteries. With no apparent riches, it had been spared the excessive colonial zeal inflicted on much of Africa. It had swamps, mountains and jungle; art that seemed crude and charmless. By the end of the nineteenth century, only the bravest missionaries and most optimistic traders had ventured forth. It was uphill work. In one Dutch mission, after twenty-five years, there had been more missionaries killed by fever and marauding natives than natives converted.

By the turn of the century, three flags had been planted on the island. Holland claimed the western half; the east was divided into German New Guinea and Australian Papua. After the Treaty of Versailles the last two became one — Papua New Guinea, governed by Australia under mandate from Britain.

For thirty years the colonists kept to the coast, trading rubber and copra. Then they found gold. Leahy, followed by patrol officers like Jack Hides, opened up the country. The world watched astonished as valley upon valley of Stone Age warriors emerged blinking into the harsh light of the twentieth century.

It had been an exhausting day. Bruised by rejection, I went to find a drink.

The bar I found seemed designed for my mood: defeated and miserable. I fell in with two Papua New Guineans — an accountant and an engineer, from faraway provinces — who, dishevelled and raucous, seemed quite at home in the barbaric surroundings. The floor was tiled, the walls rough cement, the tables plastic-topped. The barman stood behind bars. There was a gap, like in a Wild West bank, through which money and alcohol were exchanged.

The accountant was wearing shorts and lifted his shirt frequently to stroke a belly thick with dark hairs. Six empty beer cans were lined along the bar. 'I'm going to drink ten this evening,' he dribbled.

It was lucky I was not Australian, he said. 'I don't like Australians.' He peered into his beer can.

I explained about the Liawep, that I'd just been refused permission.

'Oh yes, the lost tribe,' he said. 'I bet some people in England think we're all cannibals, eh? ... Well, tell them to get stuffed!' He exploded with laughter.

He leaned heavily against the bar, reached round my shoulder and pulled my face close to his. His advice was simple enough. 'Don't listen to them. They talk a load of bullshit. Go in from the other side. You know where they live, this lost tribe? Get three or four men who know the way and walk in with them.'

'But this is a lost tribe,' I said. 'No one will know where they live.' This was partly true – the only people who would know the way would be Yasaro's men but, without official permission, I could not approach them. The only other possibility was Herod, who had set off from Wanakipa, another remote station, but he had walked alone.

I poured out my fears. They tumbled in their hurry to be heard. What about Litiki's comment that I might bring harm to the Liawep? What did that mean?

For the first time that evening the accountant looked almost sober. He stood his can on the bar, breathing heavily. He wiped his mouth with the back of his hand and prodded my chest. 'Who cares? They're ignorant. Who cares if you kill the lot?' Spittle landed in my eye.

Later, on his last can, he offered his final, bluntest words of advice. 'You watch out for the cooking pot. You watch out if they start to get hungry. And you make sure you walk the right way. There was a white man a couple of years ago who went walking in the jungle. He walked the wrong way. He disappeared. He was probably eaten. Prepare to suffer, my friend.'

Chapter 3

I stayed a week in Vanimo, watching Malaysian container ships slip out of the harbour at dusk, sunk to the gunwales with fresh timber. The weather was closing in and each morning I walked to the airstrip, only to be turned away. The rains were finally coming and cloud squatted obstinately over the jungle. There was nothing to do but wait.

When, finally, the clouds broke and the first plane was wheeled on to the wet grass, I was there with my bags. After all this waiting I had made a plan – to fly south again, to the highland town of Goroka, and meet the lost tribe expert, anthropologist Carol Jenkins. In 1984, she had accompanied the first government patrol to the Hagahai, whose discovery had spawned the usual acres of newsprint. I thought the Hagahai might prove a model for the Liawep, ten years on, and wanted Jenkins to engineer me a visit. If they now had an airstrip, hospital, school and four competing missions, the Liawep could expect the same. But I also hoped that Jenkins might offer advice that would decide my next move.

Jenkins went everywhere, afraid of nothing. I'd read her name in almost every article about Papua New Guinean tribes. Her reputation preceded her: she had a fearsome temper, reserved, I'd been warned, for the ignorant amateur. I approached warily.

Goroka sat on the floor of a high valley, surrounded by coffee plantations and, far away, mountains. Sixty years earlier, Mick Leahy had walked through here, panning for gold, the first white man the people had seen. In return for cowrie shells, warriors had heaved away huge boulders and cleared Leahy an airstrip. Goroka had also witnessed the highlands' first mission-ary push – Lutherans from Germany, who believed themselves to be the natives' saviours. As one wrote, 'The call to New Guinea came to me: Come over to New Guinea and help us that the white settlers may not drive us, too, from the land of our fathers as he has done with the American Indian and the Australian native.'

Now there were 25,000 people, three banks and an Elizabeth Street. The supermarkets sold canned soup, shiny steel kettles, leopard-print pillow cases and brown suede winklepickers.

It was a bright day. Rain overnight had given way to surprising purples and scarlets and a washed, deep blue sky. Downhill from the airstrip were streets in grids: large, modern houses with satellite dishes and razor-wire fencing, with snoozing security guards on billiard-green lawns. I had asked for Jenkins at the medical institute where she worked, but was told she had taken the morning off. When I found her house, the gates were open and a Papua New Guinean woman, sunny dress billowing, was pegging up washing. On the veranda, ten feet up, a large white woman was slouched in a deck chair.

'Hi! Do I know you?' It sounded like a threat. I approached the steps, saying I'd come to ask her about the Hagahai. And the Liawep. Her grin evaporated.

'A lost-tribe man, hey? You'd better stay for lunch.' She stood up, her thumb wedged in a Jilly Cooper paperback. She kicked open the mosquito-mesh door.

The sitting room had polished wooden floorboards and a round table with red gingham tablecloth. On the walls, propped against chairs, were shields, spears, sheaves of arrows. In the kitchen, baked beans were bubbling over.

Jenkins ran for the saucepan. She gripped it by the handle stump and banged it down hard on the sideboard, cursing viciously. 'Water!' she yelled, waving her hand in the air, flinging it under the hosing tap.

Awkwardly I looked away, out of the window. Ranks of bungalows stretched away, identical, each in its acre of garden. Two grey and pink parrots gossiped high in a gum tree. The far mountains were obscured by cloud. It had begun to drizzle every afternoon, the first sign of the rains to come.

Jenkins wrapped her hand in a wet dishcloth and spooned baked beans on to my plate. They smelled of burnt biscuits.

We talked for a while about everything but the Liawep. When I approached the subject, she bristled. She looked down, muttering, and ran her finger round the plate. She licked it and dried it on the tablecloth.

I tried to be succinct. When I mentioned the words 'lost tribe', her eyes smoked. 'Don't use that phrase in this house, young man. Who are they lost to? Their neighbours know about them, wouldn't you have said? And ask them if they're lost. What do you think they'd say? "Oh yes, that's us." I hardly think so.' She glared.

I should have known better. When Yasaro had announced his discovery, she'd been widely quoted denouncing the term 'lost', condemning its brazen certainty. No one, she said, was lost any more.

Her son Ryan, five years old but already thick-necked, like an infant quarterback, was up on the kitchen sideboard, looking through the hatch. He wanted apple juice. Jenkins swatted him away. She lifted a soft pack of cigarettes from her bag and tapped one out, filter first. She jabbed the match aggressively.

Anthropologists, she said, knew more about Papua New Guinea than any other country on earth. The first explorers, blessed with as much imagination as courage, even noticed a Semitic strain. Frank Hurley, an Australian who charted the Fly River in 1920, believed the trait 'may have been introduced by legendary mariners of Jewish or Moorish origin who were stranded in New Guinea when the Spanish galleon sank on the coral reef of Torres Straits'. Others, whose fancy ran wilder, guessed the high-boned, proud people they saw were indeed descended from one of Israel's ten lost tribes who disappeared from the Promised Land from 721BC, after the Assyrian conquest.

The Hagahai, Jenkins believed, were 'more mislaid than lost'. They did not figure on censuses because, every few years, they would move. Their remoteness meant they had distinctive habits – they laid out their dead on scaffolds, storing the bones, once the flesh had wasted, in a cave or in a high tree; widows kept their husbands' jawbones as mementoes. Yet Jenkins believed they would have had some idea of the outside world before their much-trumpeted discovery.

She conscientiously avoided using the word 'lost', yet she seemed relaxed enough with 'discovered'. This seemed a straightforward contradiction – to be found, a thing must once have been lost, or at least never known of. But she was too deep into her story for interruptions. She leaned forward towards me, smoking so hard I worried she might swallow the cigarette. Her saucer was jammed with butts.

It was not she who discovered the Hagahai, 'though you might believe so from what you read'. In 1983 a Baptist missionary saw smoke coming from a valley he believed to be uninhabited, and walked in to find 600 people, dressed in leaves, living in scattered houses. He built a church and began to learn their language.

The Hagahai were dying – of malaria, elephantiasis, diphtheria, hookworm, mumps, flu, hepatitis. Jenkins was unsure how they'd become this debilitated, but these were infections introduced by the men with whom they'd recently begun to trade, against which the Hagahai had no protection. Two elders persuaded the missionary to find help. In the spring of 1984 the government asked Jenkins on a preliminary vaccination patrol.

Other missionaries followed as soon as the story reached the press. In a pattern frighteningly common throughout Papua New Guinean history, they poured in, oblivious to the Hagahai's wishes. First Nazarenes, then the New Tribes Mission, Catholics, Anglicans and an eager couple from the Summer Institute of Linguistics, who brought soap and steel axes. Here the Hagahai drew a line. 'They told them to piss off,' Jenkins chuckled. 'They just weren't impressed.'

Jenkins had distrusted the missionaries from the start, yet had not stood in their way. She saw the Hagahai turning to Christianity, with its promises of redemption, and reasoned that they were drawn largely by the missions' wealth – their radios, clothes, money and access to a privileged world. It was inevitable and she knew there was nothing she could do to stop it.

She had become calmer, even good-humoured. Discussing

the Hagahai, it seemed, brought her a kind of peace. When I asked her how she saw herself, she grinned with evident enjoyment: 'I'm their protector.'

Now, ten years since that first patrol, an airstrip was being built, with cash provided by the Rotary Club of New South Wales. In this the Hagahai invested great hope. It would mean that medicine could be flown in quickly and that those who had died elsewhere, after unsuccessful medical treatment, could be buried on Hagahai land. Bulldozers had cut through tree roots and levered away boulders. Two Peace Corps workers held school twice a week and watched over the solar-powered fridge which kept the vaccines cold.

As Jenkins spoke, it occurred to me that she was a missionary too, bringing the gospel of vaccine and airstrip. Wouldn't it, I suggested, have been more natural to leave them be, rather than keep flying in, checking their progress and renewing contact? Her face clouded. I attempted a friendly smile. She brought her fist down on the table so hard that dust rose from the tablecloth.

'What the hell do you mean by that? Humans always alter nature. Should I have watched children die when I had medicine? Should I have just counted the bodies? I've not changed their way of life – they're still hunting the way they used to; they're not forced to come to school. I let them speak for themselves, which is more than you can say for the missions.'

Now was not the time to suggest it, but we'd been talking for an hour and Jenkins was beginning to shift in her chair. She'd already put her cigarettes in her bag and, more than once, had looked at her watch. So I said, as casually as I could manage, that I wanted to visit the Hagahai. Like it had just occurred to me.

She sniffed, then removed her glasses, cleaning one of the

lenses on her voluminous T-shirt. 'Do you have a chopper?' She poked her glasses back on her nose. 'Because if you don't, it's four days in and five days out. And who's going to show you the way? When the Peace Corps couple go in, we send a message down the bush telegraph to the Hagahai to come and get them. The Hagahai hate doing the walk but they do it because they like them. What's in it for them to collect you? You can't pay them because they don't want money. They certainly don't need you.'

I picked at my fingernail. She relented a little. She knew the strength of her arguments, and watched them work on me. Suddenly my desire to see the Hagahai seemed precipitate and unnecessary, a poor second-best. It all fell into focus. I would not have the energy for two jungle expeditions – I must concentrate on reaching the Liawep, and would have to travel without permission.

Jenkins showed me into her study. Cardboard boxes overflowed with paper, making a crazy gangway to the desk. A yellowish pot plant stood on the windowsill, the earth cracked and sandy. There was a radio beside it, littered with curled leaves, on which, each morning, she spoke to the Peace Corps workers who lived with the Hagahai.

She pointed to a box wedged into the armchair. It was stuffed with newspaper cuttings, some yellowed, some newish and still grey. All had 'lost tribe' or 'Stone Age' somewhere near the top. There was a story from the *National Geographic* – 'Diseases thrust Stone Age nomads close to extinction' – and angry correspondence between Jenkins and other anthropologists, who accused her of inaccurately labelling the Hagahai as 'lost', a charge Jenkins furiously denied. There were begging letters from journalists, typified by one from the *Telegraph Magazine* in London, asking Jenkins to verify whether the discovery of the Liawep 'was indeed a first contact'. He was interested in the anthropologist's view; the *Telegraph* had 'a well-educated readership'. She had not replied.

She filled a black leather briefcase with the miscellany of her trade – pens, a calculator, a reporter's notebook, the laptop. She was driving back to her office and had offered to give me copies of two films that had been made about her and the Hagahai. I asked for a photograph of her with the tribe – for my records – but she was reluctant. She didn't want the Hagahai associated with the Liawep, who might turn out to be 'another Tasaday'; this was a 1970s Filipino lost tribe, which turned out to be a hoax, a ruse cooked up by the Minister of Indian Affairs to attract tourism.

Jenkins' Landcruiser was twenty years old and the whole body shook when she started the engine. The rattle from the door panels was like galvanized dustbins kicked over. I sank deep into my seat, into a hole where once springs had been. Coins spilled from my pocket on to the floor behind. She charged up and down through the gearbox.

'Great engine,' she screamed, as the car collapsed into a pothole. 'Pity the body's falling apart.'

Under duress, Jenkins agreed to ask her husband, Travis, to develop me a print of her with the Hagahai. This gave me an hour, time enough to buy some medicines for the expedition. I chose Goroka's most modern-looking chemist and skulked along the pine-scented aisles, caressing tubes of Colgate and Palmolive, potent reminders of the civilized life I was about to leave. The closer I was getting to the jungle, the more uneasy I felt. Every night I counted away another day. When it rained I would lie awake listening to its steady hush and dreading the constant wet, rain hammering through leaves, the creeping dread of things unknown.

The chemist was a New Zealander in her thirties, who flirted just enough for me to buy everything she suggested – two extra packs of Band Aids, two courses of antibiotics 'just in case'. She rattled out dosage labels on an electronic typewriter: three drugs for malaria, then Betadine for cuts and purifying water. She stopped typing when she got to snakes. If I was bitten by a Papuan Black, she said solemnly, I had half an hour to get to hospital. Whatever happened, I should bind the bite and not move. Her advice on wild pigs was more practical: should one charge – run.

An hour later I returned to the institute and found the darkroom. I knocked. There was no sound, then a soft shuffle, a sliding bolt and a broad man with an Indian embroidered waistcoat stood in the doorway, blinking in the light. Travis.

In the fixer tray Carol Jenkins was swimming into focus. He fished her out with plastic tongs and clipped the print up to dry. The water shrank to beads. The shot showed her with a notebook on her knees, surrounded by adoring Hagahai tribesmen.

Travis was the institute's technological lynchpin. He had bloodshot frog's eyes from years spent developing prints under red light. He wore a Rolling Stones T-shirt, with Jagger and Richards' bruised faces, circa 'Black and Blue', mid-1970s.

'Mick gave it to me.'

'Mick Jagger?'

'I knew him.' He smiled. 'I engineered for him.'

'The Rolling Stones?'

I should have known: it was too unlikely a tale to be false. He'd played saxophone with Charlie Rich, too. Then 'did time for Elvis. But that was all a long time ago.'

Travis had not abandoned his music, even though he and Jenkins had lived in Papua New Guinea for twelve years. He'd just spent a week in Port Moresby with Sanguma, Papua New Guinea's biggest rock band. He had written the lyrics to their environmental pop song, based on a traditional Hagahai melody, about saving reefs from tourism and rainforests from loggers. It should, he said, have 'international appeal'.

His enthusiasm was a welcome antidote to Jenkins' cynicism. She had tried to dampen my spirit, and I had labelled her an anthropological pedant. She'd seen so many lost tribes, she'd lost interest. It had taken Travis, the bug-eyed bluesman, to understand my excitement.

When I told him of my plans, he gripped my shoulder excitedly. 'Go,' he exhorted. 'They'll never catch you.' He knew a doctor further west, he added, who would find me a guide. 'She knows everyone.' He guillotined off a corner of Agfa print paper and scribbled her name.

And so I left Goroka and travelled west in successive collapsing minibuses, through high passes, along the country's spine, towards the Liawep. I was in turmoil, unnerved by the wilderness, yet drawn to it. In this, I reflected, I was typical, just another European adventurer. To each generation, the country had represented one last unknown in an increasingly shrunken and proscribed world. It was a land of cannibals, headhunters and Stone Age warriors with penis gourds as long as spears. Because, for so long, so little was mapped or understood, New Guinea had been what anyone had wanted it to be.

It was on this dubious premise that the first 'explorers', such as Captain J.A. Lawson, made their names. His *Wanderings in the Interior of New Guinea*, published in 1895, told of seven adventurous months, during which he passed a lake seventy miles long and thirty miles wide, an active volcano 4,000 feet higher than Mount Etna, and a mountain higher than Everest, which he renamed Mount Hercules. This last he attempted to climb but, bleeding from the nose and ears, was forced to turn back within a hundred feet of the summit.

A precedent had been established. A spate of adventurers followed, some unsuccessful, some frivolous. It was here that Errol Flynn, later a Hollywood superstar, in between stints as government sanitation officer, plantation manager and gold prospector, indulged his quest for the perfect breast. As he later wrote, 'Often would I realize that I was staring at a honey-coloured girl of exceeding femininity . . . [with] a perfect figure and the most glorious pair of breasts you ever saw – the classic ski-jump type.' Or, of a later conquest, 'She wore a grass skirt and that was all. Her little up-pointing breasts were so symmetrical and perfect . . . I knew I had to buy her.'

For others, the country was not such a grail of plenty. Otto von Ehlers, a German travel writer who sailed for New Guinea in 1895, set his heart on an epic trek, the north–south crossing, never before attempted. To the dismay of W. Piering, the policeman assigned to accompany him, he ignored all warnings of doom. Piering's moans – 'What use are fame and money to me when I'm dead?' – proved prophetic. Within the first week, von Ehlers had lost his magnetic compass. On the thirty-sixth day, when his food ran out, he allowed his dog to be killed, although was too distressed to partake. Eight weeks in, weakened by festering tropical sores, infected leech bites, hunger and dysentery, von Ehlers ordered his two most recalcitrant carriers to make rafts. This they did, then promptly shot von Ehlers and the policeman and disappeared downriver into the jungle.

Missionaries, despite their official status, often suffered the same fate. The gruesome end suffered by the formidable Revd James Chalmers, Robert Louis Stevenson's 'volcano', was typical. It was Easter Monday, 1901, and Chalmers, scouting the south coast for natives to 'lead from the dense darkness through the glimmering light on to the full light of glorious freedom in Christ and His cross', stepped breezily ashore on Goaribari Island. He was clubbed unconscious, cut into small pieces, boiled with sago and eaten the same day.

Chapter 4

If one squints hard at New Guinea, until the edges blur and the towns and rivers disappear, a bird emerges, flying north-west towards the equator, its wings down, tail feathered over Australia's Cape York peninsula. On the coastal fringes there are malarial swamps of mangrove, sago and floating grasses. From these the spinal cordillera rises steeply, a silent place with blazing jungle flowers, razorbacks and gorges and bright green slashes where the forest has been burned.

I was travelling northwest, up the great bird's spine, along the euphemistically named Highlands Highway, a single-track road tarmacked only sporadically, towards Tari and my appointment with Travis's friend who had promised to find me a guide.

I hitched the first leg from Goroka with Trevor, a tall, silent Englishman with pale crease marks down his jeans, who ran a charity and drove a shiny new sludgebrown jeep. He drove very slowly, avoiding potholes and navigating the middle of the road where the tarmac had crumbled. He used to be a bushwalker but was married now and his days of camping out in the jungle were over.

'The first thing', he instructed me, with both hands tight on the wheel, 'is to get yourself a good guide, a school-leaver, someone who's young and keen for adventure. And make sure he's a Christian. They're more reliable. If they don't look after you, they rot in hell. That's quite useful.'

Worried about getting lost? He recommended a radio. For rations he suggested rice, tinned tuna, biscuits, peanuts and two-minute noodles. 'The only food you'll get in the jungle is sweet potato and taro, possibly a few green bananas. You'll want something you normally eat, something to remind you of home.'

He dropped me in Kundiawa, a small market town on a crest where minibuses circled for custom. As we drove into town, a train of people swelled towards us. They looked like actors in a tragedy, their faces whitened with chalk. They were in mourning, returning home after a funeral, the chalk their show of grief.

I listened to the local six o'clock news that night, in a guest house halfway to Tari. The announcer read the items in slow, careful syllables. The top item dealt with MPs' public appearance. 'Members of Parliament have been asked to look more presentable. They have been driving around in flashy cars, rather than the official cars. This is felt to be bad for their image.'

The eccentricity of this bulletin came as no surprise. For the past three weeks both national newspapers had been covering a far more bewildering story – the disappearance of the prime minister, Paias Wingti. Wingti, an enormous, bearded, hedonistic warrior statesman, had now been missing for twenty-six days. He had been reported, variously, in most of the world's vice capitals – Amsterdam, New York, Bangkok. The editorials became increasingly desperate. 'Can someone tell us where he is?' the Post-Courier pleaded. Opposition MPs began calling for his scalp. Five weeks later, he reappeared. He had been in Amsterdam with his nephew. 'Even the PM', an aide argued feebly, 'is entitled to a holiday.'

It was cool that night and I slept under blankets. Beyond the razor wire of the compound, two dogs were fighting. I awoke in the middle of the night to the rattle of rain on the roof. In my dream I had been propped up against a tree in the jungle, stricken with malaria, my bones frozen. All my carriers had left, promising to come back with help, but I knew they would not return. I was soaked with fever and the rain was stamping tiny craters into the mud around me, coursing down the bark on to my shoulders. In the distance was the yodelling of warriors on the hunt.

The drive west to Tari, a hundred miles at most, took the whole day. For long stretches the bus would stop at roadside markets and the driver would climb down, have a pee, buy a passionfruit, smoke a cigarette, have another pee, suck out his passionfruit, then ask around for a passenger to fill the last empty seat. He liked his music loud, and had screwed speakers above every seat. The radio DJ was a ham-fisted Papua New Guinean who sounded Texan and played non-stop Status Quo and Neil Diamond. Twice there was a terrible grinding as the needle slipped off the record edge.

I sat on the back seat, which was a mistake, as I was kicked higher than anyone else when we hit potholes. The tarmac ended soon after Mount Hagen and we tackled the red dirt, greasy with rain, in first gear. The landscape was six-foot grasses, higher than the bus, rising away to mountains. From the valley we climbed over a high range, up hairpin bends where the road, for safety, had been briefly metalled, with the valley far down to our right and the river winding away below, white and washed like a snakeskin discarded shiny in the grass.

In the seats in front of me sat a mother and her teenage daughter, who slid back the window and leaned right out, like a dog going on a picnic. She turned her head backwards, towards me, and a yellowy mulch splattered my window. She wiped her mouth on her sleeve, drew back inside, and lay her head on her mother's breast.

It was Friday, payday, and in Mendi, the southern highlands capital, halfway to Tari, men were strutting and spending, mostly on beer. The streets were thick with people. Men in traditional dress mixed with mineworkers. They wore bird-of-paradise head-dresses and tail feathers of stout rubbery tanket leaves. Some carried umbrellas, which blossomed open when rain fell.

The driver turned off the engine and climbed out of the cab. Two Americans, Bruce and Kelly, Peace Corps volunteers with shiny silver wedding rings, followed me outside. He looked a grizzled fifty; she was in her late twenties. Bruce was nervous. He'd never been on a bus on payday before and feared a hold-up. Kelly soothed him. They'd lived in Papua New Guinea two years and it hadn't happened yet.

Three hours later we were driving along a pitted and rocky straight when the road turned sharply and began to slip downhill. There was a shout from the front of the bus. The driver braked sharply and a string bag of sweet potatoes slid down the aisle. Everyone stood up. A line of small boulders had been laid across the road. The man beside me had his hand in his pocket, fishing for his change, the inevitable payment for a hold-up. I sat where I was. My cash was in my sock.

The driver and two others were shouting. There were three men outside the bus. They looked very young, sixteen at most. One carried a rifle with a rusted, uneven barrel. His face was mummied in a scarf and his eyelids chalked white. The other two stood in front of the bus. I could see their faces through the windscreen.

Inside the bus, a short man with army-issue trousers tucked into workboots jumped down into the doorwell and pulled the door open. He jumped out and five others followed him, screaming with anger and fright. The bandits fled into the long grass, gone as quickly as they'd appeared. Now people started shouting. Others laughed and waddled up the aisle like chickens, mimicking the bandits' escape. Two men piled the boulders by the side of the road. When we drove off I noticed a bundle of scarf, dropped in the middle of the road by the boy with the gun. It was dark blue, with white polka dots, surprisingly elegant, a gentleman's handkerchief.

On the next rise a group had gathered. They'd been watching. The driver climbed down and began asking which village the boys were from. Bruce leaned back over his seat, towards me.

'Did you see the tear-gas canister? The rascal with the rifle had tear gas. Didn't you see him fumbling? He couldn't get it to work, lucky for us. He'd have thrown it through the window.'

Violence was everyday and unremarkable. Even those who came to Papua New Guinea simply to observe, who were neither government officers nor prospectors, seldom escaped unharmed. The first journalist to visit New Guinea, the *Melbourne Age*'s George E. Morrison, arrived in 1883, aged only twenty-one. He was bullish, confident; as a schoolboy he had walked the five hundred miles from Geelong to Adelaide. He disembarked at Port Moresby, gathered a patrol and set off into the interior. Within days he was attacked and his supplies were stolen. A spear struck him in the eye – 'I pulled out the spear, which still hung from the corner of my eye, and directly I did so blood rushed from my nose' – yet he managed to fire off retaliatory shots and return, barely alive, to Port Moresby. He never went back.

Bruce's warnings were more prosaic. He believed in conspiracy. The police, he understood, were the only people with tear gas. Living in Papua New Guinea, he said, had confused his 'life plan'. Before, he'd expected to live out his life on his cattle ranch in New Mexico, bought with the proceeds from his painting. Then he and Kelly joined the Peace Corps and, for the past year, had taught basic agriculture. Disillusion had come quickly. The Peace Corps was 'Kennedy's empty dream', and his battle to persuade uninterested highlanders of the benefits of year-round carrots and running water had wearied him.

He did not envy me. 'It'll be tough,' he said gently. 'We've only been on one walk since we've been here. It was in our first week, as a point of fact. Three hours, up and down hills. And when we got to the top there was a heap of people playing volleyball.'

Bruce was keen to introduce me to the man sitting next to him: he would be able to help me. The man swung his legs into the aisle and threw a meaty hand at me – he was the one who'd chased off the rascals. He grinned, displaying a mouthful of dried beef, beached on his tongue. He'd bought a carton of bottled beer in Mendi and earlier, in preparation for Tari, where night-long rum-fuelled tribal fights had led to a complete alcohol ban, I'd seen him wrap it in newspaper and hide it in a string bag.

'So,' he said. 'Your American friend tells me you need a guide. I'm in the army.' He thumped his chest for emphasis. His name was Mark. He prodded my thigh and I moved dutifully to the window seat. He squeezed in beside me.

For the past five years he had been fighting the rebels on the island of Bougainville, and was now on six months' leave. This meant he'd been on Bougainville almost since the start of the conflict, in November 1988, when rebels stole a hundred kilograms of explosives from the mine and vanished into the mountains. It was the biggest crisis since Independence in 1975, and festered on, with still no sign of compromise. The rebels claimed Bougainville Copper Limited was poisoning their rivers and killing off the jungle. The flying fox had disappeared; crops were retarded; mangoes, pawpaws and bananas leprous; wild pigs and possums had fled; fish turned ulcerous. Girls now menstruated long before puberty; the old decayed faster. The rebels had become the Bougainville Revolutionary Army, killing for an independent Bougainville. The mine had been closed since the start of the war.

He boasted of his time in the army. It was proof of his strength; this was his pitch. He was bold and over-friendly. 'I can walk a very long way carrying very heavy weights. We will be friends.' He forced his rugby thighs wide apart, wedging me against the window. 'We are friends. I will come with you and you will not pay me.'

It had been a very long journey. It was now five in the afternoon and I'd been travelling since shortly after dawn. The road was pitted and the bus springs had lost their sponge. I wanted to tell Mark I was not interested, but lacked the courage or energy. He took my silence as encouragement. 'Tomorrow morning I come and get you and we leave, very early. We drive to Kopiago, then next morning, very early, walk to Wanakipa.'

I asked him how long he thought it would take to reach the

Liawep. His bravado, though extraordinary, gave me hope that the journey would not be as hard as I feared. He thought for a while, scratching his head like a cartoon character stimulating thought. He struck his thigh with his fist and announced, so loudly the couple in front turned round, 'Two days. That's all. Two. Maybe even one day.'

'It took the government patrol six days.'

'Yes, but I used to be a fat man. Then I joined the army. Now I am strong. Not fat.'

He was the least appropriate guide I could have imagined. I needed someone with tact and discretion, whom I could trust to help bridge the cultural divide. Mark was brutish, his view of life bald and macho.

We had arrived in Tari. I would soon be rid of him. We skirted the top end of the runway. 'That's the airstrip,' Mark pointed out helpfully, 'and that', he indicated a Twin Otter lifting off towards us, baring its muddy underbelly, 'is an aeroplane.'

The bus stopped. 'So, we meet tomorrow.' He gripped my knee. The driver had pulled over, off the main street. We were next to a huge trade store, Huli Traders, named after the local Huli tribe, with their ready smiles and photogenic hair-dos sprinkled with yellow everlasting daisies. On the other side of the street were an ironmonger, a kiosk selling fried chicken and a bank, scored off by high razor-wire fencing.

'Yes, yes.' He hefted his contraband on to his shoulder. 'We will go together. It will be good. See you tomorrow.' He jumped the three steps to the ground, waved gaily and was gone.

Chapter 5

Tari at twilight: a small town huddled round a grass airstrip, the sun slipping behind broken storm clouds. Sixty years before, with the eastern half of the highlands already opened up by Mick Leahy, the patrol officer Jack Hides had been the first white man to walk through this fertile valley. Standing atop the ridge over which we'd bundled two hours earlier, he had seen gardens laid out with a mathematical exactness, smoke drifting from a thousand homesteads, warriors armed with stone axes. For a while, to begin with, both sides stood and stared.

Hides believed in his destiny. He knew this was the last major section of jungle left unexplored and that a successful patrol would make him a hero. He loaded his carriers with beads, mirrors, steel axes and bushknives, which he planned to barter for food. Thirty men carried a ton of rice. He had no radio, and planned no airdrops. It was 1 January 1935. He would be gone six months.

Sixty years on, I was in Tari to begin my own patrol. I left my rucksack in the guest house and, in darkness, went to find Wendy. She was Travis's friend, the doctor who had promised to find me a guide.

Betty, the guest-house manager, was hard to raise. Only after persistent knocking did she emerge from her office. Bloodshot eyes rolled in her head; when she rocked towards me I smelled rum on her breath. And this in a dry town.

I followed her up a gravel road, her torch beam barely powerful enough to reach the ground. Every few steps she turned and breathed on me. 'Klostu. It's not far.' We walked for fifteen minutes and the distance never altered.

Eventually we came to three large bungalows, in their own lawns, cars parked underneath. White sodium lights flooded the grass like electric moonlight. Betty fell through a hedge and stumbled on to a broad lawn.

'Wendy, Wendy, visitor for you,' she called up, too loud. She tottered and clutched the handrail. At the top of the steps a woman with candyfloss hair was sitting on an upturned bucket drinking beer from a can. She stood up when she heard her name, handing her beer to a man beached in a deckchair. She bent over and whispered in his ear, then came down the stairs, steadying herself against the wall.

Travis had told her to expect me. 'So you're the one looking for the lost tribe,' she said. 'Prepare to be disappointed. We don't have them no more.' She had a deep Glasgow accent, furred by smoking. 'Well, hey, what do you know? Come up and have a beer anyway ... Betty?' Betty shook her head and said she didn't drink. As I climbed the steps, Betty sashayed boozily back across the grass, mumbling to herself.

Wendy introduced me to Dave. He had claw hands, polio perhaps, and held his cigarette between the upper joints of his third and fourth fingers. We shook hands but his didn't open and I gripped his fist, curled up tight.

I took a chair from under Dave's feet. The sun had set an hour ago and the mountains were black against a blue-black sky. The night was filled with the plastic chatter of cicadas, the croak of warty reptiles, geckos clicking.

Wendy was incredulous at my plans, so I explained as best I could why I was there and what I wanted. 'Well, it sounds as though you're realistic at least,' she sniffed.

Dave was more cynical. 'There's probably a Reuters bureau already set up there and the villagers are screen-printing lost-tribe T-shirts.' He was a bearded anthropologist from Towns-ville. Despite claw hands he rode into the hills every morning on a motorbike, his rucksack packed with notebooks, tapes, his recording machine and sandwiches.

We went inside to eat. Wendy had an eight-year-old daughter, Cindy, a miniature version of her, with leggings and blonde hair and a father who had left Wendy for a research student. Cindy kissed her mother goodnight and went to bed, soft-shuffling down the hallway in her slippers. While Wendy transfused blood and stitched arrow wounds in the hospital, Cindy attended Tari's International School, a 'U' of iron-roofed buildings on the road into town, each day returning with her satchel heavy with her Bible and her head full of missionary prejudice. She had been taught to be ashamed of her body and now, when she had a shower at home, would lock the door on the inside so that no one, not even her mother, could see her. When she bounced on the trampoline she wore running shorts under her skirt lest her classmates became inflamed. One day she came home and said that hell was filled with divorcees. 'I'm divorced,' Wendy said, 'and the head knows that damn well.' She drove to school the next day and spoke to the principal.

Now Wendy was apologizing about my guide. The one she had chosen, a recent high-school graduate, had just landed a job in a carpenter's yard, and would start in two weeks' time. In his place she had found Dunstan, a twenty-seven-year-old Catholic lay preacher. She hadn't met him, but knew his friends and trusted their word. Dave, however, was pessimistic. He'd never met Dunstan, but generalized gloomily about the short-comings of the local workforce. 'They're all far too eager to please. I've got two working for me and still I don't have any clue what they're on about.'

Wendy corrected him. 'That doesn't matter as long as you know what you want. Because you're paying, he'll just say what he thinks you want to hear. He won't express any opinions.'

This sounded hugely awkward. Dunstan's knowledge of the country would far outweigh mine; I would need to know his mind. When I argued this, Wendy suggested code. If I had decided to do something Dunstan judged foolish, I should ask whether it was 'dangerous'. This would give him the chance to back down without seeming to contradict me.

The next morning I sat in Betty's guest house eating a miserable breakfast – Australian peanut butter on white, cottony toast. I was alone, with my maps laid on the table, the outsize aviation chart drooping over the edge. On top was my sketch map, scribbled on file paper, a 'Y' showing the confluence of the Om and Lagaip rivers into the Strickland. This was the plan, to set off for the Liawep from Wanakipa, Herod's home, due north from here. I had marked an 'X' northeast of Wanakipa, adrift in the middle of the page, where I believed the Liawep to be. Like this, ballpoint on file paper, it looked so straightforward.

It was seven in the morning. I'd woken an hour earlier, the radio hiss of rain leaking into my sleep and feverish dreams. Outside the kitchen window there were voices. 'Where's the whitey man?' I walked down the corridor, past the locked rooms, to the door leading into the garden. A man stood at the bottom of the steps.

He was wearing baseball boots with no socks and the bottom of his slacks rolled halfway up his calves. He had a purple baseball cap with 'Papua New Guinea' across the front and a black bomber jacket, lightened with dust.

He said very little as I explained where I wanted to go. When I asked him what he thought he said, 'No problem. We can do it.' He gazed vacantly at the map, tracing his finger up the Lagaip River.

This was Dunstan. We were the same age. He was a Catholic and a carpenter who had been expelled from seminary school when he was caught making shelves for another student. He should have been in church, the principal had said.

He had a wife and two sons. She was happy he was going, he stated, unconvincingly. I wanted to discuss money, to get it out in the open as soon as possible, but Dunstan was coy and eager to say the right thing. In the end I offered to pay him two hundred kina – about a hundred and five pounds – a month. It was not an arbitrary figure. The night before, Dave had explained that a hundred and fifty kina was considered a fair price. But Dunstan did not answer.

He was far away. 'It's my wife. She told me to ask for two hundred and fifty. That's what I can earn from two weeks as a carpenter. But two hundred is good. We will be friends and we will go together. Money, it's no problem.'

It was an uncertain start. I felt we should spend the day together, talk a little, get to know each other, but this would have to wait. Today was Sunday and he was taking his family to see his wife's parents in their village up the mountainside. He loped off down the corridor into the sunshine. He had a limp and was shorter and slighter than I'd expected. His hands were soft and he had long fingernails, like a guitarist.

Later that day, I met an Australian doctor who had married a Huli woman. He lived some way out of Tari and was very thin, worn to a thread by subsistence farming. He wore a BBC World Service T-shirt and spilled instant coffee powder absently on the floor. We ended up speaking, somehow, about the American in the news whose wife had docked his penis with a carving knife. He had a professional interest. He'd treated Huli men who'd had their testicles half pulled off. 'Degloving,' he called it. One woman had peeled her husband's scrotum clean away. Nowhere, it seemed, was a man safe. A neighbour, gardening, with no woman in sight, had been attacked by a pig with a strange look in its eyes. The pig nosed up under his loincloth, bit hard and swallowed. The man lay on the floor, screaming, leaking blood. The doctor had stemmed the flow with a banana leaf.

When I walked back from his house to Tari it started to rain. Smoke leaked from the grass roofs of houses. Everyone was inside, blocking out the day. Chickens walked about unbothered, water shedding off their backs in waxy beads. Back in Tari, through the rain, the sound padded and muffled, came the dull drill of a plane circling to land. People appeared from nowhere, suddenly forgetting the wet. The plane came down through the grey, its twin propellers fanning a whirl of mist behind. Seven people climbed down the steel ladder and stood in a huddle under the wing.

The next day Dunstan and I went shopping with Wendy. We drove to the trade store, a huge supermarket without fruit, vegetables or helpful aisle signs. Wendy grabbed a wire trolley and strode off. I had made a list, but Wendy overrode everything. 'You'll need an axe,' she said, hurling tins into the trolley, 'and a bushknife. Dunstan – you choose those.' We left Dunstan running his finger along blades, waving a bushknife around in the air. Within twenty minutes the trolley was full. Blankets for Dunstan, two pots, two bright white umbrellas, enamel mugs and plates, rice, tuna, spam, noodles, soap, chocolate, PK chewing gum and peanuts. The trolley became sluggish. It needed two of us to steer it round corners. 'How about sultanas?' Wendy was strong on luxuries. Peanuts and chocolate were her idea. 'You'll need snacks. Instant mashed potato? Sounds horrible, I know, but it'll make a change from rice.' These were rations for three, possibly four – to include a couple of carriers.

Word had got out that we were going 'on patrol'. I shied from the comparison. A patrol was twenty or thirty strong, meticulously planned. On a real patrol everything was packed and checked by the patrol officer – Primus stove, canvas tent, bedding, pressure lamps and spare mantles, mapping equipment, ink for completing censuses and health surveys, rice, canned food, medicines, a prismatic compass, Australian flag, revolvers and rifles.

The food, heaped on the floor in the guest house, looked overwhelming. Dunstan had said goodbye to his family and would be spending the night on the floor of a friend's house near the airstrip. We had the rest of the day together. I bought him a Fanta and we walked down the road. We made slow progress. Everyone was a friend whom Dunstan greeted loudly, introducing me as the white man he was guiding into the jungle. When they asked how far we'd be walking, he'd say, impassively, 'Longwe tru, a long way' and there'd be admiring gasps.

'Now,' Dunstan said, when we were alone again. 'We will go to the market and meet my wife. She is selling eggs.'

Vegetables, bananas, eggs and sweets were laid out along low tables. There were few customers and the women behind the stalls were gathered, chatting. The ground was dry and dusty, despite overnight rain, and scattered with sweetcorn husks, dried banana skins and eggshell. A guard wearing a blue jacket with gold chevrons stood at the gate. He touched his cap and stood aside to let us through. In his belt was a long rubber cosh. We walked in, past the carrot bunches. Dunstan stopped at the eggs, dozens laid out pink and perfect in a dimpled cardboard tray.

'This is my wife,' he whispered as I joined him. An inch taller than Dunstan, she was heavily pregnant and rocked her weight back on her hips. She was beautiful, with a high, clear forehead. Her hair was swept back and kept in place by a faded red cotton scarf. There was dirt under her fingernails and her hands were scored with cuts and grazes.

'She hasn't sold many eggs yet,' Dunstan offered. He introduced me to her, formally, waiting for us to shake hands. 'We're going into the jungle.'

She nodded at me, and said she must get on, even though the market was almost empty and the only other two customers were fingering lettuces, nosing their insides, and showing no signs of wanting eggs. Dunstan picked up an egg and ran it down the palm of his hand, rocking it back with his fingers. He replaced it carefully. 'Well, we go now. I'm going to show Edward our village and tomorrow we go. See you. Good luck.' We walked away.

'Didn't you want to say goodbye to her alone?'

'No, don't worry.'

'But how about the baby? When's it due?'

'Don't worry about the baby. I have two babies born already. She will be OK. When we come back we will go and see the new baby. It will be a good surprise.'

He walked along, grinding a file against the bushknife blade. He stopped and asked me to run my finger along it. 'Sharp enough for cutting jungle,' he said, scything sideways, the curve of steel flashing against the dull earth.

Dunstan was obsessed by the minutiae of our trip. Why was my torch bulb so bright? He wanted to have it. He wanted my penknife, too. He snapped the blades open and shut. He pronounced Liawep as Liawef, blunting the 'p'. He was for progress, modern clothes, medicines and Christianity. But then he was a Catholic – the oldest, 'universal' church – and hoped that Herod, the Liawep priest, would be conducting a 'proper' communion, with bread and wine. It was important, he believed, 'even in the jungle'.

We walked to his village. It was only three miles but, under midday sun, seemed a lot further. It was straight down a chalk dirt road. Minibuses clattered past, forcing us into the ditch. A mile on, past the yellow Catholic church with its white steeple and red roof, we came to the Seventh Day Adventist compound.

Beside the low church was a building like a school hall. Children were leaning in through the door. Inside was a tiny office. A young man sat facing a line of small boys, a large pile of notebooks on his desk.

He was marking their grammar and preparing them for the Second Coming: 'Everywhere there are signs.' I asked if there was a Seventh Day Adventist mission in Wanakipa, but he didn't know. 'Wanakipa is a small place. Perhaps there is no one there at all.'

A mile on from the church two tree-trunks were laid side by side over a creek. 'This is where I live,' Dunstan said. 'Up there, up the mountain.'

'Can we go? I'd like to see.'

'No. It is too far and too hot. We stay here. Phew,' he added, mopping his brow theatrically. 'Very hot. We stay here.' Instead, he waved his hand in the air and led the way to a grassy bank under a low, wide tree. Four men were playing cards.

The winner of the game said he was a geologist. He had worked at the Porgera gold mine, but now they'd taken on white geologists and he'd lost his job. He'd worked in Hewa country, where we were to go. 'There's gold in those hills,' he said. 'They may be already mining.'

The Hewa people, he said, lived in tree houses. 'They build a platform first, then weave banana leaves through the branches to make a roof. They live very high up, perhaps a hundred feet. You cannot see them until they fire arrows down.'

He looked sincere, watching my face, but his friends were smiling as if I'd been gulled. Papua New Guinea was a land of stories and storytellers. Men returning from travels in other provinces told stories that stretched over seven nights, adding characters until the experiences became extraordinary. And so the Hewa lived in tree houses and carried up their pigs in string bags, tied over their shoulders. We talked about lost tribes and he told me about people he'd seen with three eyes; people who were three feet high and ate only leaves; and others, who he thought were called Liawep, but couldn't be sure, who ate only human flesh. When we left him he had begun to tell his friends about how, when he worked as a geologist, he'd often go for a week without food. 'Once,' he said, stroking his stomach, 'they left us down the mine for a month. One of the other geologists died and we ate him up. He was old and his meat was chewy.'

An hour later we came full circle; we were walking back to the airstrip. A teenager with a file under his arm ran towards us, grinning madly. 'Ha!' he laughed. 'Dunstan's looking after you. Brave man!' This was the student who was to have been my guide. He was accompanied by the soldier, Mark, who walked a few steps behind, cupping his hands to light a cigarette.

'So,' Mark said, looking at Dunstan, 'you found your guide.'

'Yes, this is Dunstan. Dunstan, Mark.'

Neither moved. Mark scratched his moustache. He looked at my fresh-white trainers. 'It's wet in the jungle. Yu baim bigpela su – some walking boots. You'll turn an ankle in those.'

Wendy had asked me to supper – 'the last supper', she joked. It was a welcome invitation, a chance to escape my spiralling worries about the journey and the jungle. I arrived early and sat on her balcony. It was a clear evening with no clouds, and the air cooled as the sun dropped towards the mountains.

Wendy had organized quite a party. While she prepared supper, guests arrived, climbing the stairs to the balcony, stepping gingerly over the pitbull terrier.

During supper, talk turned to missionaries. Wendy, who despised the Evangelical Church of Papua for its influence on her daughter, held up the Catholics as models of liberalism. 'I know this sounds unlikely,' she said, looking round the table, 'but the Catholics are OK. When we were living in Hagen, Cindy went to a Catholic school. They had kids of all ages, right up to sixteen and seventeen. They taught sex education, even though the Catholic church disapproves of contraception. As teachers they realized that AIDS had to be stopped, so they took lessons in how to use condoms.'

Dave held that missionaries had enjoyed such success in Papua New Guinea because they tapped into ancestral fears. The Huli, he said, believed the earth was supported by a delicate subterranean bamboo structure. Before the white man came they believed in their power to start the world afresh. They would start fires on the peaks of mountains and these would become a chain of beacons. When the chain was complete, a blanket of ash would fall on the earth, refreshing, renewing. The missionaries, with their stress on repentance in the face of final judgement, had destroyed the Huli belief in rebirth. Where the Huli once took care of things and were cautious in their dealings with people in the knowledge that they would be reborn, now they had no hope for the future. If the missionaries were right and judgement was imminent, they would grab all they could today. Their fragile relationship with the earth had been further disrupted by mining and industry, which tore into the earth, destroying the structures on which the earth was supported.

He talked, too, about Huli men, who, fearing pollution, steer well clear of their women. In Huli creation myths, female genitals possess formidable power. In one, Adam sees Eve squat over a pile of sweet potatoes. They turn black and smoke with the heat. Adam is violently attracted by this: he grabs her and they copulate, wildly.

It was the strangest, most unsettling evening. For two weeks now I'd worried over the immensity of the jungle, the unknown Liawep, the rain and the mud, and this cosy suburban evening only made clearer what I was leaving behind. Wendy had meant well, asking expatriates in the hope that I'd feel at home, but it gave me a sense of being on the edge, caught between two worlds.

They all had advice to offer. John, a corpulent Dutchman with a tobacco-singed moustache, said that in twenty-two years of living in Papua New Guinea he'd not once walked in the jungle. 'I'm jealous of you,' he said, 'but I'm too old now.'

Wendy waved him away. 'You could get lost,' she said, 'you could starve, and you could break your leg. More likely you'll get eaten. Just leave your wife's telephone number and I'll ring her with the news.'

Bryan, a sweating Yorkshireman who managed the trade store, could not believe the Liawep were lost. It was not possible, he said, not this long after first contact. I was no longer sure what I thought, or to which camp I belonged – the educated cynicism of the university anthropology lecturer, Carol Jenkins and Wendy, or the eager testimony of Peter Yasaro, who'd actually seen the Liawep, and trumpeted their backwardness. Besides, 'lost' was a malleable and imprecise adjective, a definition for which I had long since given up struggling; my real interest lay not in semantics but in the Liawep's moment of change. Yet whenever I tried to explain my motives, the words 'lost tribe' were thrown back at me, accusingly.

It turned out Wendy had been through a similar process of redefinition. All whites, she believed, arrived in the country with unrealistic expectations of their own novelty value. In her first week in Tari a young woman had come into the hospital with a sick baby. She'd said Wendy reminded her of someone. Wendy had read the history books. She knew how the first white men were thought to be ancestors returned from the land of the dead. She longed to quiz the woman again further. Weeks later they ran into each other. 'I remember now who it was you remind me of,' the woman grinned. 'Dolly Parton.'

It rained steadily through the night. In the gloom I could see the crouched outlines of the two rucksacks, filled with provisions. Dunstan's had split under the strain, a hernia of noodle packets which he'd tried to contain by lashing with green twine. They lay on the floor like sleeping pigs. When dawn slunk in it seemed as if I'd been awake the whole night.

I carried both rucksacks across the littered grass to the

airstrip. It was six thirty, half an hour early. The Twin Otter was there, being loaded. A crowd had gathered by the other plane, a nose-engined Cessna. There was the dull groan of wailing, the undercurrent of grief. On one of the trolleys, normally used for ferrying rice sacks from the belly of the plane, was a coffin. It was hennaed orange from cheap wood dye and the corners were uneven. Striped across the lid was an X of scarlet ribbon. Two young men in blue boilersuits stood beside it, their hands by their sides. Other men wore traditional Huli dress, face paint and wigs blooming with daisies.

Vern, the pilot, was busy weighing the coffin. He nodded at me, noting down the weight as if it was a suitcase. Two women in flowery dresses came up close and looked at the read-out. Four men lifted the coffin and walked it to the plane. The women wailed louder. The men angled the coffin through the plane door. The back four seats had been removed and still the coffin seemed too wide to fit. They fixed on the right angle, finally, strapped it in with seatbelts, pulled tight and clunked it into place.

The wailing quietened and moved rhythmically, rising and falling. Vern watched the other pilot climb into the cockpit, into the left of the front two seats. He began his checklist. Backflaps. Rudder. Radio. He flipped switches, pushed and pulled levers.

An old man approached me. 'He was my grandson,' he whispered. 'He was run over by a car. Just down the road, last week. He was only twelve, just in the high school. We're flying him back to his parents.' He had dewy brown eyes, the whites melted filmy into the pupils, making the edges milky like coffee. He looked blind, all-seeing. 'The driver was drunk,' he added, looking back to the plane. They were demanding compensation. No death went unaccounted. They would settle for twenty thousand kina, enough money for a new car.

As the plane turned to move off, blowing rain from the grass, the women raised braceleted arms to the sky. Above the hands, someone was waving a black rolled umbrella, wooden handle uppermost.

Dunstan was an hour late, which made me jumpy, but I needn't have worried as it was mid-morning before Vern was ready. He'd asked us there for seven because that was when he started to prepare himself, not when he planned to leave. I saw Dunstan some way off across the airstrip coming towards me, with the hand axe and the bushknife. The bushknife had a cheap, bright shine on it; the axe was marbled blue. He'd taken them both away to sharpen and now wanted me to test them, to press my thumb to the blade.

Vern was making radio contact with Oksapmin, his destination after Wanakipa. He was talking to Peter Yasaro, whose careful syllables I could hear swimming in the static. They needed rice, he was saying. I became edgy. I'd told Vern we were going against the wishes of the government and he'd taken it in and had seemed eager to help. I was still not sure that Wanakipa would be the right place, but Vern had said he would land there, keep the engine running while I checked.

He was nervous about the weather. The rain had stopped before dawn and the clouds were broken but there was a high wind and the threat of more rain to come. He would be flying by sight; low cloud obscured the ground and hid the mountains. He was sitting on the trolley with the map on his knees.

He hadn't landed at Wanakipa in three years, he admitted. He knew there was a strip – the Lutherans had levelled one – but had no idea whether it was navigable; planes landed there so rarely. I noticed his clear blue eyes, sandy hair, blotch-freckled hands folded calmly in his lap. I couldn't believe he was so relaxed. I pointed to the map.

'Where is Wanakipa?'

'About here.' He marked an 'X' among tight-bunched contours. There was nothing there – no reassuring dark squares for houses, only dark green denoting jungle, and the long sweep of a river. He stood up to go.

'It's true – I wish the map was more precise.' He removed his sunglasses and rubbed his eyes. 'I know Wanakipa, I'll recognize it. I just wish it was on the map. It should be simple, God willing. I'll recognize the mountains when we get there.' But this would depend on high cloud and a moderate wind, he added. If the cloud was too low, we could fly into a cliff face.

He crossed himself and replaced his glasses, folded the map and slipped it into a plastic sleeve. 'OK, then, let's go. You guys ready?' He brushed his hands down his trousers as if crumbs had fallen into his lap. We climbed into the plane and the door cranked shut behind us.

I sat on the right and could see Vern clearly through the cockpit doorway. There was a clipboard on his knee. Along the rim of the instrument panel was a long black ruler with white stickers, his safety-check reminder. At each check he'd flip down a black marker to cover the sticker. He started both engines and lowered his head. Both engines were revving; the nose was oscillating, rearing up and falling like a reined-in horse. Vern was praying. A Bible was open on his knees and I could see his lips moving, but the engine was too loud to hear the words. Involuntarily I too lowered my head. The unknown was making me superstitious. I prayed a medley of prayers from my childhood and found them soothing.

Vern taxied to the head of the runway. The ground was rough and the plane bounced along the gravel, jolting over grass hummocks. He threw a wide circle, closing off one propeller, braking and pumping the other. We accelerated down the runway and the old plane juddered and jarred. I looked out of the window and the ground fell away, the wheels span slower and then stopped. Vern flew straight, then banked, following the valley. Homesteads gave way to jungle.

Dunstan, who'd never flown before, looked less scared than astonished. He pressed his face to the glass. 'Look,' he called out above the screaming engines, 'there are gardens down there!' On the lower slopes of the mountain, sunk into the jungle, was a bright green cut-out, a speck of straw for a house. 'You see,' he mouthed, 'there will be people where we are going. Everywhere there are peoples.'

We lifted out of Tari on the morning updraughts. The plane grazed an escarpment and we were pummelled sideways, then levelled out. Down below was the heart of the wilderness, jungles that inspired even the most level-headed to claim the extraordinary: Captain John Moresby, after whom the capital was named, once recorded the tracks of a 'rhinoceros'; Dutch missionaries claimed to have seen leopards; in 1875, the Revd Samuel McFarlane returned from a short voyage up a south-coast river with tales of buffalo and a giant bird that puffed like a steam engine.

Vern was waving and pointing out of the window. Two thousand feet down were houses freckled round a lake of liquid mercury. Over another ledge, the ground dropped clean away below us and we were suddenly ten thousand feet up. Vern banked and I saw far below an oily rust-orange river, the Lagaip, its surface shredded by sun and wind.

I noticed Wanakipa as we circled, a solitary iron roof slick and silver in the sun, bright green gardens and mountains thick with dark jungle. The strip looked like a cricket square as we approached – implausibly small. The mountains made a straight landing impossible and Vern cut three tight loops. The plane banked so tight that I could see the ground out of the windows the other side. The strip ran uphill and we nosedived towards it, barely out of the spiral, the engines suddenly quiet. Then we hit the ground with the sound of collapsing dustbins, the wheels rabbiting away along the grass uphill. A crowd swelled around the plane, mostly children. Vern pulled up facing downhill, the length of the runway before him. He took off his headphones and put his clipboard on the seat beside him. 'Go on, then.' I struggled with my seatbelt. 'I'm waiting,' he said.

Chapter 6

An old man stood apart, wearing outlandish sunglasses – blue-rimmed, rising to sharp points, speckled with white plastic daisies. His legs were an old man's legs, with thinning thighs and bulbous knee joints.

'Good morning. We've come to visit a tribe called the Liawep. Have you heard of them?' The rotors turned over slowly in the warm morning air. It had been cool in Tari but Wanakipa was in a bowl, low down by the river. Vern opened his door and was watching me, headphones still on.

'Liawef?' Like Dunstan, the old man smudged his 'p's. 'Yes, I have heard of them.'

'We want to walk there. Can you direct us?'

'Yes, no problem. It's not far.'

Minutes were ticking by. Vern shifted his headphones from

one ear. He spun his finger in the air, a winding-up gesture, forcing a decision. Dunstan was standing behind me. I nodded at Vern and shoved out my thumbs, upturned. I climbed up into the plane and threw down our bags. Dunstan caught the first and crumpled under the second, loaded with rice and tins. I heaved the door back up and it shut with a greased metal clunk. Vern nodded and pulled his door closed. We stepped back from the plane and he edged up the power until loose blades of grass and pebbles leaped backwards. The plane bumped down the hill towards the river and lumbered into the air.

The old man with the sunglasses stood beside me. 'Come,' he said, when the plane had gone from sight, 'we go inside.' I looked around for our rucksacks. They were gone. Dunstan pointed up the slope to the end of the airstrip where children were funnelling through a small gate. Two boys were heaving our rucksacks away.

They dropped them by a long, low building with a veranda that stretched its length. The old man led the way inside. There was a fridge and a deeply scored wooden table with a bench and chairs. Dunstan and I took the bench.

The old man left the room and I could hear his voice, a low hum, out on the veranda. I dug out my map and notebook and pen. I wanted to listen to his advice, pick up a couple of carriers and leave. It was already eleven o'clock. I felt stupidly urgent.

He returned with three men. Children spilled in after him. He tried to shoo them away, but they stayed and stared.

'Liawep,' I said, as they each took a chair. The last, a tiny man, stood. There were no more chairs. He looked at the map I'd spread out on the table.

They talked very fast in pidgin, too fast for me. I soon dropped out of the conversation and kept nudging Dunstan for their meaning. 'Wait,' he'd say. These were not simple instructions. 'They're saying the Liawep are one day's walk from here,' Dunstan said, finally.

That couldn't be right; they were supposed to be many miles from the nearest outpost. I explained the Liawep had been contacted by a patrol officer a few months before. They were the lost tribe, I added, feeling the disapproval of a thousand anthropologists. And, I said, I thought a missionary from Wanakipa – called Herod – was living with them.

Dunstan took my pad and spelled out Liawep in large letters. They looked at the word, but it triggered nothing. A large blue butterfly was trapped in the room. It had come in with the children and was up against the window, stuck there, its wings closed together, showing electric green undercarriage.

Slowly it came clear. There were two Liaweps; 'Liawep', in fact, meant 'small tribe' in Hewa, the local language. The first Liawep was a day's walk southeast. The other was six days' walk northeast, perhaps eight days: they did not know exactly. It was to the latter that Herod was ministering.

'He is my priest,' said the old man. 'It is my church here. I sent him. I am Father Frank. I heard about them from my friend in Oksapmin. I heard a young boy from Liawep had walked there. He was dressed in leaves.'

Father Frank was a pioneer. He had arrived in Wanakipa in 1974, accompanied by two white pastors. Now only he remained, with a local wife and large family.

Other missionaries in the region had found it harder to establish themselves. Earlier, in Telefomin, a tiny outpost a week's walk west, I had met an ageing Baptist who gave daily thanks for his deliverance, forty years before, from murdering natives. It was 1953, and the patrol officers who ran the station were young, ignorant and hot-headed, helping themselves to local food and women. Revenge was swift: early one morning they were ambushed in the jungle, beheaded and their bodies hacked to pieces. The missionary had only escaped by persuading the headman's son to wait in his house until the supply plane arrived.

Father Frank was looking me up and down, eyeing my white T-shirt and spotless white shorts. Six days was a long walk. Did I realize how far?

'We could float down on a tube,' Dunstan suggested, bright-eyed. 'Float down the river.'

'A tube?' It seemed rather a good idea, easier than weeks tramping through jungle. The fantasy was sweet. Just for a moment I forgot the size of the river, its pace and fury.

'Yes,' Dunstan babbled cheerfully, 'a tube from a tyre. A big black tube. We would get there in a day.'

'But we don't have a tube,' I remembered, coming to my senses, 'and they don't have any vehicles here we could pinch one off.'

'Ah, yes,' he said, suddenly sober. 'That's right. I forget.'

'And it's upriver,' Father Frank added. 'If you got in a tube you'd end up in the sea. You want to go the other way. You've got to walk. It's a long way but there's no other way.' Worse, the only person who knew the way was Herod, and he was already there. 'And it's the rainy season, remember. You must not swim the rivers or you will drown. There are bridges made from jungle ropes but in the rainy season sometimes the bridges drown.' He drew a line round his throat with his finger, indicating execution. A pale line remained on his skin where he'd pressed.

The butterfly had unstuck itself from the window and was wheeling around crazily. 'Can no one lead us?' I pleaded. 'Someone must at least be able to set us on our way.'

Father Frank leaned across the table and gave a soft smile –

sympathy, possibly pity. 'You can have two or three men from here. Then you will find other men to take you further.' He shifted in his chair and the metal legs scratched on the wooden floor. 'Miniza,' he said – it sounded like 'minister' – 'Miniza will come with you.' He turned and pointed at a man who'd just come in and was leaning against the fridge.

I had envisaged muscled youths but this man looked ancient, tired and cynical. He had a tangled, pubic beard and a pickled face. His legs were thin and marked with glassy scars from unstitched cuts and bites turned septic. He was wearing a shirt that had once been white but was now greeny-brown, and the top button was done up, an odd affectation in the tropics. The back of the shirt was rucked up, and rested on a bunch of leaves from the rubbery tanket bush – the uniform cover-up throughout the jungle. His loincloth was a folded T-shirt.

He did not look happy to be proposed. He pushed himself to a standing position and the fridge rocked on the uneven floor. 'Will you go and fetch Dison?' Father Frank said, sensing rebellion. He turned to us. 'You'll need two.'

Miniza left the room without looking up. He looked far too old. I explained I wanted men to carry our packs as well as guide us. Father Frank looked solemn. 'He's very strong, and he is a good man. Trust me.'

We sat in silence waiting for Miniza to return. Father Frank stood up, looked under the table, walked to the door which was flapped back against the wall. He looked behind it. 'Ha!' He pulled the door away. There was a long, pale bamboo staff leaning against the corner. 'This', he said, taking it in his fist, 'is for you. You must walk with it. It was made for me and every time I walk in the jungle I walk with it. I have never fallen. You take it. It will bring good luck.'

The wood was cool and polished smooth at the thicker end

where his hand had been. Regular knots divided up the sugar-cane lengths. It was the colour of pale straw, and heavier than I'd expected.

'Thank you,' I said, touched. 'I will look after it.'

Miniza returned with Dison, another small, uninspiring man with heavy-hooded eyelids who looked at my chest when he spoke to me. They took a rucksack each and levered their arms through the straps. Dunstan and I wore baseball caps; his was purple and had the peak reversed to cover his neck. Father Frank wished us luck and shook hands. We stood on the grass in front of the building, Dison and Miniza leaning forward to counter the weight on their backs. The veins in Miniza's temples stood out and sweat beaded on his hairline.

We walked through the village Miniza leading the way. Since he'd been enlisted he'd not said a word. We trod through the front yard of a house where a woman was boiling a pan of water on flattened, glowing logs. Despite the intrusion, she smiled at each in turn and, as I passed, beat the ground with the flat of her hand. It made a thin noise and she laughed, flashing blackened teeth.

Lower down the hill, near the river, the dry grass became longer and covered the path. Miniza was clearing ahead with his bushknife, leaving sheaves of grass that were flattened to a copper carpet by the time I walked on them. As we passed the last house there was the breathless rush of someone running through the grass behind us. 'Masta! Masta!' a voice called out. We stopped and turned. A smiling man caught up. He'd addressed me with the old colonial form of respect which spoke of starched shirts and scrambled eggs on toast on tropical mornings, outdated and irrelevant. 'Can I come?' I looked at Dunstan, even though it was my decision.

His eyes were large and eager, but he smiled ceaselessly, certainly an improvement on the funk of the other two.

'I don't have much money to pay a lot of people,' I apologized. 'I was only counting on taking one or two.' In Leahy and Hides' time, I remembered, carriers were paid in tobacco slugs and often died on patrol.

'Money is OK. Let me come. Please? I will carry and I will lead. I am young and strong.' I had a feeling that boredom, more than anything, had driven him to join us. Wanakipa was a quiet place.

We stood in the grass, twenty yards from the edge of the jungle, introducing ourselves. The newcomer was Andrew. He did not know how old he was, but believed he was born around Independence in 1975. This made him nineteen. His eyes bulged froglike, as if he was continually surprised. He said he would carry Miniza's rucksack, and Miniza put up an unconvincing act of wanting to keep hold of it. 'No,' Andrew insisted, 'I'll carry it. Let me.' He held it from behind and Miniza unsnaked his arms. It was hot in the sun and there was no wind. Miniza walked on ahead and we followed. Andrew walked behind me for now. He sang to himself, the same phrase over and over.

The jungle was terrifying. It was endless and extraordinary, everything outsize. I felt so new, so green, and this place so dark and vast. It was everything I had dreamed and feared, only more grotesque, monstrous: butterflies as fat as soup plates; tree trunks so wide that, up close, they could have been walls. There was sunshine only on the riverbank, where the jungle thinned away. Under the canopy it felt like underwater – two hundred feet down, cool and dark and green, with the surface shimmering far overhead. The path was cut through creepers, spiky ferns and bone-thin saplings that shot upwards, leafless, towards the light. Orienteering would have been pointless. We could only see through the trees when we broke on to a ridge, and then the mountains looked identical, dressed in forest, broken only by banks of steaming cloud. It felt impossibly big and unknowable and my glasses steamed up.

I was less fit than I'd thought, and this walking required concentration. For the first three hours we skirted the river-bank, but the water was fat and swollen and the path along the sandy shore, just under the steep bank, was three feet under-water; under the fast, blind, greedy river. This meant we had to walk along the bank, but there was no path and it was a sheer drop into the river.

'There are ropes, here,' Dunstan kept saying to me. I was edging my way along very slowly, leaning too heavily on the staff, which sucked into the mud. Dunstan urged me to grip creepers with my right hand, to let them take my weight. I would reach forward for a thick creeper, which hung in loops, take a step forward and wedge my toe in above a root or deep into the mudbank. It was slow and painful and we covered little ground. They waited for me. Once, when I caught up, they were halfway through home-made cheroots. I had covered twenty yards in five minutes. But they were uncomplaining and always, even though they'd been waiting and were impatient to move on, asked if I needed rest. A fat man running a marathon.

The canopy blocked out the sun. The river, in contrast to the darkness inside, the thick wet black tree trunks and rubbery sawtooth leaves, was almost too bright to look on. I'd noticed it before, its dangerous rusty orange, but now it seemed like thick cream gravy, chicken with apricots. It was opaque, even a scoop of water in the palm of a hand obscured the skin completely. It boiled and churned like Swiss cheese.

After too long we climbed off the riverbank and back up into the jungle. Behind us the river began its long sweep round to the north. We were back on a path which had cut up from the river. We came round a shoulder and in front of us, sitting against the huge buttress flanks of a pandanus pine, were three men. They were eating taro, a pale, cottony root vegetable, its innards bruised with tiny purple scars. They were dressed in leaves, small men with mud caked on their shins. They had tiny chests and splayed toes. I expected them to back off, suspicious, but they did not seem worried about ambush, which would have been an everyday threat in the years before colonial law was imposed. Their bows and arrows lay at their feet.

They also spoke a broken pidgin, a sign of how fast change had come; in 1935, when Jack Hides had cut across the Great Papuan Plateau, forty miles further south, each valley contained a tribe with distinct language, beliefs and customs. One group would be segregated into sexes, living in longhouses perched on high ridges; another would survive by cannibalism, ambushing not only rival warriors but also their women and children. Revenge was the only constant.

Dison and Miniza greeted the men with shouts. They had been in the jungle three days, they said, offering us each a taro tuber. They were heading back to Wanakipa. They'd killed only one pig, but it was a baby and too small to take home, so they'd eaten it. One pulled out a tiny femur, white like a clay pipe, as proof. They'd seen an emu, and fired arrows. He mimed its escape, his hands flapping, feet slapping on the wet earth. He asked if we'd been in the river. No, Miniza said, it was too high to walk in. 'We walked along the bank,' he said. 'Difficult for the whitey man.' Dunstan and I watched them talk.

The shorter man turned to us. 'You must not go near the river.' He shook his head in emphasis. 'The water is bad. People have died from swimming in it and drinking it. The big gold mine is killing us.'

This was the first time I'd heard this, and it would be repeated again and again by people whose lives centred on the river, heard like a refrain against all that was new and poorly understood. Much later I met a Port Moresby lawyer representing a group of Hewa people, who claimed that one hundred and three people had died, poisoned by the river, polluted by tailings from the Porgera gold and copper mine fifty miles upriver. The lawyer had been impressed by the thoroughness with which they had prepared their case. Those who'd died, they claimed, had been in contact with the river shortly beforehand. They could account for each death. The victims had either crossed, washed or swum in the river.

The mine had its defence prepared: the levels of mercury and arsenic came out below the permitted minimum. The lawyer, however, suspected the line had been drawn 'where it was cheap, not where it was safe'.

We were some way back from the Lagaip now, a distance from its roar, and we came to another, smaller river. The bank down was very steep. The track had slipped away and there was fresh crumbled earth from the landslip into which I dug my heels and slid. A rope bridge looped low across the water, suspended between two trees on either bank. The trees took the weight and between them the structure sagged, its belly almost on the water. The handrails were wrist-thick vines: the footrail bamboo was lashed in place by rope bark. It looked very unsafe.

I let the others go first. I took off my shoes and socks and found grit between my toes. My feet were already soft and grey and wrinkled and felt very tender. Dunstan offered to carry my shoes and I accepted gratefully, giving him the walking stick as well. He tied the laces together, wedged the socks down into the toes and slung the shoes over his shoulder. Andrew, Dison

and Miniza had already crossed. Although heavily laden, they'd
trodden gently, feeling their way across the bamboo, and were
now sitting on the other side, handing round tobacco.

Dunstan climbed the ladder between the two trees and
levered himself up on to the bridge. He bent low underneath a
strut and took his first step out over the water. He moved
slowly, like a tightrope walker, his arms stretched out, feeling
his way along the vine handrails. He looked up and across,
never down. I waited until he was halfway across then climbed
the ladder. Joints were secured with knots of slender green
vine that bent easily as nylon rope and had not split apart, even
though doubled back on themselves.

Twice I'd asked Dunstan what would happen if I fell and
broke my leg or arm, and he had replied, patiently, 'I would
carry you back. But please be careful. You would be heavy.' I
had begun to see meaning in everything – an upturned leaf, all
its veins showing, was an omen; crossing a muddy pool in one
stride guaranteed a safe return. I was unused to being so ruled
by superstition – at home I would only walk round a ladder if
I saw a workman wielding a paint pot above – yet had begun
to measure out the hours in portents. I would set myself
meaningless goals, holding my breath until the next stream
crossed the path, and draw disproportionate succour from the
achievement.

This time I crossed the bridge with surprising ease. It felt
strong underfoot and industrial, even though, in the middle,
the river slopped over the bamboo and reached to my ankles.
As I climbed up to the other side, the curve lifted clear,
shedding water. On the other side we stopped to rest. Again I
looked at my watch, taking comfort in its steady mechanism,
trying to gauge our progress. It was four in the afternoon and
we'd been walking since eleven.

'How much further today?' I said, for the fourth time. I

could feel them wanting me to relax, but I couldn't. I had a compulsion to collect facts.

By now I should have been able to predict the answer. It would be either longwe (a long way); longwe-tru (a very long way); or longwe liklik (not too far). When I'd asked before, it had been first longwe and then longwe liklik. Now it was longwe again, which made no sense.

We were heading for Maleili, a cluster of huts in a clearing up the mountainside where a friend of Miniza's, named Titus, lived. Apparently he had walked to Liawep before. If he wasn't there they weren't sure what to do, as none of them had ever walked further.

My worry about the distances and the lack of landmarks was not just empty paranoia; even the most experienced explorers had got lost on occasion. Leahy's first expedition saw him end up on the south coast, when he had believed himself to be crossing the island westwards. Twenty years before, Miles Staniford Cater Smith, the administrator of New Guinea, had set sail from Port Moresby to explore the unknown regions between the Purari and Fly Rivers. There was an ulterior motive: he wanted the job of governor, and believed a successful expedition would secure it. The trip was a disaster. In four months he lost more than a third of his men and, like Leahy, came a fruitless full circle. He turned barbarous, beating his carriers. The sitting governor, whose job Smith coveted, admitted he was 'heartily sick' of him. He never did get the job.

But it was the success stories that I read and re-read most hungrily – the men who entered this new world and made great discoveries. For Mick Leahy and Jack Hides, gold prospector and patrol officer, they were driven as much as anything by the thrill of discovering tribes who, for thousands of years, had lived in isolation from neighbours even a mile away, separated by different languages and by a revenge culture with no concept of forgiveness. Papua New Guinea had hundreds of languages, and no one, for fear of certain ambush, travelled beyond their own valley. Small wonder that Leahy and Hides, the first white men, were greeted with such incomprehension.

Dunstan nudged me out of my dream. 'Don't worry about the jungle. It's OK. We're all alive; the sun is shining. This is an adventure; we're off to meet the lost tribe. Don't worry so much.' And we walked on.

His guileless optimism affected me, and we walked on faster and lighter on our feet. He stopped me at one point and said, 'See that?' Up above, in the sunlit leaves of one of the topmost trees, was a cackle of pure white cockatoos, fat like little chickens, screeching and clucking and shaking the branches as they jockeyed for position. They were watching us. They'd been silent until we walked underneath and then stopped and looked up at them. Now they were shouting at us, making me laugh. Dunstan clapped his hands and hollered and they tumbled into the air.

I walked along the path, trying to mimic the cockatoos, feeling relaxed for the first time. The path turned sharply and ran alongside the river again. It narrowed and the drop-off was sheer, fifteen feet down, unbroken by trees. I missed my footing and crashed down. I grabbed out wildly but there was nothing to hold on to. My leg caught in something, an overlooping vine, and I was tipped upside down. The bank rushed towards me and I threw out my arms to break the fall and plunged headfirst into deep mud, up to my neck in it, grey and thick and wet like potter's clay in my hair and my ears and my eyes as I sucked my head out from the mud. I tried to stand but was on my knees and sank in again, up to my waist. My glasses had somehow stayed on my face but were smeared with mud. I took them off and Dunstan loomed in, blurry, leaning over the edge at me, saying, over and over, 'Oh, my God, oh, my God. I'm sorry, I'm sorry.' The shock made me start crying and, worse, I couldn't get up from the mud. I floundered and grabbed for the bank and sank further in. Dunstan scrabbled down the bank towards me, holding out my walking stick, like a plank to a drowning man. I would have thanked him, praised him, blessed him, had my mouth not been wedged with mud.

There was a justice, I suppose, after the months of planning, my worship and emulation of the early explorers, that it should have come to this: my tearful struggling in a mudbank. Reading books, it had been easy to imagine myself a hero; Leahy and Hides' own memoirs had exercised a powerful hold on my imagination. They were the real-life *Lost Horizon* or *King Solomon's Mines*. Even those books written about them and their kind, *Knights Errant of Papua*, *Papuan Epic*, *Behind the Ranges*, were couched in heroic rhetoric, and Hides and Leahy understood themselves in these terms.

The natives, by contrast, were considered backward and untrustworthy. The whites found them lazy, careless and irresponsible; customs such as polygamy, female tattooing and cannibalism were incomprehensible and abhorrent. Leahy, typically, was an undisguised and unrepentant racist; Hides became one under pressure. Both men led from the front, certain of their place in the hierarchy.

It was another two hours before we stopped for the night. There was a straw house, on low stilts, beside an earthy little river, a tributary of the raging Lagaip. I had not expected to sleep in a house and was flushed with relief when I saw we were alone and had it to ourselves. It sat clear of the jungle on a grassy nub of land around which the river turned.

The house seemed new. The roof was made of long, oval

saksak leaves, woven together with vine and overlapped like slates, and was flawless, falling to a trimmed fringe over the door. At the edge of the clearing were two pawpaw trees heavy with fruit. Most were green with flashes of yellow but two were soft orange, the colour of half-ripe tomatoes. Dunstan took my stick and shoved one heavily sideways. It swung like a breast and collapsed into the grass. I picked it up. It was smooth and warm and almost hairy.

The house had been built for travellers, Andrew explained: 'People like us.' Anyone on the move could use it. I asked who had paid for it. Andrew shrugged. 'I don't know. No one pays. No one has money.'

It had started to rain and we sat on the ground outside the house, sheltered by the roof overhang, watching the rain turn the grass heavy and silvery. Darkness was coming. Dison made a fire. Whoever had come before had left a pile of logs in the darkness just inside the entrance, and they were dry and burned easily. Miniza disappeared into the jungle to find Titus, his friend who knew the way.

Dunstan opened my rucksack and dug out two packets of rice: he gave Andrew a knife and ordered him off into the rain to cut the large, disorganized, papery leaves he called pumpkin top. His authority made me wonder about the precarious balance of power between us.

Should I have been more in control? Did it matter? As much as I knew it to be a spurious comparison, I could not help sizing myself up against the cool leadership of Leahy or Hides. On their expeditions, everyone had been sure of their role: the police made sure the carriers kept in line and did not raid natives' gardens or plunder livestock. The patrol officers, who enjoyed the luxury of personal orderlies to clean their laundry and heat their bathwater, were left with the logistic decisions – where to go, how long to stay. I, in contrast, fretted endlessly.

As the light faded, I slipped away through deep, wet grass to the river to wash. I took off my clothes and sat on a rock in the muddy water as the rain smoothed and dimpled the river.

It was dark when Miniza returned with Titus. They appeared through the gloom, their legs swishing through the under-growth. Titus was about five foot ten and towered over the others. He looked stretched, rather uncomfortable in his height, and his belly, entirely without fat, bulged like a balloon.

They sat down beside us. Titus shook my hand. He'd decided to come with us. He seemed very reserved, but gazed longingly at the rice stuck to the bottom of the saucepan. We'd boiled it dry by mistake and this last caking had proved immovable. 'Go on, have a go,' I offered. For men used to unrelieved sweet potato and taro, rice was a delicacy. He lifted the saucepan and I handed him a spoon and he began chipping away at it, excavating hard, bubbled chunks.

I asked him about himself. He didn't know how old he was. Earlier he'd said he had ten children and, despite having been recently baptized, two wives.

We spoke in pidgin. I'd learned none before leaving, yet after a few days found I could understand other people's conversations. A simple language, constantly changing, a bastard blend of English and Papua New Guinean tongues, it has only one thousand three hundred words to six thousand in English. This produces some fantastically unwieldy constructions – Prince Charles is *nambawan pikinini bilong misis Kwin* – and countless words that need no translation at all: *bagarap* ('bugger-up'), for broken; *apinun* (''appy noon'), for good afternoon. Generations of whites have dismissed it as broken English, using it as a tool of colonial condescension, explaining western objects in baby pidgin – a helicopter, thus, becomes a *Mixmaster bilong Jesus*.

Dunstan was asking Titus for his verdict. How long did he

think it would take us to reach the Liawep? Titus crunched on his rice. He opened his mouth and spat a burnt lump on to the grass.

'How long? Yes, I wonder. Two weeks?' His pidgin was as halting as mine.

'Two weeks?' I said, dismayed. 'Two weeks and we could walk to the coast. It can't be that far.'

'That's what I hear,' Titus confirmed, confidently. 'It takes two weeks.'

'Have you ever been there?'

'No, but I know someone who has.'

'Who's that?'

'Well, he's not my friend, but a friend knows him. And he says it takes two weeks.'

'How far have you been, then?'

'One day. I have walked to Wanakipa from Maleili where I live and I have walked to Kinalipa, one day towards Liawep. That's all.'

'And after that?' It seemed ludicrously haphazard.

'We ask.' He looked to Miniza for support. 'People will know.' He picked up the rice chunk he'd abandoned earlier. He sniffed at it and nibbled the corner. Miniza smoked silently.

I knew then that I would have to stop asking for precise distances by which I could pace myself. This was a place with no clocks and no calendars, where distances were approximated in adjectives rather than miles.

Dunstan approached me sheepishly. He'd forgotten his mosquito net. I suggested he share mine – there'd be enough room if we stretched it.

The rest of the baggage seemed to be intact. I had a sleeping bag and he two red railway blankets I'd bought in the trade store in Tari. I cut my roll-up sleeping mat in half and while the four carriers sat round the fire, smoking, we tied the mosquito net by its corners. I laid my half of the sleeping mat under my back and shoulders. Dunstan did the same. We lay down. My face was six inches from his. When he said goodnight, I smelled the warm fug of the jungle on him.

Chapter 7

Dunstan said grace before breakfast, giving thanks for the crackers we were to eat, for each other and the beauty of the jungle. He prayed for the Liawep and for our safe arrival. 'Baby Jesus,' he mumbled, his head upright, back straight, eyes closed, hands clasped over his lap, 'encourage them to welcome us. We pray for your blessing on our journey and that we may bring happiness to them. Amen.'

All night I had lain on my front, with my arms under my body. I had been hot in my sleeping bag, but it was dry in the house and I'd fallen asleep quickly. I had awoken with other worlds painfully present. I had been swimming, naked, in shallow water off a clear beach. I dreamed of Mother Teresa, of scouring a shopping mall for an electronic pager that I could bleep when lost, of sitting in a café, to be greeted as Nick by friends who'd known me all my life.

My joints were stiff and my muscles ached as though I'd been punched. My neck hurt between my shoulders where I'd fallen in the mud. It was barely dawn and Dunstan was already outside, boiling water for tea. The other four had woken long ago. They had slept outside, in the damp, round the fire, even though there had been unlimited space inside, on the slatted bamboo floor.

I had been rolling up my sleeping bag when the carriers returned. The bridge across the river had been washed away and they had been building a new one. They had finished it, and I was only just getting up. I sat beside Dunstan with a mug of hot water in my hands. An inflated tea bag and fungus spread of powdered milk, not yet dissolved, floated on the surface.

The night before, by the fire, they'd been chewing over the Liawep, discussing their feelings about walking there. While none had been, all had an opinion. All were superstitious and highly religious. Three American Lutheran missionaries had passed through this area in 1975, setting up churches and installing indigenous pastors. Miniza, Dison and Titus had all been baptized in a mass cleansing on the muddy banks of the river. Andrew was christened as a baby.

So, like Herod, they were Lutheran. I had asked them why they'd found Luther's teaching more attractive than, say, that of the Roman Catholic church, but they could not say. The Lutherans, who'd been based in the country since the turn of the century, had been the first to reach them, that was all. It might have been anyone. They knew nothing of Martin Luther or the Reformation. They had no idea of the scorn which Luther had reserved for the magical transubstantiation of the mass. But they sang, and believed in evangelism, of which Luther would have approved. Unlike the German, however, who had pushed for the re-establishment of Christ as the centre of the faith, they were more at home with the Old Testament, its rudeness and its threats, its rule by fear.

Dison had wondered whether the Liawep were the only heathen left. He imagined their lives. 'Perhaps the men still live in big houses and have many wives.' He sighed, dreamily.

'Not any more,' Dunstan had corrected him. 'Not now the missionary is there.'

Sitting together before breakfast, they fell to prayer so zealously that it was easy to forget how recent an innovation Christianity was, that until a hundred years before, only a handful of pioneering missionaries had set foot on the island, and that the Bible had been in this region less than twenty years. Missionaries held that the nation had been, in a sense, 'waiting' for Christianity; evangelists, they argued, were answering a real need. This is reflected in the wording of the constitution, composed for Papua New Guinea's independence in 1975. Here the people pledged to 'guard and pass on . . . our noble traditions and the Christian principles that are ours now'. So much, in such a short time.

Yet, and I came again and again to this – how much did they really understand? How much was accepted, unquestioned? As frequent as the stories of missionary triumph were examples of hopeless misinterpretation. In 1961, a Catholic archbishop visiting coastal villages was asked by a village leader to sacrifice a black rooster (blakpela kakaruk) to cleanse the inhabitants' sins. The archbishop refused, shocked by the barbarity of the suggestion. The leader then ordered the killing of one of his men. The sacrifice of a black 'Jesus' would, he believed, bring his people the same benefits whites had gained from the crucifixion of their saviour – cars, aeroplanes, good clothes.

We were off by seven; keen to move on, I'd been eyeing my watch nervously since dawn. The bridge they'd built was two tree trunks, wedged from a boulder-island in the middle of the river to the mudbank the other side. The boulder was a yard from our bank and the gap was bridged by two smaller trunks, lashed together. Over the longer stretch they'd built a handrail, bound in place by vine-hatching. I walked it, slowly edging sideways, both arms outstretched, hands held by Dunstan and Andrew.

It was very steep the other side. The path ran straight up and there was no way of taking an easier zig-zag. I followed close behind Andrew and watched his bare, callused feet. He walked with his toes, curling them round roots and jamming them into mudbanks when there was nothing else to grip on to. There was just the noise of his feet in the mud and the rasp of my breathing. There was no view and no way of telling how far we'd come. Only occasionally did we look back to find a break in the canopy at eye level, enabling us to look out to the other side of the valley, down which we'd scrambled the day before.

Three hours up, we had climbed the worst. The jungle gave way to a clearing and we walked up through hot grass between banana trees. There was a house built in a small dusty plateau, ringed by a wooden stake fence. A black-and-white hornbill with a dragon-claw beak sat on the roof, fixing us with a malevolent yellow eye. Everything else was Technicolor – demerara grass, straw-roofed house, fat fistfuls of green bananas, the random jerking of a peacock-blue butterfly and the bleeding orange flesh of the pawpaw Dison had carried up the mountain. The house was built as a wedge on the mountainside, the downhill wall five foot deeper than the uphill. Halfway up was a dark square of window from which a boy with bumpy adolescent skin idly watched us. His face was as dark as the shadow from which he emerged. Below the window were two drawings – a helicopter with a flat-petalled rotor and a plane, both scratched on the wall in charcoal.

Far over the valley there was a break in the jungle and smoke rising. Dison said a man lived there, on his own. 'He lost one arm fighting, and the other is crippled. It is very hard for him.'

We stopped walking two hours later. It was only afternoon – we had four or five hours' more light – but the carriers would not move. They sat on a log and said, 'Tomorrow, tomorrow we go.' This was Kinalipa, apparently. None of them had walked beyond this point. The house belonged to Titus' friend Malolo, who pressed us to stay. We must eat together, he said. We would have a feast. We could sleep in his house, and tomorrow he would guide us on. It was out of my hands.

Malolo sat with us on the steps of a lean-to where tobacco was drying. The leaves hung from the eaves like strips of cured beef, blackened by sun. Malolo may have been as young as twenty but his cracked, flaking skin made him look old and diseased. He had an upturned cockatoo's claw pierced through the end of his nose. He took it out to roll between his fingers, revealing a snug, dark hole.

There were three other buildings: the house, with different entrances for men and women; a miniature longhouse, three foot high, where the pig lived; and a smaller, roofed structure on a mound a little way up the hill – a mausoleum, where Malolo's brother-in-law and niece were buried. They'd died of malaria the year before. Malolo's sister had not come to greet us. I'd glimpsed her earlier, digging out ginger, her face still chalked with mourning paint.

Dunstan kept apologizing. He knew we should be walking, he said, but there was nothing he could do to make them go on. I shrugged and went to wash in the stream. It was a cold and reedy trickle, teased off a banana-leaf spout. I sat in the pool under it and washed with one hand. The other, patched with plasters covering cuts, I waved fussily above the water.

Malolo had heard about the Liawep. He'd never been there but he'd heard the stories and the next day promised to take us to a man who knew the way. Liawep, he said, was not only the name of the people but the name of the mountain. He said that a man and a woman lived on the mountain, whose taste for human meat made the Liawep's lives dark and miserable. I asked if anyone had seen the couple, and Malolo shrugged, annoyed at being doubted. Stories, it seemed, went unquestioned, judged by their power to amuse.

We moved on to pigs – their size, cost, beauty and taste. Pigs were the currency; they bought wives and influence. Malolo had two large sows and two healthy piglets: scrubbed, pink and aggressive. They had their own house, too carefully made to qualify as a sty. Alongside was another, built the same, but its entrance clean of pig hairs and hoof prints. It had a small, square door tied back with twine. There was a partition halfway down, dividing the two sides. I walked over and leaned in; behind me, angry voices bubbled up. I retreated and stood up, brushing away mud from my hands and knees.

Malolo had forgotten the fire and was standing up, pointing at me. He had replaced the claw in his nose.

'It's the women's house,' Dunstan explained, when I walked over. 'Half is for the pig and half is for the women, when they are pregnant. They sleep in there. They must not go near the men when they are pregnant. It is dangerous.' This was not a surprise. Elsewhere in the southern highlands, men believed that the proximity of women sapped their power, and they lived in separate houses to protect themselves.

When night fell we moved into the main house. There were four fires inside and little room to move. From the corner of each fireplace poles rose from floor to ceiling. They were bound into squares with bamboo, from which leaves of tobacco were hung to dry. Malolo smoked incessantly and scratched his scaly knees.

He had stories about the Liawep, warnings of how to behave when we arrived. The tribe lived under a mountain; if we looked at the mountain, we would die. The superstitions were endless: to dream of one's own death while staying in the village was another sure intimation of doom.

Titus warned against whistling: this, too, was unwise. It was also not exclusive to the Liawep. In Tari, if you whistled, they thought you were a witch. In 1935, when Jack Hides had walked through, one catcall from his deputy, Jim O'Malley, dispersed warriors gathering to attack. In Liawep, however, the reaction was aggressive. If you whistled, Titus said, they would put a spell on you.

Malolo was beginning to fidget. 'One last thing,' – he looked around – 'you must not sleep with any Liawep women. Otherwise you die.' He fixed me when he said this, pointedly. I chose not to protest. What would have been the point? There was a history of this kind of thing, white men buying native women – Leahy fathered three mixed-race children by nameless 'harlots' he met on patrol.

When Leahy and Hides had begun their expeditions, they, too, knew nothing about the people they were to meet. Those whom they encountered were similarly astonished. They stared, mute, as Leahy, 'more than a prospector, a genius', according to one awe-struck government officer, marched through the eastern highlands in the early 1930s, with his Leica camera, American high-laced walking boots, Mauser rifle and Italian lightweight tents. In 1935 they made as little sense of Hides forging through the jungle further west, this 'volatile and restless [man], a born storyteller', whose 'apparently extravagant tales were often true'.

The white men were mysterious, terrifying, divine, so pale they were the returning dead. Did their shorts hide colossal penises? Did they sleep or eat? The open-mouthed highlanders who witnessed Leahy's first patrol assumed, because they were from the spirit world, that these pale strangers did not defecate. Then they discovered the latrine. 'Their skin may be different,' one later confided to an anthropologist, 'but their shit smelled as bad as ours.' Even away from the latrine, they found the white men's smell unbearable, and covered their noses with leaves from a medicinal bush. The disgust was mutual. 'Nigs pong woefully,' Leahy wrote in his diary.

With Hides, further west, the welcome was more ominous; one tribe even believed they had foreseen his coming. The appearance, two or three months earlier, of the first steel tools, traded up from the coast, had confused them and made them fearful their 'owners' would return to claim the strange objects. Hides's appearance, preceded, by grim coincidence, by plague, was the prediction fulfilled. Those tribes who guessed he was a benevolent spirit returning from the dead revised their opinion when he opened fire on them. The scars remain to this day: a favourite expletive of one such tribe is 'towmow hundbiy', pale-skinned ghost.

We shared tea from the blue enamel mugs, prodding the dried milk under. Malolo gave Dunstan three hornbill beaks

and a ball of fur, tied with twine, from the *cuscus*, or tree
kangaroo. He pulled these treasures from the eaves. They were
wedged in and smelled foxy, of smoke and taxidermy. He
brought them out just to show us, but when he saw Dunstan's
excitement and his fingers twisting the fur, he stood up and
reached under the roof again and pulled out a spray of emu's
feathers, skeletal, with oily, dark-blue feathery fingers.

It was a long night, broken by Malolo's coughing, like his
lungs were full of broken sponge. He shuffled logs in the fire
and smoked, and the rain tapped on the papery roof. As I went
to sleep, Dunstan, lying beside me, was asking Andrew about
Christianity. Andrew, the youngest and keenest, had become
his favourite, and Dunstan made sure they walked together.
Andrew also laughed at Dunstan's jokes.

'Do you know about Jesus?' Dunstan asked. His voice was
growly, blurred with oncoming sleep. 'He died to save us. Did
you know that?'

'Yes, I know that,' Andrew answered, patiently.

'Have you been baptized?' The other side of the room a pig
squeaked and was soothed to silence by Malolo.

'When I was a baby. *Mi oltaim bilipim long Jesus*. I always believe
in Jesus.'

'Then you know he died to save us. I will tell you more
later.' Andrew didn't reply. A log hissed. 'Goodnight everyone,'
Dunstan said. There was a ripple of goodnights. Only Andrew
stayed silent.

It took me a while to fall asleep – I was thinking about what
Andrew had said, his blanket acceptance of Christianity, that
blind faith that distinguished modern Papua New Guinea. It
astonished me and made me uneasy. Why did they make such
happy converts, such apparent pushovers?

Weeks later, when I returned to Port Moresby, I looked up

an old Englishman, David Hand, who for forty years had been the country's Anglican archbishop. He was a warm, open man who looked like an antique teddy bear and was something of a local celebrity – on the way to his house there were banners looped high above the road congratulating him on his 'golden jubilee' in Papua New Guinea. He had grown up in Yorkshire and studied history at Oxford. All his family were priests. He came to Papua New Guinea at the end of World War II and had brought the Gospel to thousands of previously uncontacted people.

He was scornful of the ignorant and opinionated outsider – he was too tactful to finger me directly – who 'comes to Papua New Guinea with some fantasy of the happy savage. It's not like that. People live in fear of their neighbours and of evil spirits. Christianity delivers them from that fear.'

The approach best designed to deliver converts was, he believed, to first learn the local language. This might take five years. 'Then see how Christianity crosses with their beliefs – at how many points is it necessary to explain there are different ways of looking at things?'

Yet not all missionaries, he felt, improved lives. 'How can people who've just been contacted make an informed choice between Rome, Canterbury or Geneva? When I think of the scramble that goes on now, I thank God I'm retired.'

Many of the missionaries I met in Papua New Guinea still lived in the nineteenth century, believing themselves to be heroes of the stature of the Reverends Livingstone and Chalmers, who would return from their tours in the 1880s to fill lecture halls and make headlines. Papua New Guinea, with its malleable population and absence of government controls on mission activities, now boasted a burgeoning lunatic fringe. From the long-established New Tribes Mission, with its 'consistent passion for souls', to the bewildering Have Christ Will

Travel, Door of Hope International and Habitat for Humanity Incorporated, the ranks keep swelling.

Their techniques have always varied. The first missionaries found tobacco the most effective inducement to prayer. Today the bribery is more subtle. Often the missions provide medical help, making it only prudent to attend church. Elsewhere the locals believe that, by turning to God, they will become as rich as the missionaries. They fill the churches, expectant.

Yet whether radical or liberal, each missionary I met argued the same. They claimed to offer redemption to people locked in a cycle of war and revenge. Christianity released them from fear.

In a century, the country has capitulated to Christianity, a rate of conversion so blind in its speed I found myself worrying for future generations, their certain resentment when they discover how quickly their heritage has been betrayed. Will they, too, trust the pastor when he explains how Jesus freed their parents from fear? Or will they look closer and find that this has simply been replaced by something worse, the dread of hell?

It was a gruesome night. The pigs, starving and irritable, had foraged round the corners of the room and the dog, scaly and mottled and almost hairless, peed ceaselessly against the wall. The pigs heralded the dawn, screeching and squealing for their feed. It was five in the morning and there was only the faintest edge of grey leaking over the mountains into the blackness. Malolo lay asleep, hands on his belly, the rattle of loose machinery coming from deep inside. He woke finally and poked at his eyes and scratched his skin. The pigs and the dog followed him outside. I heard the splatter of his early morning piss, slapping into mud.

The morning was heavy to begin with but then the cloud started to break and lift. It had rained all night and nothing was dry. The mud was thick and sticky and impossible to get a grip on. Grass and bushes were bent over with water.

As we ate breakfast – crackers for Dunstan and myself, sweet potato and *kaukau*, for the rest – Dison asked how long we planned to stay with the Liawep. From his face it was impossible to guess his concerns. Had the stories unnerved him, or was he already homesick? He was a small man but his hooded eyelids made him look dangerous, brooding. The question irritated me unaccountably.

'Two days? Two weeks? A month? I don't know, Dison. We'll see when we get there.'

Dison nodded and looked at his yellowing ball of *kaukau*. There was a cigarette behind his ear, kept in place by tight curls. He put his *kaukau* on a flat stone and pulled out the cigarette. He reached to the fire and picked up a long stick that glowed red at one end and held it to the cigarette tip. The tobacco was homegrown and often smoked before it was dry. Dison had his own supply, folded into a wad like a clip of banknotes. When we walked he, or one of the others, would carry an ember from the last fire, smoking like a snuffed torch. When they stopped they would peel a leaf from the wad, dangle it over the cross-hatch of glowing wood, first one side, then the other, until it darkened and smoked. Then they would flake it into a greener leaf, roll into a cone and lick along the edge. Somehow the cigarette managed to stay together. Between thumb and forefinger it was held to the orange of the burning wood and the tobacco caught fire, blistering round its tip. Once alight, they blew on the end, rather than toke it, until it glowed all round like a well-lit Havana. Only then would they put it in their mouths, drag, turn the cigarette ninety degrees, drag again, turn another ninety degrees. The ritual was always identical. The smoke was strong, uncured, and blue exhaust curled from their nostrils and leaked from their mouths when they spoke.

Malolo led the way when we walked on. Despite his appearance, his coughing, his diseased skin, he walked fast, in a half-run, so his weight was always moving on. He never slipped. The sun had come out and Malolo too was buoyant and sunny.

From his house, high up on the mountainside, we climbed down into the jungle again amid the yabber of cockatoos, perched in their treetops two hundred feet up. It was very steep and I descended very slowly, like an old man climbing down stairs. My legs juddered.

The others were jubilant and whooped by turn. Malolo started it. '*Yaiiee!*' And the others took it up, until it passed back and forth faster and faster and we walked faster, stirred into exuberance. It was a song relayed in the jungle, a war call, a warning that we were coming. Not that anyone would have heard – since starting, three days before, we'd run across five people. It was not hard to see why no government patrols had come this way. The few people who lived here could easily have moved by the time the next census patrol came by.

We came to a stream. The other side the mountain rose up sheer again, as steep as we'd just climbed down. I sat on a rock and watched the water. It was mid-morning and the sun burned hot on my neck. The water was a clear emerald over grey-metal rocks, quite different from the rusty soup of the Lagaip.

Andrew was walking upstream, the water round his calves, sun flashing in the broken mirrors. He was a silhouette against the sun. Suddenly he screamed out, splashing his hand on the water. He looked back to us and screamed again. The other four ran after him through the stream, cartwheeling spray. The sound came back on and they were hurtling out of the stream, on to the bank, back into the jungle. 'Yaiiee! Yaiiee!', the noise beating up to a climax. Then there was silence and the crashing of the undergrowth stopped and I could hear their voices, raised in triumph.

'Wild pig,' Dunstan said, standing beside me. 'They chase wild pig.'

Their prey was tiny, no more than three months old, and can't have put up much of a fight. Miniza came back holding it in his hands. They looked like creatures from different times, Miniza's old, scarred face and the piglet's tiny button eyes, dark and new. He held it like a rugby ball, one hand round each side of its tight belly. The piglet was breathing in and out very fast and little pearls of wet dripped from its snout. Its skin was pinky brown with a haze of black hair.

'You like it?' Miniza said.

'It's too small to eat.'

He looked at me, then back to the piglet. Nothing was too small to eat. He squeezed it tighter and the pig squeaked. He held it in front of me. Titus giggled into his hand. The piglet looked up at me with its little dark eyes. Its tail had uncurled and stood upright, an antenna scanning for news of a reprieve. It tried to run, then stopped when it realized its legs were pedalling in mid-air. Miniza said something to Andrew, who took the bushknife and walked to the edge of the jungle. He cut out a two-foot strip of springy twine, slashed from round a sapling. Miniza made the piglet sit up in his hands, its legs sticking straight out, its underbelly, twin rows of tidy nipples, huffing out in fast short pants.

Looking it in the eyes, Andrew wrapped the twine round its neck. He wrapped it loosely, then tighter until the twine bit into the soft skin of the piglet's neck. The piglet kicked its legs outwards and Andrew tightened his grip. Titus was bent double in laughter, clutching his stomach. His humour was infectious. Everyone started laughing, cackles of delight and pride.

The piglet went limp and stopped kicking. Its head slumped sideways and its mouth fell ajar and a corner of pink bubble-gum tongue peeped out. We all gathered in close and its eyes changed colour, from a clear dark to an opaque smoky blue. Miniza lay it on a cross of banana leaves and squeezed its little body up tight, pressing its snout down into its belly and pushing its legs up round its ears. It was so small like this, not like a pig at all, more like an oversized gerbil, barely a handful. Miniza flapped over one leaf, then the other, and enclosed it. He tied it with a cross of twine, through which he looped a longer strip, to serve as shoulder strap. When he walked, it swung from him like a long-handled handbag. The green bundle was tight and the leaves were shiny, almost plastic. I put my hand on it. It felt warm.

We would eat the piglet later, Andrew promised: because I had shared my food with the carriers, they offered to share the meat with me. Leahy and Hides, proud imperialists both, never stooped so low. They had special food – flour, tea, sugar, tinned meat – separately prepared. There is a photograph, taken by Mick Leahy in 1934, which eloquently demonstrates this divide: his brother Dan slouched in a canvas chair in front of a linen-covered trestle table, a carrier lowering a tray of tea and biscuits, two hundred staring highlanders.

Away from the table, the white men used their novelty to their advantage: Michael Dwyer, Mick Leahy's companion on his first expedition, enjoyed dispersing nosy onlookers by ostentatiously spitting out his dentures. Leahy, too, like the tourist, was interested only in the surface – oiled bodies and dismayed faces – and his photographs reinforce his belief in white superiority: a rifle shattering a tree stump at fifty yards; highlanders puzzling over a wind-up gramophone or their first mirror; warriors with sardine-tin head dresses. Yet amazingly, considering what was to follow, this first trip, in the spring of 1930, was bloodless.

The jungle was a blur of sensation. Looking across, high up, it seemed a dark forest, unbroken, like Europe five hundred years ago. Inside, it looked much brighter and the bright papery green hurt my eyes. Everything grew so fast, there was no ground cover, just warm decay and thin saplings that had seeded and shot upwards, leafless, towards the light. It was a strange, terrible place, which felt so warm and was so full of colours, yet so foreign. I recognized orchids, occasionally, blowsy pink candelabras in moss by streams and hornbills yakyakking overhead. We never saw an emu, but by every stream picked out their giant three-fingered prints in the mud.

From the stream we climbed again, falling into silent, breathy single file, back on a path. I'd expected there to be no paths but, so far, except where the way had crumbled with a landslip, we were following where others had gone before. At points the paths would diverge and we'd stand while Malolo, as this was his territory, would try to remember which route to take. Often, too, the paths would have grown over and the only sign that this was the rot, or road, as they all called it, were oval wounds where saplings had been hacked off with a bushknife. If they'd been cut only a week before they would already have lost their keen creaminess and turned off-brown, and soon the tree would begin to grow back. So when we lost the path we'd look out for signs that people had come this way before – scars in trees, grass trodden into mud, cold circles of ash where fires had been. Alone I would have become quickly lost, and often, when I was walking far behind them, inching down paths that fell off vertically, and they were way ahead out of sight, I'd take the wrong fork and find myself in deep bush round my face and my ears, and have to retrace my steps: muddy, waterfilled footprints. Whoever was in front hacked away constantly, cutting with a sideways, downwards chop. The next man slashed away what was left. Dunstan, who followed behind, just in front of me, carried a handaxe sharpened to a razor edge. The clearing had been done, so he used this for gratuitous destruction. When we stopped he'd chop into trees that looked far too big for a handaxe, excavate a deep 'V' and then start working away at the uphill side. The wound bled clear resin, dripping from his axe, and he'd cut out cake slices of wood. Slowly the tree would begin to give way, creaking and aching. It became a ritual, marking our passage through the unknown. The tree hinged from its wound and toppled, crashing through the canopy, taking an armful of smaller trees with it.

My glasses steamed up constantly. We'd cut from a clearing into the warm damp of the jungle and they would mist over like a windscreen on a frosty morning. When it rained they streaked with water and I took them off to wipe on my shirt only to find them now damp and striped instead with mud and sweat. So I left them on, and peered through the gloom, and in the evening polished them on my underpants.

We were climbing. From the stream where they'd caught the pig we climbed two hours. It was more of the same, and I was learning to switch myself off from the drudgery of it. I thought of the Liawep, when we'd get there, what we'd find, how easily they'd talk to me. I had a strange picture which could not resemble the reality. They were feared and revered by their neighbours, who invested them with dark powers. On what was this based? No one knew, or would answer.

At last we crested the ridge. The others had waited for me and I rested, sinking my staff into the mud and sitting down in a dip of dead leaves against a tree.

'There's a house not far on,' Malolo said. '*Longwe liklik*. We stop there.'

He was keen to move on. He'd replaced the upturned claw in the end of his nose and was itching the soft skin on the inside of his elbow, which had not curled into tissue-paper flakes like the more exposed skin, working it with his long dirt-ridged fingernails into a pale, dusty graze.

'Liklik,' he encouraged, sensing my reluctance.

I stood up. I was very stiff and my legs shook when they bent. Only when I locked my knees did the spasm stop. Although we were on top of this particular mountain, I felt like a baby who has learned to crawl upstairs but who hasn't yet worked out the more complicated motor movements for negotiating descent.

Malolo was right. It was liklik after all. We broke into a clearing, bounded by a stream which had cut a sharp groove, fifteen feet down, over which a tree trunk had been laid. Malolo sprang on to the trunk. It was greased with rain and slime. He skipped along the top, into a depression where the bark had decayed and there was a dusting of soggy chippings. From there the trunk was whole again, a perfect curve, polished, fifteen feet across. It demanded confidence and surefootedness, neither of which I had. The other had bare feet, and I watched their toes splay wide, suck the wood like geckos up a door. Dunstan took my stick and went on ahead. The trunk was thick and he couldn't climb on to it in one step. He found a foothold, a fist-thick knot, sticking from the side of the trunk, and stepped from that.

'You all right?'

'Yes, yes,' I lied. 'You go ahead.'

He walked slowly, stick in one hand, the other held out for

balance. At the far end he jumped down and threw the stick to Andrew. He fumbled and dropped it and they both laughed.

They waited for me. I stepped up to the trunk. Its cross-section came up to my chest. I considered scrambling down into the gully, wading across the stream and fighting my way up through the steep mud the other side, but thought better of it. It would save me having to negotiate the slick tree trunk, but they were waiting for me. My pride was at stake.

'Come on,' Dunstan coaxed. 'It's easy. Do you want to take off your shoes?'

'No, I'll leave them on.' I looked at my shoes. The lace ends were frayed and mouldy water squirted through pinholes designed for aeration. I would treat it like a narrow path, like walking along the lines in the middle of a road. I would not think of the drop.

I had always thought of myself as fit and strong. Coming here I realized my rambling had only ever been recreation. Malolo and the rest walked because there was no other way. They understood the size of mountains and had never flown or been driven. Travel took days or weeks and was undertaken on foot. Titus once said to me, 'You never walk, do you? Your feet are soft and your legs are weak.' I could not argue.

I put my hands on top of the trunk and felt round the side to the knot from which Dunstan had propelled himself. Under my skin the trunk felt slimy, like rain on an oily road. I levered myself on to my knee, pulled the other knee up and was stuck, kneeling, on the trunk. I could see their heads the other end. They were watching, silently. I pushed myself up from the log, one leg at a time. Everything went quiet. The hornbills stopped clacking. There was only the rush of the stream below me in the gully, fifteen feet below. I could hear my breathing and blood banging in my ears. Dunstan smiled nervously.

I took my eyes off my feet and stepped on a comatose gecko. It was softer and slicker than any banana skin. My foot kicked out to the side, a skid of gecko pasted to the sole and I snatched out at the air as I fell. I tried to grab the trunk as I came down but I was already falling round the side and caught the descending curve on my ribs. The pain was so blinding that the rest of the fall was like a dream, a soft rush of leaves and the blur of sun on water. Only when I stopped sliding, at the bottom of the gully, did the sound come tumbling after me. It felt like I'd been run over. I didn't dare touch my ribs. I was winded, bruised, but more than anything shocked at my failure of nerve and co-ordination. It was the second time, as well. It did not bode well.

'Oh, my God, oh, my God. I'm sorry.' Dunstan's voice came over the edge of the gully, but I was buried in a bush. I lay on my back while he struggled down the bank. I could hear the shickshick of bushknife slicing through soft fibrous under-growth. It was lucky, I reflected, that I'd fallen early on. If I'd toppled in the middle I'd certainly have broken something. As it was, I felt bruised but intact. Dunstan sloshed through the stream and I could see him, behind a wall of leaves, looking from side to side.

'I can't see you.'

'I'm here, Dunstan. In the mud behind the bush.'

He slashed away the leaves between us, great drooping heart-shaped leaves on rhubarb stalks. The stumps were gritty and white like pearflesh and oozed transparent glue. Dunstan gave me his black hand, into which I placed my white one. He leaned back and I pulled on him and inched back up the bank.

The country was overwhelming me. The present was becoming so powerful that I was losing sight of the goal. Climbing could have been a time of contemplation, but often my exhaustion or fear of losing my footing made intelligent thought impossible. And then, when everything was spiralling downwards, something astonishing would happen. Once, when we sat down to drink and wash, a large purple butterfly landed on Titus' head. Its wings were shiny as if stitched with bright silk thread. When we pointed and Titus shook his head, the butterfly lifted into the air. When we turned away, it returned. After a while he forgot it and it sat on his head, on the dark spongy curls, its wings flat for balance. When we walked on, it flipped over into the air like a leaf knocked by the wind.

In comparison with what the first explorers had suffered, my journey was shamefully mild – a stroll in the woods, nothing more. A photograph survives of Jack Hides, four months into his patrol. His beard is patchy and distressed; his belt is hitched tight over a contracting waistline; his legs are wasted and scarred. And it had all started so hopefully; to begin with, his judgement on the natives had been faultlessly generous: 'The Papuan, taken quickly after the civilizing effect, will become just as good an industrialist as he is today a cannibal, a fighter and a likeable gentleman when you get to know him.' Fumbling for meaning, he believed the warriors' hostility to be betrayal, unable to see that it might simply have been their way of keeping him off their land. The people rejected his gifts of axes and knives, believing that to accept them would be to precipitate disaster. The fault lines, the unbridgeable gulf between his world and theirs, were beginning to emerge. By the end, exhausted, starving, dependent on the local people for food they were reluctant to barter, he became delirious. 'I imagined these big black Papuans with wild boar tusks through their noses, killing and burning ... They would show no mercy on the lives of the weak.' His certainty that he was next on their list led him to rely, with increasing frequency, on his rifle.

For Mick Leahy, bounty hunter, the novelty of first contact wore off in days. 'The kanakas', he wrote in his diary, 'murder each other with as much compunction as they kill their favourite pig.' They were 'foul-mouthed bastards ... who badly want a lesson'; 'kankas, coons, niggers, apes' who were, depending on his mood, 'thieving, godless, sneaky, cruel, murdering, merciless, disgusting, wicked, cruel, shiftless and immoral'. They were the enemy of all that was civilized, wholesome and white.

We came out of the gully into a windless clearing. The sun, after the rain, came down unfiltered and burning. Down to our left was a wide valley, thickly forested, and on the far side was a huge mountain, its summit smudged by cloud. The edge of the clearing through which we were walking had been allowed to grow over, and the path ran along the spines of felled trees, above long, drying grasses. A stake fence separated this, which the jungle was busy reclaiming, from the polite potato-mound cultivation of kaukau and rubbery banana trees. There was a crowd of people, naked children, and adults in tanket-leaf bumcover. We climbed over the fence, up a plank wedged in between two stakes, and down another on to the dusty earth. Everyone watched us.

I let the others walk on and make their greetings. I sat back in the shade of a banana tree. It was too hot in the sun. Two sprays of green bananas lay on their side like petrified grass skirts. Dunstan was talking to one of the men. He had a string bag slung across his chest. His nipples were shiny and oiled. He was pointing across the valley, at the mountain lost in the clouds. They were too far away to hear. Dunstan turned round.

'Edward!' he shouted. He grabbed the peak of his baseball cap and tore it from his head, waving it about in the air. 'Come here!'

I walked over and a crowd gathered round us. 'You see that?' he said, pointing his cap at the mountain. 'That's Liawep.' He was speaking English. A little boy laughed and scuttled away sideways.

'The mountain?'

'Yes, the mountain is called Liawep. The Liawep people live below. You see?'

I could see little through the gunk on my glasses. I rubbed them with a leaf. 'Where's the village?' The far mountainside was unbroken, dark green jungle. The mountain was enormous, the only one I'd seen high enough to be obscured by cloud. Only its shoulders were visible, rising steadily. Just below the cloud-cover the incline accelerated. It looked close, but could have been eight or ten miles away.

Dunstan ran his finger up the contour, up its shoulder, and stopped. He made me look down his arm, pointed like a gunbarrel. There was a dusting of brown, a scratch in the dark green jungle, specked with paler brown dots, six, perhaps seven, the roofs of houses.

This was it, then, the place I'd come this far to see: home of the lost tribe. I felt relief, after so long of estimated distances, that I could finally see it; I knew, now, that we would get there. I understood, too, a little of Hides' elation when he stepped into the Tari basin and saw for the first time 'a population such as I had dreamed of finding'.

Just two days more.

Chapter 8

A crowd had gathered round us in
the sun, women in bustling grass skirts, men with whippet-
scrawny chests and skin gone powder-white with malnutrition,
like old chocolate. A little way off, two men were lighting a
fire, spinning sticks into smoking dry grass. The rest looked up
at me, hoping for a lead, a word.

I looked around. One man stood apart, distinct and proud.
He was a young man with a beard confined to the underside
of his chin, where it spread straggly and unnoticed. He was
much darker than the others, and looked almost African. His
nose was flatter and his forehead higher, exaggerated by a
headband of old cloth pushed back against his hairline. He was
short and strong and had thick rounded shoulders. He wore
leaves over his behind and a string bag, lumpen with sweet

potato, across his chest. The overhead sun elongated his muscular breasts into shadows that pointed down his belly. He was standing beside me, looking out across the valley to the Liawep village.

'Hello,' I said, and then, in pidgin, '*Apinun*.' He ignored me.

'He's from Liawep,' Titus said.

My first encounter with a member of the lost tribe; so unexpected, so casual. He puffed on a cheroot and looked at me as we discussed him, thick blue smoke spilling from his mouth. I was desperate to quiz him.

He spoke no pidgin so I spoke to him through Titus, who understood the dialect. He didn't know how old he was and couldn't remember the arrival of Peter Yasaro last year. This seemed extraordinary. Yasaro's patrol and Herod's arrival must have been the biggest events in their lives.

'But you must remember. Lots of men came with clothes. They had books, and they shot a pig with a gun.'

No, he insisted, he didn't remember. He shook his head sadly and looked at the ground.

'And Herod? You know Herod, the Lutheran missionary?' I suddenly wondered if I'd been taken to the right place. If there could be two Liaweps, why not three, or four?

'Yes,' he agreed after some hesitation. 'I know Herod. He makes a church. He gives us shirt and trousers.' He looked away anxiously towards the fire. The men were blowing it alight, smoke backing into their faces.

'So where are yours?'

'This is my trousers.' He pinched his loincloth between finger and thumb. It was a pair of pale shorts never washed and now discoloured a dingy beige. Rather than wearing them as they'd been intended, he'd folded them double, like a dishcloth over a washing line. They'd grown dirty that way, and it was clear from the way he'd strung them, with dirt all on one side, that they'd never been worn as shorts.

I said we were on our way to Liawep. He looked up at me, his expression caught between amazement and fright. He pushed at the ground with his foot and dust puffed up. Was there anything we should take? He answered very softly: salt. But I had only one canister. I had brought matches and soap, but no salt. I kicked myself; it would have been so easy, and the Liawep, as I discovered later, would trade almost anything for salt – bows, arrows, pigs and bananas. Mostly the salt was traded up from the coast, but there was also a method, which no one seemed able to explain, of extracting it from plant pulp. It may have been an apocryphal plant, or indeed an apocryphal process, as it was always done by the people over that mountain, or in the lowlands, never those I asked.

All of which would have pleased Carol Jenkins. If the Liawep had begun trading with their neighbours, however recently, how could they be described as lost? Lost people would trade with no one, because no one would know of their existence. The Liawep, by contrast, seemed well-known in the neighbouring valleys: it was only to the outside world that they were lost, and the reason they had remained thus for so long was, it seemed, the fear in which they were held. No one had dared approach.

Tiring of my questioning, the Liawep man sat down, leaves tucked under and knees pulled up, looking out across the valley. The sky was clouding over again and beyond the mountain great banks of cloud were massing on the horizon. The wind had died with the stillness of coming rain.

It was midday, and I was keen to move on. We might, if we left now, reach the river by nightfall. By the end of the next day we could reach Liawep.

I should have known better than to try and rush our departure. These people among whom we had stopped, who lived here in this leaf-roofed barn, were insisting we eat with them. They were baking bananas for us, the fat green skirts I had noticed lying on their sides when we arrived. The man who had made the fire gestured us over; the bananas were spitting and bubbling in the flames, their unmarked skins cracking open.

I agreed to wait, though I hardly relished a meal of unripe banana. Even when baked until the skins were charred and flaky, the flesh still tasted chalky. They stuck, bitter and obstinate, to the roof of the mouth. The thought that, left a few weeks, they could have ripened into a sweet mellow fruit, made them impossible to enjoy.

We crouched round the fire, chewing drily. The man who had made the fire sat beside me, watching me pass the food to my mouth, as if nervous I was about to toss it in the fire. I smiled and smacked my lips as best I could. He turned to his own banana, shaving away the charcoaled skin with the point of his bushknife.

I asked him about Christianity. Had it come this far? Had he met Herod? I spoke through Titus and the answers I received were often answers to different questions. He had met Herod, he said. He'd come through a few times, on his way to Wanakipa.

'Are you a Christian?'

'No.' His teeth were caked with banana.

'Is anyone here Christian?'

'They are all my family,' he answered, strangely.

'But when Herod comes through, do you talk about God with him?'

'Herod is going to build a church.'

'Here?' There was only one house and fewer than twenty people, half of whom were children. Hardly enough to fill a church.

'No, on the hill up there.' He pointed to where we'd come from. They would clear the jungle. Then Herod could build the church. 'He says if we build the church they will send us our own priest.'

I asked him why he wanted a church, but the question seemed to anger him. His expression turned cool and he looked to Dunstan, who spoke for him.

Dunstan leaned towards me and delivered the stock missionary response. 'Because God's word is good. Before, they were killing each other. He knows God's word is good.'

My hypocrisy had begun to worry me. While questioning the benefits Christianity had brought, I was also praying feverishly. Prayer had underscored the whole journey, and it was impossible to remain immune. Vern had prayed when we'd flown to Wanakipa; Father Frank had prayed for us when we set off. Now I, too, was offering prayers, sometimes hourly, whenever a new paranoia entered my head. Before each meal we would pray. Usually Dunstan would rattle off the grace, but last night I'd said it. I'd thanked God for the food and then I'd asked Him to lighten our darkness. The words were soothing. They reminded me of Sunday evenings in my dressing-gown as a small boy and I enjoyed them as much for their rise and fall as for their meaning. Dunstan and the others believed completely.

Later that evening, conscious I was in danger of losing my detachment, I begged Dunstan not to let his Christianity stand in the way of my research. I needed straight answers, what they really felt and believed.

'But are you a Christian?' he pleaded.

'I am,' I hedged. 'But this is about more than just that. I want to hear them talk.'

He mumbled his answer, said he understood. He gave me his hand and we shook over the fire, with the other five watching. Malolo laughed a laugh which turned into a wet gargle, turned, spat into his hand and rubbed it in the dirt.

We left the next morning with one extra – a teenager called James who had an adolescent's tactless curiosity, who stared at me when I dressed or peed. But he was astonishingly fast and claimed he knew the way. When Dunstan said he could come with us he clapped his hands and shouted and ran to the house. He had been wearing leaf bumcover and a scrappy denim sporran. Now he appeared on the narrow balcony of a house in an unexpectedly chic red T-shirt and blue shorts. He stood there for a second, smoothed the shirt self-consciously, then jumped to the ground.

Now we were eight – six carriers, Dunstan and myself. A momentum was building. We still had three hours to walk. On the last climb the rain, which had held off this far, came down on our heads. The path cut straight up the jungleside and as the clouds gathered it became very dark under the canopy. Everything turned the colour of the black mud and the dark green leaves. The brightness, the orchids, butterflies and cockatoos all disappeared. It was just a noise at first, a rattling on the jungle roof, two hundred feet up. For a while I heard the noise and knew it was up there and because it hadn't come through yet I thought we'd stay dry. And then it split the canopy, beating on the leaves and falling heavily, ripe berries tipped out of the sky, squashing in my hair and on the path. Dunstan stopped Titus, untied the umbrellas from the rucksack he was carrying and passed me one. It arched open and the rain drilled on it but it was impossible to scramble upwards holding it upright, and before long I caught it on a thorn creeper and tore it open. The path was running with water and I kept slipping onto my knees and onto my side.

Near the top the rain eased and there was a slight breeze. It blew in my wet hair and on my T-shirt which clung to my back and chest. It was almost dusk and the brightness had gone from the sky. We had walked for ten hours, yet, inexplicably, I felt I could have walked more. For the first time I didn't complain or ask how far we had left to walk. When the others stopped and waited for me I smiled and leaned on my stick. The sight of the Liawep village had made everything real again.

We waded through grass chest-deep, a slashed-out garden now grown over, and came to a house in a small, fenced-off enclosure. This house, James said, belonged to his father and we could stay. Everywhere there was other travellers' debris – sweet potato husks and chewed bones which had been heaped on the fire as it was cooling and hadn't burned, only curled blackly and were now sodden and molested by hard black flies.

The house was smaller than Malolo's and was the first I'd seen not built on stilts. Inside it was completely dark. There were no windows, and the doorway gave on to a passageway, down which another hatch opened into the house. Inside, two fireplaces used most of the floor space. We would have to sleep around them.

Andrew made a fire outside. He used the dry wood stored under the eaves, replacing it, once the fire took, with wet logs. We sat round and the light died. There was no sunset; the colour just fell out of the sky. The orange uplight of the fire turned noses upside-down, lit necks and cheeks and made dark pools of eyes.

Titus took the piglet, still wrapped in its tight bundle of banana leaves, and cut the twine with a bushknife. He unfolded the leaves and the piglet looked smaller than before. Its hair was flattened to its skin and there was a cross pressed in its flesh where the twine had been bound. Titus tried to uncurl the animal, but it had frozen in the foetal position and would not move. He lifted it up by a back leg and lowered it onto the fire. Anxious not to burn himself, he dropped it six inches into a whoomph of ash.

Flames lapped round the piglet and its hair crackled and smelled of burnt tyres and fizzled away like short fuses until it was hairless. In the heat its body opened and one of its legs stretched outwards, sleepily. Titus reached into the fire with two long sticks, pinned the small body between them and levered it over to cook the other side. The exposed haunch was black and hairless. In places the skin had burned and contracted, and holes of grey flesh had torn open. He let it cook for a while longer and then lifted it from the fire. Its eyes had blackened and its ears had burned down to crumpled field mushrooms. Titus laid it back on the banana leaves and, when it had cooled a little, lifted it up and with the bushknife scraped off the brittle burnt hair, the remaining dusting. He wiped the black edge from the knife on his shorts, where it stayed in a dark tidemark. He wrapped the piglet in the leaves again.

'Aren't they going to eat it?' I asked Dunstan. I kept my voice low lest Titus heard and felt obliged to offer me some.

'They will eat it later, tomorrow perhaps. They have other food for today,' he added, which seemed unlikely.

So where we could have nibbled on roast piglet, we ate green banana and kaukau again, tempered with boiled rice and cold tinned mackerel. The food I'd brought was almost exhausted. I'd shopped for three and we were eight. They ate the rice and fish eagerly and I was too timid to impose rationing.

The night was cool. The sky had cleared and the stars were an extreme white, like neon city streets viewed from satellite. The moon was not yet up but we could see the mountains, dark and silvery like the sea and deep in their own shadow; only the very top of the jungle, the fish belly leaves, caught the starlight. It was silvery like the spines of grasses or silver birch leaves turned by wind; a steel sheen on black treacle oil.

This was remote country, across which these people now moved freely, without fear of enemy ambush. Here, though, in the furthest jungle, life had always been freer than in the densely populated eastern highlands. There were fewer people, and families moved every three or four years. Few missionaries and still fewer patrol officers had bothered with them.

The change had been sudden and recent. In the past year the Liawep had had their first missionary, their first brush with bureaucracy, their first church. In the eastern highlands there had been more tribal fighting because more was at stake. More people lived in less space, with homesteads surrounded by deep ditches, on prime, fertile land: rich, red earth.

It was this, the fact that every acre of bush was owned, that precipitated the bloodshed on Mick Leahy and Jack Hides' expeditions. Each tribe guarded its boundaries jealously, and was constantly prepared for war. What they took time to comprehend, of course, was that their spears and arrows were useless against rifles. This did not them stop them trying − in May 1931, Leahy's camp was attacked by tribesmen and Leahy himself was clubbed over the head. The casualties, however, were typical: six natives shot dead. As Leahy grew more experienced, so he hardened. Once, walking into a village, one of his carriers was grabbed by a hysterical woman, convinced this was her son, killed in a recent tribal skirmish, returned from the dead. Leahy remained untouched. His diary mentions only his hopes for striking gold: 'A couple of very fine colours out of the top layer of wash ... It looks good for the country further on.'

*

Stretching his hands towards the flames, Dunstan was warming into one of his favourite stories. I'd heard it before, the first day we met. Now it was the carriers' turn. Did they know, he teased, that missionaries were often eaten? They stared at him, not quite daring to smile. I puzzled over Dunstan, this uneasy union of devoutness and blasphemy.

'The mumu and the missionary,' he began. It sounded like a Just-So story. 'It was in the 1940s or 1950s. In Erave, or perhaps southern highlands province . . .' He paused, knowing he'd not started convincingly. 'Lots of people know the story,' he added. 'Somewhere near Erave.' He smiled, punchline in sight.

The missionary was a white man, venturing unwisely through cannibal territory. He had been speared to death and eaten. Dunstan began sniggering. 'Then they mumu his shoe. It was a brown boot, a brown stockman boot. They cooked it a couple of times, maybe three or four times they mumu it. But the shoe was still the same.' He paused, and looked around. Only I was laughing; the carriers were silent, embarrassed. 'Yes, very funny story,' Dunstan mumbled.

Titus, with awkward haste, unwrapped the piglet he'd taken so much trouble to cook. I'd assumed the leaves to be for storage, but now it seemed they were part of the preparation. He took a bushknife and laid the piglet on its spine on the bed of leaves. Its back was still curled up and Titus put it across his knee. There was a crack like bamboo cane snapping and the little body hinged in the middle of its back. He laid it on the leaves and traced a line down its belly with the bushknife tip. He then ran the knife to the sternum and pressed into the flesh. It sank in easily, like into butter, and he pulled it downwards, slitting the belly, between the nipples, tiny pink moles, until he reached the pelvis. He laid the knife down and pushed his fist through the envelope and pulled out a red tangle of spaghetti guts. He forced the thighs apart and used Dunstan's handaxe to cut through the joints. He cleaved the neck with one blow and the axe bit into the earth. He held up the head, its ears frazzled, snout puckered and crinkled black, hairless, with the eyes burned to dust.

Because I had shared my food, they now shared the pig with me and I was given a slab of skin and flesh off its back. It was mostly fat, with strips of meat clinging. It was difficult, in the dark, to tell whether the meat was red and bloody or tender and perfectly done, but it had a coldness which made me suspect the former. It tasted like frog, or underdone trout, the flesh dissolving. There was barely enough to go round. The others' lips and chins were shiny with juice, glistening like massage oil. It had leaked into Dunstan's beard, making it dark and lacquered. They slurped as they ate, breathing heavily through their noses. The cicadas were angry and electric in the jungle all around us.

We packed early the next morning and made tea over a soggy fire. For three hours we climbed down to the river. No one mentioned the bridge, superstitious, perhaps, that this might somehow precipitate its collapse. As we neared the valley bottom, the far mountainside came closer, cutting down towards us to meet the far bank. Finally we rounded a corner and were on top of the river. It was fuller, more orange and more poisonous. It boiled and curled and folded.

The path James had taken two weeks before was now submerged. It had run along the muddy beach, but the river was now full to the bank and there was no other path. We felt along, blindly, for flattish rocks to walk on. Even right in close to the banks the water was warm and deep, well over my knees. I felt along the bank with my hand, my feet moving from rocks to mud into which my ankles and calves sank. At points the river sank away underfoot and became too deep to wade and we would climb up the bank.

It was quite a way to the bridge. We waded along the submerged bank for another hour or two, the river curling slowly to the north, where it narrowed to a point and vanished into the jungle. I kept expecting to see the low loop of the bridge, but there was only the endless undulating green of the jungle, the riverbank, the river's orange drive. James had forgotten how far it was. 'Just round the corner,' he kept saying, but the curve of the river was one long corner.

We heard voices across the river. James yodelled back. I couldn't see them; the jungle was thick and unbroken, but James was waving and pointing and shouting upriver. He beat the water with his hand and moved on again and, sure enough, before long, the bridge came into view. I had prepared myself for it, the sagging arc, its belly on the water, and the real thing was exactly how I'd seen it, only smaller, from this distance. We were half a mile away, in water to our waists, and it looked like a cat's cradle, an insubstantial toy.

Up close, it was the opposite – twice or three times as big as the bridge we'd crossed four days earlier. It was a major work of engineering, a suspension bridge built without steel girders or bolts or joints, just bamboo, creeper rope and two strong trees as pylons. We sat in silence at its base. From here it was a day and a half to Liawep. I took off my shoes and socks. My feet were doughy and soft from too long compressed into damp shoes. James saw me examining them, parting my toes gingerly to see what lurked there.

He stuck out his index finger, advanced towards me, and prodded the sole of my foot. His touch was very soft. My feet were crumbly, like feta cheese. 'Ooh,' he gasped. 'Strange feet.'

The voices from the other side materialized into two boys, crossing the river. The bridge bounced and heaved as they came across, one starting the downhill slope when the other had almost reached the other side. The boys were a little awkward, yet graceful, with long fingers and long legs. They wore tanket leaves, with bows strapped across their chests, and stood gawping at me, waiting for action. Tentatively, one stuck out a hand, and shook each of ours in turn, pausing when he got to me. His handshake was boneless and I held it, afraid to squeeze. He had a charcoal smudge of hair on his upper lip, a fine downy dusting, too flimsy and foal-like to qualify as a moustache. They were out hunting but had caught nothing; they'd seen an emu, but it had run away. The smaller of the boys imitated the bird's waddle, putting his hands on his hips and wiggling his bum.

They spoke no pidgin. Dunstan communicated with them through Titus. 'Edward, this white man, wants to meet the Liawep. He has got permission from the government.' Dunstan had not told me he'd spin this one, but the lie was effortless and he did not flinch. 'You remember Peter Yasaro, the government man who came last year? He said Edward could come.'

The boys did not reply. When Dunstan finished talking they sat down with us. I shared out a packet of medicinal glucose tablets. They waited until I'd put mine in my mouth, placed the orange square on my tongue, then they did the same, looking sheepish. We sat by the river, in the shade, at the edge of the jungle. The sun was on the river, catching as the river folded, and we were on a worn circle of earth, sitting at the base of the ladder that led up to the bridge. It was still, but not quiet. The river roared like a distant motorway.

Were these Liawep boys? They were darker skinned than the carriers, and wore the same high headband as the man we'd met earlier, but because they would not speak to us, I did not know. I was prepared for reticence; much of the excess, the murder, the blind hate of Leahy and Hides' expeditions, had been caused by a simple failure of communication. Too often, the explorers misread a welcome as a threat, and opened fire.

The bridge was a long, pulsing thing. We crossed one at a time. It seemed a long way across as I stood at the top, contemplating the crossing, the dip into the river and the climb up the other side. And it was a long way – twenty, perhaps thirty metres. The bridges were built in the dry season, when the rivers were half the size, made on one side of the river and swung across on rafts. They were continually patched as the rains came, but when the rivers were high, maintenance was impossible. This one was badly in need of repair. In the middle, where the bamboo dipped under the water, there was only the occasional strip of twine holding the 'V' together. Any more rain, and the bridge would go. It would tear apart in the middle and the two halves would hinge away under the weight of water, pulling away from their trees, and that would be that.

I worried, as I crossed, about the return. Another night of rain and we'd be trapped the wrong side of the river. In the middle, for a six-foot section, the bamboo went unsupported, and I crossed it in two big strides. As I stepped up the far side, the belly of the bridge lifted out of the water and the bridge swung with my motion. I could feel it, heavy under its own weight, borne down with the water in the bamboo and shearing from the strips of twine trailing up from the water. It felt like I was walking the spine of a huge, sleeping snake, or was a dwarf on a horse's back, underfoot its breathing and the subterranean thud of its heart. I stood at the top the other side, between the two support trees, the legs of this pre-metal structure, and looked back. It would not be in place when we returned, I felt sure.

Chapter 9

James waved us forward. This was his father, in whose house we'd stayed the night before. The old man was unsmiling and seemed far too old to be James' father, although ages were impossible to guess. He cut an extraordinary figure, rendered more comic by his unbending earnestness. He lay on his back, regal and languid as we crouched, in turn, to shake his hand. It was as if he was king of these miles of untamed jungle, with only sweet potato to feed his subjects. He had a large fleshy mole in the hollow of each cheek and wore two necklaces of miniature cowrie shells, with two larger, fist-sized cowries as pendants. The nylon of his green Converse baseball cap was peeling away from the cardboard peak. He spoke solemnly to James, who stood with his head bowed.

It was early afternoon, the rain had stopped and the sun was burning. We had walked away from the bank up a well-worn path, coming before long to a newly cut clearing, with raw tree stumps still oozing sap and the ground littered with curling leaves. There was a shelter, a roof which ran to the ground and underneath ten people huddled from the sun.

Would we stop here? I wanted to move on; we were so close. Dunstan had taken off his cap and was leaning against a tree. His hair was glossy with sweat. He wanted to stay here the night, and climb to Liawep the next morning.

A hot afternoon stretched out before us. I said I wanted to walk to the river to wash and somehow this became a sign for everyone to do likewise. James warned us away from the Lagaip. It was a bad river, he said, repeating what we'd heard before — that those who washed in it died. So instead we walked on, through the clearing, and down to another river. It was a cloudy green, stirred up with grey mud and glittering. It ran shallow over rocks and, at this point, near the confluence with the Lagaip, it forked. We waded through the first fork, where the water was shallow and raced in the sunlight. In the middle we stopped on an island where a long tree trunk lay beached. The other side the water was deeper and greener, cool and sweet. I kicked off my shoes and was undoing my shorts when Dunstan shouted my name.

He was hopping from foot to foot, a towel bundled chaotically under his arm. 'Wait a minute, please.' He scuffled over. His anxiety was perplexing. Was nudity forbidden, even in the wilderness? I wanted to wash. My skin felt suffocated with mud and sweat and the build-up of salty fear.

'Please,' he said, when he was up close. 'Keep your sports-wear on.' He clasped his hands together. My shorts were round my ankles.

He jerked his head. The carriers were a few yards off,

undressing carefully. 'It's the missionaries. They say it's bad to take off your clothes.'

'You don't believe that, do you? We're in the middle of the jungle.' I was overheating.

'In Tari, yes, I take my clothes off sometimes. But here you have to be careful.' He insisted and got his way. I left my underpants on.

Perhaps this modesty, ludicrous though it seemed, should not have surprised me. While missionaries have regarded Papua New Guinean cultures, with their nakedness, exotic, 'primitive' ways and casual violence, as the embodiment of devilry, the natives themselves have accepted the missionaries with a trust that has bordered on gullibility. In the early days of the administration, villagers were charged a mission levy. One day a beachcomber, a white man with a long Messianic beard, passed through, claiming to be Jesus; he'd come for his tax. The people, assuming generosity would guarantee salvation, gave everything they had.

James and Dison were in the water, fully dressed. James was swimming across the current which hit out midstream and picked him up. He flailed through, doing a frantic wheeling crawl, with his head, like a dog's, held out of the water, neck straight up. He reached the far bank, laughing and panting, twenty yards downstream. Dison stood knee-deep, a comb and a mirror in one hand, my bar of soap in the other.

I heaped my clothes on a flat rock and hobbled across the shingle. The water dropped away into soft, cloudy mud that turned it from green to slate grey when my toes sank in. The beached tree trunk stretched across the water, its belly flat on the shingle island. I hung my towel and soap over it and lowered myself into the current. Out of respect, I washed with my underpants on, a complicated manoeuvre that ended with my buttocks slippery with soap. Dison, I noticed, did not attempt to wash underneath his. He scooped up handfuls of water and splashed them over his chest and face, leaving his armpits and legs. He sat on a rock to dry himself and then dressed in a clean T-shirt and from his pocket pulled a candy-pink crucifix, bearing a silvery Jesus, hands and feet pinned with tin tacks. He scrubbed his beard with clothes soap.

We returned to the clearing and sat down beside the lean-to. James' father now wore an ivory emu claw in his nose and lay propped on one elbow, his face turned towards us. He spoke about the Liawep in reverent, hushed tones, savouring the drama. We should be careful when climbing up to the village; we should say we were 'going down', rather than 'climbing up'. But more important, we should carry up armfuls of firewood, dry and ready stripped. 'If you don't,' he said haughtily, 'you will be crippled.'

Dison tapped me on the shoulder. 'That's everyone,' he said. 'Everyone must bring firewood. Even you, masta. Dunstan, you, each one, or they will cripple us.' He tucked both arms in, folded tight, to his chest, and curled his wrists back. He made a slick scaremonger.

We sat with the old man in the windless clearing as hot afternoon turned to warm evening. There were long periods of silence. Before dark fell, Dunstan stood up and stretched. It was time to build a shelter. The sun slanted sideways, red and lazy, through the jungle. Butterflies and dragonflies jerked about erratically, silhouetted against the sun. A little boy was squashing ants against a tree trunk with a wooden mallet. He had perfect dusted nutty skin which glowed. The ants poured from a hole and funnelled in single file round the top curve of the trunk. The boy struck as soon as a new troop walked out. The mallet face was sticky with the dark squashed fruit.

Dunstan was standing, shirt off and shorts rolled up, leaning on my stick, ordering the carriers about. They were making the shelter at the edge of the clearing, with two trees as the upright wall. From there they lashed diagonal poles to the ground and tied down the blue tarpaulin tightly. It filtered a bluey shadow on the ground. Andrew was inside, tucking leaves round the bottom edge to make a seal, and the blue made his skin grey and deathly.

We sat under the tarpaulin and the old man joined us. He had dressed up and now wore a nylon dress with a fine steel zip down the front, neck to hem. It was quartered into pastel ice-cream shades – strawberry, vanilla, lime, milk chocolate. He wore it with pride.

When I asked him about the Liawep again, he seemed guarded. Questions he'd previously been happy to answer now seemed intrusive. I asked him what religion they followed and heard Dison mumble something. The old man said he didn't know and sat dumb.

In an attempt to smooth over the rift, I asked him about his family. How many wives did he have? He laughed, regally. 'Three.'

'I thought Christians were only allowed one wife.'

'I am quite recently a Christian. Two years only.'

'Shouldn't you change your ways?'

'I love them all. It would not be Christian to leave them.'

Two of his wives had been at his feet earlier. Three was the minimum, he said. A man could not manage on less. They had different roles. One tended the garden, one cooked, and one shared his bed. He loved them all.

He was fortunate to have been able to sustain such a decadent practice. In communities where missionaries exercised a tighter stranglehold, there was no such luxury. In 1936, the *Pacific Islands Monthly* reported the case of a native charged with killing his wife. In defence, he had pleaded that he had wanted two wives, as was the custom. When the missionary had forbidden him to take a second, he had solved the problem by murdering the first. He was hanged.

James' father, getting into his stride, began boasting of his pigs. Women and pigs. Men's talk.

'I have ten.' He grinned a mouthful of blackened teeth.

'Ten! And are they all fat?'

'Very fat!' He squeezed a plump, imaginary buttock.

I felt an unexpected surge of affection for him and fished out my chocolate-chip biscuits from Dison's string bag. They were imported from Australia and were enormously expensive. I had only two bags, supposedly for emergencies. I pulled at the seam and the bag tore open. I held them out and he grabbed the bag. He clutched it to his chest and I could hear the scrunching of biscuits. 'No,' I said, suddenly regretting the impulse. 'Have one, then pass them on.' I pointed round the widening circle, faces expectant in the firelight. Clutching the bag close, he stuck a hand in and took out two. He pressed them into his mouth, powdering his cheek with demerara crumbs.

He passed them on, eventually, and the bag rustled round the circle. I took one, and was preparing to save the rest, when he snatched it, scooped his hand into the bottom, sweeping up crumbs and crushed remains. He lowered his head to his hand and licked the chocolate off his palm. He funnelled the bag into his mouth with a shiffle of crumbs. He nodded once, folded the bag in half, in half again, placed it inside his hat and put the hat back on his head.

It was dark but far from quiet. The insects shouted insolently in the gloom. From the jungle there was the crash of under-growth and a man's voice, calling out.

'It's Herod and the hunters,' the old man said. I strained my eyes where he pointed.

'What's he doing down here?' I was stunned by the coincidence – to meet the Liawep priest here, by chance, in a jungle clearing, after such a journey.

'He likes to hunt wild pig. He likes to kill. Here he is!'

From out of the darkness came a slight, boyish man, picked out by the orange firelight which brushed his face and chest as he walked over. In his right hand he held a snake by the jaw. Its eyes popped and mouth hung open. Herod had thin, contortionist's legs which he folded under him and sat down, laying the dead snake by the fire.

He looked softer than Yasaro's photograph. The image I remembered gave such an aspect of fury that I was astonished by this man, who looked so gentle and mild. His eyes were alive and bright and he seemed intrigued rather than suspicious. Perhaps I had been too quick to judge.

He was nervy and excited, and had very little, very dark brown eyes. He breathed noisily through his mouth. A scarlet flower was caught in his damp, scratchy beard. He saw me looking at it and rubbed it away, rolling it into a crushed velvet smudge.

He shook my hand firmly, though he seemed astonished to see me. I wasn't sure how to begin. Meeting him here, a day before I'd expected, had caught me off guard. All this way I'd been planning introductions, working out the right mixture of tact and persuasion, but was taken aback by his sudden appearance. I decided to bring up the Liawep indirectly, as if they were only part of the reason I'd come to the jungle, but as he stared my resolve slipped. He leaned forward, smiling like an eager child, asked what I was doing, and I blurted it straight out: 'We've come to meet the Liawep.' He edged back and his face closed off. He looked around for the men he was hunting with, but they were sitting on a log a few yards away.

'You are not the first,' he said, finally. His eyes were cold, like oil. He shifted away, turning his back to me in a gesture of calculated dismissal. He looked out into the night, the warm, deep jungle. I leaned round, trying to catch his eye, but he only swivelled further away, crumbling tobacco into his palm.

The two men with whom he had arrived were watching me warily, sitting on a tree trunk a little way off, dangling little-boy legs. I asked Herod who they were, but he shook his head violently. Ignoring him, I waved them over.

Firesmoke was trapped under the tarpaulin and they sat down, screwing up their eyes. One was dressed in tanket leaves but the other, shorter and thicker-set, wore a red T-shirt with cutaway sleeves. There was a steel badge in the middle of his chest, clipped on with an outsize nappy pin.

'What does that say?' I said. Herod grunted, just loud enough to halt the conversation.

'Luluai,' the man answered. 'Luluai, Oksapmin District.'

'*Wanem samting i min?*'

'Leader,' Herod snapped, swinging round and rapping the badge with a dirt-ridged fingernail. 'Peter made him leader of the Liawep.'

So this was Jack. It had been a bewildering hour. One after the other, quite by chance, I had met the two central characters in the story. First Herod, who had first excited Yasaro to the possibility of a lost tribe. Now Jack, without whom there would have been no story, no jubilant Yasaro proclaiming his discovery, and no newspaper articles. He was the reason I was here. Without his journey, I would never have begun mine.

I leaned across to shake his hand. Yasaro had described him as a boy, but he looked older. He was balding, both temples cut away in smooth, hairless paths from his forehead. Thirty, I guessed. His nails were bitten right down and feathery.

'*Nem bilong yu Jack?*'

'*Jeeyck*,' he said, his voice gentle.

I told him I'd come to meet the Liawep. When I mentioned Peter Yasaro he smiled dreamily. 'Yes, Peter.' I asked him how it had happened. I'd heard this so many times, from so many sources, but it was Jack's story. I had to hear it from him.

Herod, unable to pretend uninterest any longer, turned towards us. He stared at Jack; the carriers, sensing drama, moved closer in anticipation. Dison passed Jack a cigarette, token of respect, and Jack took it and grinned back. He lit it and pulled hard, flattered by the audience.

'I was scared because I lived in the bush and I never saw those type of things like plane and cars.' He described the long walk through the jungle and his astonishment at reaching Oksapmin. It was an odd feeling, hearing this story again, like stepping back in history and speaking to kings and queens I'd only read about in the classroom. It was a long way from the fantasy I'd first read in a newspaper. The Liawep were not nomadic; they did not worship a head-shaped rock; they had not been discovered by Baptist missionaries; they had not, at least not yet, been rounded up.

Jack had walked to Oksapmin because his grandfather was ill and because he'd been told there were doctors and hospitals there. Peter Yasaro had taken him in and given him clothes. When, six months later, he returned to Liawep, his grandfather had already died. His family blamed him, saying it would never have happened if he'd returned sooner. When their anger was exhausted he told them what he'd seen. 'I said there was rice and aeroplanes and it was better living in the town than in the bush like us. But they were frightened. They said, "Will they kill us if we go there?" I said, "No, they are the same people as us."'

So, until Jack discovered Oksapmin, the Liawep had known nothing of the outside world. This pleased me – despite the barrage of cynicism, I still believed in the possibility of lost, or at least isolated, tribes, and Jack vindicated my faith. Yet it was extraordinary, too. How could this small jungle tribe have remained so ignorant and incurious for so long?

Jack stared at me as if I'd shone a bright light in his eyes. 'Nobody came to tell us these places existed, so how could we know? It's six days' walking.' He looked round at the others, with his eyebrows raised, as if expecting support, but no one spoke.

I asked him if he'd walk to Liawep with us the next day, but he shook his head. He was travelling to the other side of the valley and would be gone a week. This was a blow – to have had the support of Jack, Liawep leader and pidgin speaker, would have been invaluable. As it was, this might be the last time I'd see him. I needed to know what he felt about the changes and hear his hopes for the future. So I asked, but halfway through the question Herod interrupted loudly, 'Tell him about the patrol, Jack.'

Jack, confused, addressed the fire. 'Peter brought clothes for us. He gave me short trousers and shirt, because he was my friend. The others got one thing or perhaps nothing.'

A gecko started up on the pole above our heads. It had been sitting quietly enough, but now started rattling crack-crack-crack. Dunstan struck the pole with my stick and the gecko raised its square head, jerked it to either side, then vanished. Jack stroked his badge. He looked suddenly tired and far away and his fingers felt round the machine-stamped grooves. I tried to persuade him to change his plans and accompany us. Herod was coming, I said, unsure whether this was a reason to come or go. Stories of the Liawep's volatile temper and the weight of their neighbours' superstitions had worn away at me and I was keen to arrive in the village protected. But Jack was adamant.

He was taking news of a birth to a neighbouring tribe and could not turn back.

Herod had been concentrating so hard on Jack, so anxious he'd somehow be tricked into revealing all, that he'd let his cigarette go out. It hung, cooling and soggy, from the corner of his mouth. I pressed on, afraid I might not get another chance to talk to Jack. I explained why I'd come all this way. 'I heard about you in my country and wanted to meet you. I wanted to hear your stories.'

Jack grinned, but before he could reply, Herod snorted and cracked his knuckles. 'Stories!' he spat.

The prospect of Herod looming over every conversation as prompt and censor was depressingly bleak. I could only hope that, once at Liawep, he'd be too busy with other things to worry about me. Now, when I bent forward to ask Jack a question, he leaned with me. I persevered, swallowing my irritation.

'You're the leader, Jack,' I said, ignoring Herod. 'What future do you see for the Liawep?'

'I want them to move closer, to make Liawep a bigger place. If we move to an airstrip then the government will help us. That's what Peter said.'

'And do the people want to move?'

'I tell them to, because I am the luluai, but they are not so sure.'

'What about Peter? Is he coming back?'

Jack looked away. 'He has not yet come back. He said we should move, but he has not yet come back.' He scratched away at a scar on his knee, itching it to dust with chewed nails. It was starting to rain again, the first drops ticking on the tarpaulin drumskin. Dunstan, Herod, Jack and I edged over to where the others sat close to the fire. Titus was drying tobacco over the embers. Steam lifted off the leaf.

'He will come back,' Jack mumbled, smoothing out a banana leaf to sit on.

Jack had seen the promised land and could not forget it. He repeated 'aid post', 'MAF'(Missionary Aviation Fellowship), 'trade store', 'airstrip', over and over like a mantra. Perhaps they would materialize if he said them often enough. He'd seen the modern world and had had to return to mud and artless poverty and he knew which he preferred. The gulf was deeper and wider for him than for the others. He wanted action and his words were coloured with an unvoiced desperation and choked resentment that nothing had yet happened. He remained loyal to Yasaro but as the months passed this became harder and harder.

What he did not know was that, to Yasaro, he was nothing special. Jack knew nothing of the system whereby, since exploration of the highland jungles began in the 1930s, patrol officers had adopted young boys from newly contacted villages, taught them pidgin and used them as interpreters and go-betweens. Yasaro had gone one step further – he had appointed Jack leader, presumably over the head of the existing chief, thus establishing government control. Jack was a useful tool of power, little more.

But he was also wiser than I credited; he had not invested everything in Yasaro's return. The gold company represented a possibility for improvement, too. In the hope that the gold diggers would return, Jack had ordered a helipad to be built, and was convinced this would guarantee a delivery of medicines and clothes.

The year before, in the dry season, the prospectors' helicopter had come down in the riverbed. The Liawep ran down through the jungle and saw it land. 'Pooff!' Jack threw his hands in the air to simulate the beaten dust. The prospectors dug in the river for two days, panning the water, then took off upriver.

Herod, finally, had bored of our conversation. I had deliberately avoided any discussion of religion, and the tactic seemed to have worked. He had grown listless and moved off; now he was lying on the ground, his head on a rock. He blew smoke upwards where it flattened and spilled against the tarpaulin roof. I moved closer to Jack and lowered my voice, anxious Herod should not hear.

'When I asked you earlier about your religion,' I whispered, 'Herod said you didn't worship anything. He said you went round in the bush hunting and killing. Em tru?'

'Enemies.' Jack looked anxiously at Herod. 'We were frightened of our enemies.'

'Yes, Herod said that. Didn't you have any God? When you needed strength, did you pray?' He looked at me quizzically. 'Did you ask help from anything?' I closed my hands in mock prayer and looked heavenwards. Jack laughed. I looked anxiously at Herod, but his eyes were closed.

'Our ancestors', Jack said, labouring the word, 'worshipped things like fat-growing bananas and taro. And we worship the mountain. It shakes the earth when it is angry and it helps us in battle.'

Chapter 10

We never did bring the firewood, and I'm sure we said we were climbing up rather than going down. The only hint that we were getting close was Herod's acceleration. We were still in dark, deep jungle, when suddenly, like a dog that has smelled its supper, he broke into a trot. When I came out over the rise he was nowhere, and around me the jungle started to thin. Fifty yards ahead I saw him disappearing into waist-high grass, the sun on his back. He was climbing to a crest.

He shouted, his voice thin yet commanding, and I heard the word 'patrol'. He was warning people of our approach. Buoyed by the nearness of our goal, I hurried after him, then waited, in a sunny patch of jungle, for Dunstan and the others, who had slipped way behind. I did not want to enter the village alone.

It was hot and still. They took ages to arrive. 'We there?' panted Dunstan when he reached me. He stood beside me for a few minutes, his beard oily with sweat and his eyes blank.

It was late afternoon when we came over the ridge. The jungle had been cleared here, and we walked through deep grass, along fallen tree trunks, up towards a clearing. As we reached the crest I looked around for Herod, expecting to see him waiting, but there was no one, just the hiss of sun lifting rain off grass.

Ahead, in the clearing, was the village, this place it had taken six days to reach. It was built on a shoulder, three hundred yards long and a hundred wide. At the edges of the spur the jungle dropped sheer away.

I could see six houses – each scattered about the perimeter, save one which stood alone in the middle of the clearing. There was little neighbourliness about this; each occupied its own territory, fringed with sprays of wild green shrubbery.

I climbed out of the grass and looked around. The spot on which we stood was distinctive: a circular plateau, free of weeds. The ground was smooth, as if levelled and flattened by hand. In the middle was a circle of green leaves, three foot across. This, I felt sure, must be the helipad Jack had built, and the leaves the marker for pilots. The earth was the colour of flapjacks and sticky from the rain.

From here, looking uphill towards the mountain behind, the village looked established, permanent. Hardpacked paths crossed the spur, the result of years of padding feet. At one edge, as the slope dropped away into the jungle, trees had been cleared and there were staked enclosures and fresh-turned earth: people lived here and worked the land. And yet, despite feeling like a 'proper' village, with its centre, its houses, it felt strangely displaced, too, so high and isolated. The drop-off into the jungle was so sheer I imagined myself launching off the edge into effortless flight, immediately a thousand feet up.

The houses themselves, though, were falling into disrepair and looked as if the next storm might wash them from their perch into the jungle below. The walls were insubstantial, of thin planks whipped together, held in place by vine rope. Roofs were dried leaves, overlapping like slates. All stood on stilts, except for the lone house in the centre. Their roofs were blackened with age and firesmoke and, from the biggest, at the far end of the village, thick grey smoke leaked, spilling from under the eaves, tarring the pale leaves black with soot. That house, unlike the others, had a window, a tiny handkerchief-square high up on one wall.

I walked forward, past the first house, expecting to find people talking or cooking, but there was no one. I came to a wooden fence, sturdy and thickened with logs, laid between posts to form an impassable wall. It looked like a pig fence, and in places the mud was stamped by hooves, but I could see no pigs.

Bright green shrubs grew in careless corners: these were tobacco plants, their leaves hairy and sticky, heads heavy with seed. From the jungle canopy a cloud of cockatoos exploded, screeching. By the fence I noticed a heap of *kaukau* tubers, just harvested. When I touched them they were warm, as if they had been hurriedly dropped, just minutes before. I had a feeling of being watched from the shadows, but when I turned there was no one. Far below, in the valley, the river whispered.

Where the ground was not beaten hard, bushes of weeds grew furiously, as blowsy and unkempt as the tobacco. At the edge of the clearing, where the ground began to slip away, they billowed like an old man's beard. Further on, past the house in the middle, there were signs of life − a circle of grey ash, smouldering logs, footprints in the mud.

It was ghostly quiet. While the carriers stood together, as if for safety, I took a few steps on. I could not understand it. The village was bleak and abandoned. Never had I felt so foreign. For the first time, I found myself longing to see Herod, anyone.

I returned, bewildered, to Dunstan and the carriers. They had their backs to me and were pointing to the mountains and valleys across which we had climbed. From here, high up, the landscape looked almost tame; to look across the jungle, at the mountains cloaked in deep green, gave no clue of what lay under, the difficulty of the land we had crossed. The view, this unassailable height, made Liawep seem a warriors' village in a stronghold position, hard to surprise, simple to defend. Ahead, over four or five ranges, was Wanakipa, six days' walk. The Lagaip River folded and curved, bluey, into the distance.

The village was not what I had expected. For weeks I'd carried Yasaro's photographs in my head and built an image of a low-down scrubby place in muddy colours. I'd pictured the village down by a river, but in fact it was isolated high on a ridge, with a view for miles on all sides. It felt like a holy place, higher than every mountain except the one under which it stood. It had a bold simplicity – these small, wooden houses, the forested peak. We were here, finally. Dunstan grinned at me crazily.

The mountain was obscured by cloud, the only cloud on this still, blue-late afternoon. I stared at it and found the others were staring, too. We'd heard so much about it, how the Liawep feared and worshipped it, and were now seeing it for the first time. It was impossible to gauge the distance – two miles away, perhaps ten, it rose steep from the far end of the village where the clearing ended and the jungle began again. Thick, dark forest ran up into the cloud. The slopes climbed sheer: it seemed alive, brooding and malevolent. In my apprehensive state, neither here nor there, having arrived and not yet welcomed, I did not find it hard to imagine why the Liawep revered the mountain. It seemed to have a power all its own. It made me shudder just to look at it.

Yet there was no one. The wind had dropped and the sun beat down. The stillness made me uneasy. Where was everyone? The arrival of Yasaro's patrol had been a big event – he'd shown me photographs of his men entering the village, shaking hands with each Liawep in turn. So I'd expected a reception committee, or at least an excited hollering, but there was nothing, just the murmur of a distant waterfall. Apart from the smoke leaking from the eaves of the furthest house, there was no sign of life. The place felt eerie and deserted, as if the people had been driven out by plague.

At the far end of the clearing, where the jungle was beginning to grow back and tree stumps stuck up like stubble from bright new growth, smoke curled up thinly, rising straight in the still air. Looking closer, I saw two women crouched over a fire, both with shaved heads and grass skirts. Until now they had been hidden from sight by the central house, but when I moved to one side I could see them clearly. One was bent over a cooking pot; the other poked the fire.

Dunstan nudged me and giggled. Their breasts were naked, he sniggered, gesturing crudely, mimicking their pendulous droop. The women, hearing him, turned towards us. They fled, knocking over the pot, spilling steaming water on to the hissing mud. They ducked into a grove of banana trees, their grass skirts rustling, and were gone.

I turned to Dunstan, confused and frightened. Was Herod, too, in hiding? It was hot out here in the sun, standing on the flat circle of the helipad, lost. My neck was burning.

Dunstan suggested I cry out. This seemed too violent – the sound would carry for miles. As if in answer to my bewilderment, there was a clatter and creaking from inside the nearest house. I looked round. The house was built on the edge of a shoulder, the back wall twice as deep as the front to compensate for the drop-off. A shallow roof spread wide, giving the house a skirt of dark shadow.

On to the veranda stepped a man with a sprouting of tanket leaves over his behind. In the shadows he seemed slight and very old. Only when he stepped into the sunlight did I see it was Herod. Without his clothes there was nothing to him; hairless, hollow-chested, he looked pitiably fragile.

But his face was hard and set. He leaned on a stick and eyed us, half smirking. He moved back into the shade and drummed his fingers on the balustrade rail. For a full minute we looked at him and he at us. He let us wait. No one spoke. I looked away at the smoking house further uphill. A black bird wheeled slowly overhead, its shadow skating across the mud. Titus whispered something to Andrew. When Herod shouted, his voice was rude and shrill. 'What are you doing?'

I stared at him, incredulous. We were doing nothing, he could see that. It was hot. I needed shade. He shouted again, for us to come over. It was an order, not an invitation.

Herod waited until we had all filed along the veranda, then followed us inside. The floor was made of planks softened by the ceaseless rain and was springy underfoot. The door, at the far end, was narrow and low; I had to duck my head and twist my shoulders to pass through. Inside, the darkness was thick and suffocating. The room was gritty with warm smoke.

We stood awkwardly round the door while our eyes adjusted to the blackness. Herod, the last in, pushed past and I could hear him talking in pidgin, explaining to someone who we were, these eight displaced strangers.

The room was low and square and cramped. When I moved forward my forehead brushed against something papery. I reached up. It crackled: tobacco hung to dry.

In the centre of the room was a fire, sunk six inches below the level of the floor. With the door closed, this gave the only light. On the far side, brushed in orange light, sat a woman in a blowsy floral dress with ruffed short sleeves, like the paper socks on roasted chicken legs. Herod was bent over her, whispering low.

She sat cross-legged. In the bowl of her skirt was a tiny naked baby. While she listened, she stroked the baby's head. It mewled quietly, a little moan every time it exhaled.

Herod stopped speaking and sat on the floor beside her. Together, very slowly, they looked up at us. Herod bent over the baby and tickled its ribs. It stuck out a pink tongue and gurgled.

'Well,' he muttered, without looking up, 'you'd better sit down.'

I chose a spot close to the fire, opposite Herod. Behind me Dunstan and the carriers shifted heavily on the floorboards. Herod, with studied indifference, began to roll a cigarette, crumbling tobacco into his palm.

'Herod,' I began tentatively, '*olgeta Liawep* – where is everyone?'

He jerked his head upwards. His eyes were lost in shadow. He spoke so softly I had to lean forward, screwing my eyes against the smoke. It was my fault, he whispered. They had never seen a white man before and feared me. They had known of our approach for the past day and had watched us from the shadows as we neared the village. This meant they would have seen me struggle in the mud, lose my footing, fall on my knees; no one could believe me dangerous after witnessing that, surely?

But Herod insisted. I could see it in his cold, hard eyes, black and unblinking. He pulled on his cigarette until the tip fizzed. A spark leapt towards me.

I distrusted him, but knew I would need him on my side. It felt impossible. I explained that I wanted him to translate – I did not yet know whether Titus spoke Liawep well enough – but regretted it immediately.

'They will not talk to you. *Ol no tokim.*' He gave a sly smile.

'*Bilong wanem?*' I was struggling to keep calm.

'Because you are a white man. But don't worry, I will tell you what they think.'

Still smiling, he turned to stroke the baby's head. She was his child, he said – Evelyn – and the woman, Elisa, his wife. These were not names they had been born with but, as with himself, Dunstan and the carriers, names given them on baptism. Elisa blinked when she heard her name. When Herod pulled away she slipped her dress off one shoulder and cupped the baby's head close to her nipple. It whimpered gently, its face submerged.

Tobacco smoke gathered in the rafters. As we talked I searched for a way into Herod's confidence – I had to make myself useful to him. In return, he might loosen his grip. So I asked him about his church, even though it was now dusk and too late to explore it and praise his craftsmanship.

He had started to build it the day after he arrived, telling the Liawep that the mountain they worshipped was less important than God. 'God made the mountain, so we must build him a house.' Herod stopped and looked at me with his head tilted to one side, eyebrows raised, waiting for my next question.

I wanted to know what the Liawep made of it, this sudden upsetting of their beliefs and imposition of Christianity. But Herod sidestepped the question. Instead, sensing a sympathetic ear, he began to unburden himself.

He did not have an easy life, he complained, not easy at all. He had not, initially, wanted to come, fearing the lost tribesmen would turn out to be cannibals. But Father Frank had reassured him: cannibals did not eat men of God. Now, though, the Lutheran church had abandoned him. They'd given him no money, no kerosene for his lamp, no nails to build his house and no hinges for his doors. 'Look,' he said, his lips wet with anger. He stood up and walked to the door. 'No door.' He stepped out, and back in again. 'Just a plank we put across at night. This house was built without nails. Very hard.'

The house, in fact, was typical bush. None of the other jungle houses were nailed together, all were lashed with twine, but Herod came from Wanakipa, where there was a solar-powered fridge and a radio, and he expected more.

'And that's not all!' He was shouting now. 'I have no medicines. A few pills maybe, but no medicines, and the people die all the time of malaria and fever and what can I do? I am just a priest.'

His mood changed as quickly as sun followed storms. His volatility seemed like a madness. One moment he would be sweetness and gratitude, the next, frothing indignation. There was something adolescent in him that age and responsibility had not mellowed. He made me uncomfortable and when he turned his head away I edged back from the fire, away from him.

He complained bitterly of the battle he had fought with the mountain, his struggle to persuade the Liawep that it was his God that had made their mountain, and so was more deserving of veneration.

He had resented the coming of Yasaro's patrol. Yasaro had brought clothes for the people, but this had only complicated Herod's ministry: to teach the Liawep not to covet each other's possessions had been easy when they had none. He frothed as he spoke, spittle suspended in the firelight.

Three missionaries had accompanied the patrol; all planned to return to build their own churches. The Seventh Day Adventist had brought a Bible and a big poster chart, like a wall calendar, which told the Bible story. God was pictured as tall and American, with a toga and flowing blond hair. 'In heaven,' he had told the Liawep, 'people have white skin.'

The patrol had disrupted Herod's relationship with the Liawep. They now knew what lay beyond the valleys and the knowledge made them restive. Hardest had been Yasaro's insistence that they should move. Here Herod was caught – he wanted the people to have access to medicine, yet did not want to see them forced from their homes.

Herod fumbled over his words, laying open his confusion. While, initially, he had resented the intrusion, he now wanted the patrol to return, and looked forward to a helicopter carrying everything Yasaro had promised – soap, malaria pills, rice and salt – but every day the sky was still and the only sound was the distant whisper of the river and the tick of axes on wood. Almost a year had now passed, and Herod could not forget it. It seemed a shame, almost like a grief, how reality could fall this short of expectation, and it made me see the Liawep in a new light. Until now I'd imagined them besieged by the twentieth century. The truth might be the opposite – that their first contact had given them a taste for the trappings of civilization that was never going to be sated.

But it was not that simple. In the past year there had been one other visitor, a stranger who had walked down from the mountain wearing a blue shirt and a yellow badge on his cap. He had explained that he worked for a gold company and was prospecting on the mountain. It was too early to say whether there was any gold, but he had reports of an evil man and woman living up there. One of his men, on a foray, had come face to face with them, naked and smeared in black mud. They had long spears and long oily hair; they snarled like dogs and had blood on their teeth. His man had crashed up through the jungle, not looking back. The man from the gold company said he'd come to warn the Liawep to keep away from the mountain.

The fairy-tale element to this story was at once astonishing and yet also what I'd come to expect. So often, cliché and surprise ran side by side. Later, I met the government official responsible for the region in which the Liawep lived. Until then I had doubted Herod's story about the 'company man'. Herod had mentioned it often and it always struck me as a fiction, designed to lure my attention away from his work with the tribe. Yet the official had nodded and unfolded an application from BHP and Kennecott, two multinational mining companies, for an exploration licence, the first step to mining. When I took out my map and showed him where I believed the Liawep lived, he became excited. The story of the evil couple was a device, he believed, to prevent the Liawep from snooping.

Suddenly Herod fell quiet. When he spoke again his voice was low and menacing. 'I think the Liawep do not listen. Some come to church and then they don't come again. And the ones who do come do not remember the words. I tell them the same prayers every time, to make it easy, but still they do not remember.'

This surprised me. Despite the stories we'd heard of their

EDWARD MARRIOTT

love of war and their taste for blood, I pictured them in feeble
capitulation to Christianity. That was the pattern elsewhere: at
the 1966 census only seven per cent of the population said
they still followed the religion of their ancestors. But here was
Herod, admitting to a struggle. It cheered me.

Yet, statistics aside, there was no reason to assume the
Liawep should have been a pushover. The first missionaries
had dedicated their lives, while Herod was a product of the
modern world – impatient, expecting quick results. He disci-
plined them fiercely, yet had no thought for consequences. I
couldn't help feeling he should have taken more care; the
modern missionary needs only to study his history to realize
the need for tact. In 1935, a missionary, who killed a pig to
punish natives who refused to help build his church, was
hacked to pieces. Why was Herod, who betrayed an equal
arrogance, so sure he would be safe?

His tirade over, Herod brightened. He sat upright and placed
his hands on his knees. He glanced round at the carriers, who
had fallen asleep, and beckoned to me to lean forward. He
looked excitable, boyish.

'Tomorrow,' he whispered, 'I have church. You will come?'

I had not expected an invitation, especially one this eager,
but Herod wanted me there for a reason. The testimony of a
white man, he figured, would impress the Liawep more than
his preaching could ever do. Could I stand up and explain how
I'd come by my faith?

Naturally, I wanted to help – Herod might pay me a favour
in return – but I worried about the dishonesty. I had no faith
to speak of, only a tealeaf-counting superstition. And besides, I
was an Anglican, and Herod a Lutheran. I offered this in
apology, secretly relieved.

But Herod was having none of it. He waved his hand as if

shooing away flies. 'No problem!' He grinned. 'So, tomorrow morning, early. Tomorrow is Sunday.' This I'd forgotten, but Herod explained he had a calendar. 'Last year's, but I keep on counting.'

His admission that the Liawep sometimes did not listen was the first time he'd shown any weakness. It made me warm to him, but surely, whatever Herod's protestations to the contrary, Dunstan was the right candidate, not me? Dunstan's faith was robust and did not, unlike mine, need fear to kick it awake. For me to stand up in church and tell them how I'd found God would be straight hypocrisy. I looked at Dunstan, hoping he'd offer himself in my place, but he was asleep, his head lolling against the wall, his mouth open, gargling. Reluctantly, I turned back to Herod. 'What do we have to do?'

'Just come and talk to the people. We're all brothers. It's no problem.'

He reached across the fire with a long stick and prodded Dunstan's knee. Dunstan woke with a start, his head jerked forward and a pearl of dribble catapulted from his open mouth into the fire. 'Dunstan,' Herod coughed, 'you must come, too. You and Mr Edward.' Dunstan grunted and closed his eyes again. 'Dunstan!' Herod raised his voice. 'I want you to read from the Bible. Tomorrow, in church. It's a pidgin Bible, so you read it out and I'll translate into Liawep.' He reached behind him and took out the Bible. The spine had collapsed and it had long ago lost its hard cover. The pages were curled and splayed. Dunstan took it, gazing blankly at the flyleaf: Buk Baibel. The passage Herod had marked was from Paul's second letter to the Thessalonians. Herod's theology was not a delicate, precision instrument, more a length of lead piping which he wielded, insensible. The reading was heavy with the threat of eternal damnation.

Dunstan delivered it slowly, his finger tracing each line. He read aloud and Andrew, Dison and Miniza bowed their heads in automatic reverence. Herod nodded and smiled and looked at Dunstan with something approaching love. 'And to you who are troubled rest with us, when the Lord Jesus shall be revealed from heaven with his mighty angels, in flaming fire taking vengeance on them that know not God, and that obey not the gospel of our Lord Jesus Christ: who shall be punished with the everlasting destruction from the presence of the Lord, and from the glory of his power.'

Herod touched the back of Dunstan's hand. 'Very good,' he said. 'Yu ritim gutpela.'

Across the jungle, night had fallen. There were no stars, no moon, no shadows.

Outside the house was the sound of footsteps. I heard their slack tread in the mud and felt the vibration through the floor, from the veranda. Herod, suddenly agitated, grabbed the Bible and darted his head towards the door.

The steps were slow and heavy. I expected Herod to stand, even walk to the door, but he stayed sitting, his eyes fixed on the opening. The floorboards squeaked, swollen by the wet.

A figure filled the doorway: Herod's baby started to scream. Herod, stunned to silence, let her wail. Lit only by the dim orange of the fire, the figure seemed only half there, so black that, but for its size, it might have been an apparition.

From the size of the chest and shoulders, broad and shining dully, I could see this was a man. He looked unlike any jungle people we'd met so far – his ribbed stomach and forearms with spaghetti veins reminded me of a bodybuilder, not a tribesman weaned on kaukau.

He moved his head slowly, taking us in. When he turned away I could see that his jaw, up to his eye socket, was smeared with a pitchy stickiness, oily like molasses. His eyes made pale goggles. His hair, a wiry bush, was held back by a dark band, similar to that worn by the Liawep boy we'd met the day before, on the other side of the valley. His eyes bulged, the black pupils furiously alive.

Herod twitched as if to get up. The big man stepped forward, threateningly. In his hand was a steel axe, its blade worn thin and jagged. Unexpectedly, he offered it to Herod, handle first. Herod reached up and took it, nodding thanks.

Somehow, the presence of this man had silenced Herod like nothing before. He fidgeted, fussing with the fire and with the baby, crying more softly now, but said nothing. The big man's presence filled the room. I could smell him, too – rich and heady, burnt yeast.

As he turned to leave he noticed me. He leaned over, through the smoke. I offered my hand – this man seemed important, perhaps a key figure, someone I should impress.

He looked down at me, at my outstretched fingers. He squinted at my feet, at my trainers, then swivelled and stepped out of the door, leaving monster mudprints on the floor.

Herod breathed out deeply. His hands were shaking. I could feel his relief. 'That', he said, his voice quavering, 'is the chief. Bigman. He has never come to church. I gat samting nogut. You watch out for him.'

Chapter 11

I woke to an extraordinary noise —
long, curling arcs building and fading away. It sounded like a
hunting horn, as if the master of a fox hunt was standing in
the middle of the village in his red coat and black breeches, a
single-coil brass hornet to his lips. It came again, four, five, six
times. Beside me, in our tiny cupboard partition, off the main
room, Dunstan moaned grumpily.

After a night of rain, the sound carried clear and bright
across the still morning. It sounded urgent, like a call to arms,
yet I could hear no voices, no gathering crowds. Still half
asleep, I believed this was Herod calling the Liawep to church,
but how many hunting horns could there be in Papua New
Guinea? More likely a gourd, blown to announce some dim-
remembered ritual.

It was barely dawn. I dressed in a hurry, hoping to catch the musician, leaving Dunstan snuffling in his sleep, his head back, mouth agape. The carriers had relit the fire and were sitting around it, trying to warm themselves. When I stepped through them they looked up like ghosts, their faces ash-grey.

Outside, the light was choked and groggy. The mud was slippery like potters' clay and, as I struggled up to the level ground, I could see pure white clouds, the rain wrung from them, breaking up in the valleys below. The mountain that rose up behind the village was sunk under cloud. The light was pale and early, seeping into the day.

The sound had stopped. I looked around. Across the helipad from Herod's house I saw another straw dwelling, its roof smoking; even at this hour, people were awake, beginning their days. Uphill, the village disappeared into mist. I walked on up towards the smaller, central house.

As I neared I saw a man on the log fence that divided the village, sitting with his head bowed. I crossed the flattened dirt slowly. Only when I came close did I see it was Herod. He stared at his hands, mournful like a little boy parted from his friends, an old baseball cap turned backwards on his head.

Without looking up, he held out the object in his lap. It was a beautiful brass horn, three feet long, with a thick-lipped silver mouthpiece – the kind that demanded dedication, the musician standing with his feet set wide apart and hands halfway up the stem. At the end it widened gently, flowering into a lily mouth. But he'd not looked after it. Its surface was scratched and dull like tin cutlery; the perfect glide of the trumpet sweep was flawed by a dent where it had been dropped.

'It's lovely. It was you playing?'

'Yes.' He stared blankly at my knees. 'It means I am holding a service. They can all hear it.'

'So where are they?'

'I do not know. Perhaps they think I am still away hunting.'

'We'll be there,' I said, suddenly sorry for him. I climbed on to the logs and sat beside him to wait. He handed me the horn. It was warm and sticky where he'd held it.

We sat together a while. Elisa, Herod's wife, ducked out of the house and looked about her. Her string bag was slung across her chest, and when she came closer, up the hill towards us, I could see the curled back of the sleeping baby, filling out the belly of the bag. She looked us up and down and climbed the logs, past Herod, laying a hand on his shoulder to steady herself.

'My baby,' Herod said, getting up to follow his wife, 'she is sick. This morning we pray for her.'

'Sick?'

'Malaria. She cannot sleep or eat.'

Elisa wore the same dress as the night before, scarlet with turquoise flowers. She was a butterfly in the desert, flapping up the hill towards the church, marked out against the wet clay earth.

We followed her, picking our way round a thistle clump of sinewy tobacco plants, their stalks frizzy and leaves like trowels. Further over, towards the edge of the clearing, I noticed other plants, which I did not recognize, their great heart-shaped leaves drooping from rhubarb stems.

Ahead of us Elisa stopped. She was standing by the smaller house, which stood in the centre of the village. At her feet was a tangled heap of ivy which she began weaving in and out of the planks that formed the wall, threading it, ordering the leaves so they hung prettily. Herod led me past her, to the door.

When I looked inside I could see my mistake – this was no house, but Herod's church, the size of a suburban garage, built without nails, steel or iron roofing, perhaps twenty feet long.

Each joint was a criss-cross of vines. It was empty. Herod gestured me in, caressing the air before me.

There were eight pews on each side of the aisle, planks raised six inches off the ground on blocks of wood. The wall stopped two feet below the roof overhang, giving a view across the jungle on all sides. It was cool and shaded inside, and the breeze washed in. Its simplicity made it beautiful. I said so to Herod.

'Thank you,' he said, clasping his hands together. 'I'm going to build a bigger one. If it is bigger, more people come.'

The altar was made of bamboo, a string of flowers skirting the top lip. It was built flush against the far wall, with a step in the middle. Perhaps it doubled as pulpit. Herod laid his Bible on one corner.

Dunstan appeared at the door. 'Where is everyone?' he asked. Herod shook his head and coughed. He looked hard at Dunstan who turned and glanced nervously up the hill behind the church, towards the mountain.

Dunstan asked for the Bible; he needed to practise the reading. Herod handed it over and Dunstan sat down on a pew, reading it through in a stagy half-whisper, labouring his pronunciation, his back a curve of concentration. He cleared his throat continuously.

Herod was standing by the altar, sniffing the flowers. I asked him why he chose this lesson. Why the New Testament? 'Because,' he said, with perfect logic, 'this is a new place.'

A man appeared in the doorway. Herod had his first worshipper. He looked magnificent, with bulbous wicker bracelets into which tiny orange flowers had been woven just above the bicep on each arm. On his head was a crown of red ivy. Tanket leaves, so glossy and rubbery they looked like Sunday best, covered his behind, and what looked like chintz curtain material made up his loincloth. He knew he cut a figure. He stood just outside, his arms folded, the hazy morning sun turning his skin milky gold.

'Come in, come in.' Herod sounded a little over-anxious. The man stayed where he was. 'OK, you stay there.'

Behind him more appeared: a younger man with a pair of shredded shorts and a woman in a grass skirt and spider tattoos on each temple. They hid behind him and peered at us. The woman tittered when she saw me, covering her mouth with her hand. They'd brought a gaggle of children – eight or nine, almost a congregation.

'Right!' Herod clapped his hands and moved outside. I sat down next to Dunstan, facing the altar. It couldn't help, my staring at them. They looked so shy and insubstantial, like creatures in a dream.

Herod shooed them into the church, clucking with his tongue. Three adults, nine children, Dunstan, myself and Herod. From a total of seventy-nine, this was a poor turnout.

It started with a procession, the children following the adults up the aisle to the altar, where each placed a taro or sweet potato in a pile against the wall. One little boy struggled under a fan of green bananas. He laid them down and looked at the ground with studied humility as the grown-ups had before him. None looked at me and all chose seats at a safe distance.

Dunstan and I were marooned on a middle pew. No one had spoken since stepping through the door and when I tried to catch their eyes to smile or shake hands, they turned sharply away. It felt increasingly like a religious cult, and I the outsider. Their silence felt like a code; their stillness, as they waited for Herod to begin, a shared secret.

The two men sat on the left, the woman on the right, settling in quickly, as though they had rehearsed the moves. Like an

English village church, everyone had their place. All sat in the front two rows, the children jammed tight on to the pew in front of the woman. A cockatoo landed on the roof, its claws scrunching the papery leaves as it scrambled for a foothold. It stopped above me and I could hear it muttering to itself, its clog beak clacking.

Herod strode up the aisle. Five steps and he was at the altar, turning on his heel, looking us over with his hands on his hips. He was wearing his Sunday best – flared jeans and a purple sweatshirt. He'd changed his baseball cap for a black cotton skullcap, embroidered in blue and green. He wore a necklace of red beads, the pendant a varnished wooden cross.

He started shouting. It was a violent beginning. People who'd hung their heads, awaiting the start, sat bolt upright. Herod was full of resentment and in church his anger found a legitimate, righteous outlet.

In front of us, the men whispered something to each other. The smaller man, who wore tattered shorts, turned and looked me straight in the eye. The contrast with the others' timidity could not have been balder, and it gave me hope. When Herod began yelling again he turned to the front, nudged the other man, and hung his head. Across the aisle the children, pressed shoulder to shoulder, were leaning forward as if in prayer, their heads between their knees. But they were so close they could have been doing anything – camouflaged by Herod's shouting, they might be plotting, joking, chatting.

Herod addressed them in Liawep – unlike the eccentric babble of pidgin, this language had no music to it, the words dragged along the voicebox floor – and Dunstan and I sat dumb, uncomprehending. I picked up 'Dunstan', 'whitey man', but no more.

Herod windmilled his arms and rolled his eyes in furious

ecstasy: sweat began to darken his shirt. Thinking he was too transported to notice me, I whispered in Dunstan's ear. What was Herod saying? Did Dunstan understand anything?

'Quiet!' Herod barked. He glared at me, his hands planted on his hips. In front, the man in the shorts sniggered; his shoulders juddered. One of the little children turned to me – a boy, his naked body cracked with dried mud. His mouth hung open, dribble stretched elastic from his bottom lip.

'I'm saying,' Herod went on, tapping his foot impatiently, 'about you. I explain who you are and that you walk across the jungle to meet them.'

'Thank you,' I said, unnecessarily, but he was already off again. He shook his fist at the sky, then brought it down with a thump on the Bible, but no one started this time: perhaps they'd seen the device before. We were still on his opening address, his words of welcome, when his speech slurred to a halt. He feathered through the Bible and pulled out a scrap of paper. It had been folded into quarters and he unfolded and smoothed it out. He breathed in deeply before starting.

'Mambau . . .' he read. The word fell into silence. 'Lasawi?' No response. 'Fioluana?'

'Yes,' mumbled the man in shorts.

He read through the roll-call with a painful slowness, making those who had come suffer for the heathen others. He did not once look up. He barked out the names and each time he struck on one who'd come, they'd answer very quietly and timidly. Outside, for the first time in days, the sky had cleared to a pale snow-blue over the mountains, arching to a deep Mediterranean blue overhead. The sun caught on the water in the ditch-moat Herod had dug round the church and reflected in a yellowy ripple on the underside of the roof overhang. Unlike night – an endless battering of noise, the electricity of a million insects competing to be heard – the jungle was now quite still.

The only sound was Herod's voice, audible valleys away, God's word pounded out.

He announced every name. The woman rested her head against the wall. She looked exhausted. One of the girls clambered on to her lap for attention, then stopped, leaned forwards over her knees and squirted bright yellow vomit over the pew in front. The woman looked up, checked on the buttery splash, nodded slowly, then rested her head against the wall. Her hair was cropped close to the skull. Herod looked at her, then at the child, its mouth wet and dribbly, and then at the spume, darkening at the edges. He raised his eyebrows, folded and tucked the paper back into his Bible, turned round and placed the book on the altar.

His back to us, he started singing, his head high and his voice loud, clamped-up and nasal, as if he'd plugged his nose with paper. The tune, I could have sworn, was 'Oh My Darling Clementine'; the words were Liawep. He swirled his arms, indicating we should all join in, and there was a low grumble as everyone lifted their voices. They spoke rather than sang the words, looking at their feet, or their hands, anywhere but up. If it was 'Clementine', perhaps Herod had learned it from an Irish missionary. Certainly there were phrases where the tune took a wrong turn. There were five verses, and it dragged interminably, more funeral dirge than hymn of worship.

Herod looked round each of us, as if checking no one had fallen asleep or was otherwise distracted. His eye fell again on the hardening vomit. He pointed to it and muttered something curt. The woman shifted on her seat, tore a handful of grass from the back of her skirt and scraped at the sick. It came away in long gluey strands. She turned her grass sponge the other way up and cleared the rest with the dry side, then laid it gingerly on the pew beside her and rested her head against the wall.

Herod turned to Dunstan and me. He flashed a saccharine smile. 'Please come up here. You must talk to them now.'

It was a tortuous process. I was nervous, which was ridiculous, as there were only twelve of them and they seemed more afraid of me than I of them. Herod wanted me to explain myself, and I'd told so many different stories that I was unsure which version would be appropriate here. This was my first public address to the Liawep, and I wanted it to be good.

The children leaned forward again, pressing their faces into their hands. The men watched my shoes. The woman, oblivious to Herod's fury, had not lifted her head from the wall.

I stood up, telling myself not to forget to mention God. 'Hello,' I began, which Herod translated into two or three longish sentences in Liawep. What was he telling them? He could say what he liked and I'd have no check on him. Was this an extended ceremonial greeting or something more sinister? Halfway through the translation everyone looked up from the ground, curiosity replacing their shyness. The small girl who'd decorated the pew in front of her had a crust of egg yolk round her bottom lip. She looked at me and grinned. Her nose had been running and the dried snot was blackened with dirt.

Herod turned to me, expectant. He held his heavy cross pendant in his hand, weighing it. The beads caught the sun and glinted in my eye. 'Well,' I began again, wondering whether Herod minded what I said, so long as I was seen to open my mouth, 'I'm from England.' Herod looked at me hard and delivered another two sentences. He did not mention England. It felt hopeless. All eyes were on me.

'I heard about you, the Liawep people, in my country. People said you were a lost tribe – new people – so I wanted to meet you.' I could feel Carol Jenkins sitting behind me, her breath on my neck, muttering 'ethnocentric', cackling cruelly. I was running out of steam. Herod spoke for a minute and I noticed that the man in shorts, sitting in the front row, had fallen asleep. Twice now his head had fallen on to his chest, to jerk up sharply when his chin made contact. The third time he cupped both his hands forward and lay his forehead in them. It looked impossibly uncomfortable, but it did the trick. Very gently, he started to snore.

Herod pretended not to notice. He smiled relentlessly. I had forgotten my speech and knew it wouldn't be long before I sat down again, cornered and confused. I began again.

'We walked here from Wanakipa. Six days through the jungle. We walked all this way to meet you. Thank you for welcoming us. We're very pleased to be here.' This time Herod used fewer words. When he looked round for more I was already halfway back to my pew and Dunstan was standing, ready to say his bit. As we crossed, he whispered to me, 'You forgot to talk about God.'

His first words were apology for my omission. 'Edward', he said, 'is Anglican. I'm a Catholic.' Herod beamed. Dunstan continued, striking the pose of devotion, which pleased Herod enormously; he illustrated the words with flamboyant hand gestures. Dunstan explained how he was a lay preacher in Tari – omitting that this was a career from which he'd since been ejected – and how he was married, with two children. He wooed them as I'd failed to do. He told them how we'd walked through the jungle to meet them; how it had rained continually; how we'd thought the bridges would be washed away; how it was the first time either of us had climbed in the jungle. We did it, he said, because God gave us strength.

Herod moved closer to Dunstan. He was a few inches shorter but now their shoulders were almost touching. He looked up into Dunstan's face and I saw them as an evangelical double-act. Hard man, soft man. Herod the pummeller; Dunstan the seducer.

Two children peeped round the door, one head above the other, and stared at Dunstan and me. When I turned they withdrew their heads and spied on us through the slats. They were naked. They whispered so loudly we could all hear.

Herod, ignoring them, lay the Bible in his left hand and thrummed through the pages with his right. He found Thessalonians and opened the book out flat, handing it to Dunstan. He read slowly, stopping after each sentence for Herod's translation. In pidgin each word was simplified; what had been subtle in English became playschool compounds of simple words. So there was no word for testimony, presence, vengeance: instead there was 'what we say', 'where we are', 'do bad things back'.

The mechanics of translation meant that St Paul's terse instruction took far longer than it should have. The man in shorts started to snore loudly. For a moment I thought it was the hornbill on the roof. The other man, the one with the floral wicker armbands, noticed my puzzlement, dug an elbow into his friend's ribs and whispered something sharp. The man stopped snoring, spluttered, coughed, wiped his mouth with the back of his hand and looked at his friend. They both exploded into giggles, which, stifled, turned into snorts and moans. Dunstan stopped reading; Herod's evil stare only convulsed them more. It took some time before they unpeeled their hands from their mouths. They sat, breathing heavily.

My bottom was numb. An hour and a half in, Herod gave no sign of whether the service was nearing its end. As he badgered on, I couldn't help thinking his approach was all wrong. He had to make God an attractive option, to praise those who came to church rather than blame them for the others' absence. Even the length of this service seemed in some way vindictive, a punishment by proxy to those who had not come.

He pressed right up to the wall behind the bamboo altar, his back to us, and poked his nose through two planks. He prayed in Liawep, very fast, short prayers, announcing 'Amen' every ten seconds. We concentrated on the back of his head and repeated 'Amen' after him. Only the woman with the pukey girl did not pray. She rested her head against the wall, exhausted by sickly children and lazy men.

Herod started shouting again. It sounded like a question this time, a test, something we needed to pass if Herod was to let us leave and get on with the day. He yelled out. The sleepy man flinched. The woman with her head against the wall muttered something that sounded insolent. Herod yapped out one short word and she lifted her head and gave him a sour look. He repeated the question. This time a little boy answered, and Herod listened like an uncle and smiled. 'Yes,' he said, turning to all of us, 'whatever you need, put it in God's hand. If there's no food in your garden, or your children are sick, you must not fear. Ask God.'

There was a shuffling in the dust by the door. Herod, who had not heard, continued his prayers, his back to us. I looked round, but sun flashed in my eyes and all I could see was the silhouette of a big man standing, feet apart, filling the doorway. He moved, blocking out the sun, throwing the aisle into shadow. Herod, registering the change, span on his heels.

Everyone forgot their prayers. The woman sat up, gripping the pew either side of her. Her eyes flashed over me, then to the figure in the doorway. Herod, squinting against the light, clutched his Bible to his chest.

It was the black face paint that marked him out, even though the sun was behind him and his features were lost in shadow. That and his size. It was the chief, this man who had interrupted us last night, of whom Herod had warned me, who never came to church. He was here.

But his was not a friendly curiosity. He did not look around him; did not take his eyes off Herod. When Herod, attempting a reconciliation, walked forward, scooping the air in welcome, the chief tilted his head back, looked down his nose, turned and walked out as suddenly as he'd come.

Sunlight filled the church. Forgetting their reserve, everyone leaned into the aisle to watch the big man retreat. He trudged along the hardpacked earth, uphill towards the mountain. He had a boxer's neck, as thick as a tree stump. The leaves that covered his behind swished from side to side, comically feminine.

His entrance had ruined Herod's crescendo. The priest's mouth crumpled, tearfully. He raised his hands, gesturing us to stand.

He weaved among us, shaking hands, his eyes liquid with disappointment. To the boy who'd answered his question he spoke with a quiet warmth, pointing to the heap of kaukau and banana that had been deposited by the altar earlier. The boy scuttled sideways, with one eye on Herod. He tore off a green banana with a crunch, slalomed through us out of the door and was gone.

Herod led the way from the church. I'd not noticed it before, but he had a loping, long, equine stride, with high arches, dragging his toes. His paltry congregation filed after him, the children silent and demure. Only when they were outside did they relax, their voices chirruping relief.

I waited back awhile with Dunstan. He clicked his tongue at me, oddly, and smiled, but both of us were too bewildered by the service, the force of Herod's barrage, the sheer inappropriateness of Christianity in this pagan wilderness, to say anything. Outside, the people were gathering around Herod.

A few feet from the door was a wooden cross that I hadn't noticed before. It was ten feet high, its base ringed with polished black rocks. Behind it the village climbed, past the big house, its roof tattered and sooty, into the jungle, towards the mountain.

The cross was pale, waxy wood. Herod leaned against it as though it was a lamp post, as if demonstrating that it was a sturdy thing, made to last. His congregation closed round him. An older man walked up. No one looked round at us. They seemed lost in themselves.

The girl with the snotty nose was flirting with the old man. She can't have been more than five or six, but she shone and danced, turned her face into the sun and held his hand. He was much older, with hair gone white round his temples and the skin loose over his chest. She wore a little dress, yellow with brown birds, and pulled at his tanket leaves. He pinched her nose in reproach; she turned away, giggling into her hand, watching him.

I walked towards the door into the sunshine. Far up the hill, where grass and new jungle growth billowed over the edge of the village clearing, I saw the chief. He was walking away, very slowly, picking his way towards the giant trunks and greedy void that marked the start of the jungle. His head was bent forward and above his broad shoulders I could see a thin fuzz of hair.

Herod raised his head, watching us emerge, then pushed himself upright and walked over to the old man. He coiled his arm round the man's thin shoulderblades, jutting like a cow's back in drought, and whispered in his ear. When the old man turned towards us, so did the others, the men and the woman, the little children. Construing this as a welcome, an invitation to introduce myself, I stepped forward. My movement seemed to spark panic. The woman began to hustle the children, chivvying them like sheep; the two men followed. As they bundled away, uncertain on their feet as antique machinery, two turned to take one last look: the younger man twisted his face into a smile: the girl with the snotty nose and pretty dress raised her hand, as if to wave. When the woman saw it, she slapped it down. She looked disgusted.

Chapter 12

Herod smiled at me, a sickly, smug grin. He held his Bible in one hand and feathered the pages lazily with the other. He did this with such malicious casualness that I felt like tearing it from his hands and stamping it into the mud. But to see me lose control would have pleased Herod more than anything else and so I smiled back instead, and complimented him on the service. I enjoyed it, I mumbled insincerely, especially the singing. He nodded and looked past me, down the hill towards his house. He started to move away.

'But there was one thing I wondered about,' I added, suddenly angered by his conceit. 'Why didn't more people come?' I stepped into his path. 'Haus lotu i pinis – empty.' I shrugged my shoulders in mock innocence.

Herod squared up to me. 'Because of you.' He coughed the

words. This was a shock. I'd expected him to forward the explanation he'd offered before – that their hearts were still made of stone and that this was a new place; that they hadn't yet renounced their 'old ways'.

I wanted to see him admit his failure again. But here he was, turning the blame on me. He talked fast, stroking his thumb over his crucifix. 'More people would be here, but they are hiding in the bushes. Just now they tell me. They will not come out until you are gone.'

He elbowed past me and strode off downhill. I ran after him. He did not turn his head to speak to me. 'You are whitey man. They never see whitey man before.'

'But that's simple enough. I'm just a little paler than you, that's all.'

'No,' he said. 'that's not all.' He stopped and turned, jabbing his finger at my chest. Even though he was smaller, I recoiled, wilting under the burn of his self-righteousness. 'They do not understand why you are here. They think you are from the government. They think you are here to lock them in prison, behind bars.'

Herod scuttled away towards his house, slipping on half-dried mud. He seemed rat-like, hunched over, his precious book clasped to his chest.

I couldn't bear to follow him, to sit in his house and listen to his pious grumblings. So I walked back up the hill, up the beaten earth to the church.

The village was deserted once again. It was nearing midday and the sun was high. Across two valleys black storm clouds were building. From far off, they looked beautiful: charcoal-black, strangely precious.

I leaned against the church, shaded by the roof overhang, and looked up the spur towards the mountain. For the first time that clear morning, the peak was visible. It was jungled, dark and jagged. The summit had the metal shine of wet rock; a tiny wisp of cloud was snagged there, like cotton on a thorn bush. Like this, in sunshine, it seemed hardly worthy of the Liawep's fear. It was a big mountain, no more.

I was confused by the way the Liawep appeared to have shied from me. Were they nearby, in the big house further up the spur, or were there other houses, hidden in the jungle, in which they were gathered? I had expected so much more – more bustle, movement and interest. I had expected to be the centre of things, for them to bubble over in their eagerness to be heard. But this had not happened. There was much I did not understand.

My expectations stemmed in part, at least, from historical precedent. In 1933, when Mick Leahy, exploring the eastern highlands, had pitched camp every afternoon, the highlanders were so inquisitive that Leahy ordered his carriers to circle the tents with string, a waist-high barrier which marked the edge of his territory. The warriors sat the other side, sometimes hundreds of them, in brave head-dresses and oiled skin, scanning the white men for clues. Because they did not understand the white men, because they had no place in their world, the highlanders were not afraid. Only when Leahy began to open fire on them did they approach more warily.

Two years later, treading the explored jungle further west, the patrol officer Jack Hides was greeted by singing and dancing, wailing voices and the wild flapping of arms that seemed like the unrestrained joy of welcome. The difference between them and me, of course, was more than the passing of sixty years. In the year since Yasaro had announced his discovery, the Liawep had become suspicious. They now knew about white men, and believed they brought trouble.

But they seemed equally wary of Herod. A hundred years ago, the Revd James Chalmers had introduced tobacco to New

Guinea; those natives that came to church were given a free smoke. Chalmers admitted the bribery openly: 'Today's Gospel with the natives is one of tomahawks and tobacco; we are received by them because of these.' Herod, reined in tight by the Lutherans, had no sweeteners to offer the Liawep. Success depended on drilling fear into the people's hearts; only a few, so far, had succumbed.

Perhaps I dozed off – the heat made my head go heavy, and it was so quiet and still sitting against the church – because the next thing I knew, Titus was by my side. I hadn't heard his steps or seen him approach. He tapped me on the shoulder. I jolted awake.

He had news, he said, sitting beside me. To his surprise, he had found he could speak Liawep with near-fluency – it was close enough to his dialect to have much similar vocabulary. He'd observed my difficulties with Herod and wondered whether he could help translate.

I could have kissed him. Tied to Herod, I had foreseen a grim, sycophantic future for myself – laughing at his jokes, expressing sympathy with his problems – solely in order for him to act as interpreter. Now Titus, unprompted, was offering me a way out.

That was not all. He had been talking to Fioluana, the younger of the two men who had come to church, who'd looked me in the eye and had sniggered openly at Herod. He claimed to have something to show me. I followed Titus up the village, through the backyard of the big house at the top, then through a thicket of tobacco plants, their leaves furry and sticky, up into an old garden. When we reached the banana trees he looked puzzled. He swivelled his head, bending down as if checking for something lost. He turned to me, his bottom lip stuck out, his face blank.

In front of us, someone coughed. Titus looked again. A fan of banana trees parted and Fioluana's grinning face appeared. He stood up and, beckoning us after him, walked on uphill, into deep grass, towards the edge of the jungle, twenty yards away.

He stopped only when he reached the tall trees. Under the canopy, he squatted against a smooth olive-green trunk, as wide as a house. When we caught him up he was still grinning. He could have been fifteen or sixty, and his knees were scaly with dirt. He had an indented mouth and his teeth pointed inwards, miserably, as if his childhood had been marked out by railtrack braces.

He spoke so softly we had to bend over to hear him. Suddenly serious, he said, 'What I show you, you won't tell Herod?' He waited till I promised.

He walked very fast, looking round all the time, as if afraid to be seen with me. His feet were fixed outwards, a duck's splay, and he walked from the hips, his torso twisting, looking round, checking the way. I slithered behind him along a path seldom used and overgrown. Fioluana had no bushknife, so pushed through where creepers fell across the way, holding them back for us. We crossed a stream which, despite the rainfall, was brackish and reedy, coaxed over a curled leaf into a drinking spout, then we climbed the bank and cut away from the path, heading straight up the mountain.

It was cool and dark under the jungle canopy. Fioluana and Titus went ahead, pausing for me, breathing heavily. Leaves mulched underfoot. Before long the jungle thinned and it seemed we were coming out on to a crest. Fioluana disappeared ahead and we followed him into the open. It was a clearing with rough-cut stumps and wet grass, fifty feet across. The sky, far overhead, was clear and, to the right, if I strained my neck upwards, was the peak of the mountain, dark forest and black rock. Again I felt its presence, something almost evil in its dark overhang, the way it drew storms across the valleys and attracted lightning like the devil's own cathedral.

'This is it,' Fioluana said. He kneeled down in the grass. 'We pray here.' He looked up, almost vertically, to the mountain. 'This is where it speaks to us.'

Ever since our arrival I had wanted to talk about the mountain, this brooding presence that cast a shadow over the village in the evening sun and was so sheer at midday that its slopes were in shadow. Jack and Yasaro had both told me that it was worshipped, and I could see why. Herod claimed smoke issued from its summit; sometimes the ground shook; when storms came, it bristled with lightning. It was colossal, and standing in the village it felt like the centre of the universe. It stirred in me a peculiar paranoia. I feared, ludicrous though I knew this to be, that it was in some way evil. Perhaps, I reasoned, by understanding it as the Liawep understood it, I might be able to defuse its power.

I also wanted to know what happened behind it, whether it fell away sheer on the other side, too, or flattened out. Perhaps the smoke Herod had seen came from the fires of another tribe that lived up there, in the rarefied air, but I was unable to pinpoint it on my map so could only guess. I had aviation charts – the best available – but the cramped contours, gradual green, and misleading thin blue curve of the Lagaip, like a mountain road, meant nothing to anyone but myself. Over this whole area was a white square marked 'obscured by cloud cover'. Although the maps were the best there were, they were still useless.

And now we were here, in this private place, this shrine of which Herod, it appeared, knew nothing. I sat in the grass with Fioluana and Titus. Even though we were an hour up from the village, Fioluana still seemed edgy. I put my hand on his shoulder, trying to calm his nerves, but he flinched and pulled away.

Fumbling his words, twisting grass between his fingers, he told me about the mountain. It was two brothers, with two different personalities; one lived on the summit and was the mountain at its blackest and most unpredictable; the second lived on the lower slopes.

Fioluana waved his arm in a wide circle. 'The one who is underneath is a kind man. The other brother gets cross easily. He is a man of violence. He likes to kill people when they come up the mountain.' He jabbed his finger in the air, towards the summit. His eyes were fixed on the ground.

Unbelieving, I asked who had been the last person to die such a death. Fioluana did not know, but was adamant. I twisted my head upwards. I could just see the summit, where the jungle cliff disappeared into cloud. It did spook me, the size and the taboo of it, however intellectual the line I put forward.

Emboldened by my example, Fioluana looked skywards. A black-bellied cloud was lumbering across the summit, drawing shade over the clearing. Fioluana turned to me. With the sun gone, his skin was cobwebbed with tiny lines, hairline fractures. There was mud on his neck.

'Before Peter Yasaro came, we still fight our enemies, we praise the mountain. We praise it before we go and fight. Then we win the fight; the mountain tells us when to fight and when to stay at home. We yell out the names of our enemies. Our enemies have heard about our mountain. They are frightened of it.'

So the mountain talked: it had a voice. What did it sound like? Did the mountain utter words, or was the noise more like a sigh or a groan, perhaps like wind in the tree-tops?

Fioluana looked pityingly at me. He shook his head. 'How

should I know? Only one man at a time talks to the mountain, so no one else hears it.' He added irritably, 'Ask the chief, he has heard the mountain speak.'

He got to his feet, keen to be off. Titus, too, appeared uneasy. He was standing up, cupping his hand to his ear. He kept saying he'd heard something – breaking branches, people on the move.

He waded through deep grass to the edge of the clearing, vaulted a rotting fallen tree trunk sprouting weeds and grass, and jumped on to the path.

Titus and Fioluana stopped ahead of me. They stood side by side, staring, immobile.

Advancing up the path towards us, brushing aside creepers, was the chief. His chest was heaving with the exertion, sweat was running off him. I remembered seeing him climb towards the jungle after church, yet we had arrived here before him. It made no sense.

Without looking up, he climbed past us and stepped on to the tree trunk in one stride. He eyed us, one after the other, with a look that managed to combine contempt with uninterest. I'd not seen his face in the light before, but now I noticed one of his eyes, like Fioluana's, was cloudy, as if the pupil had been punched out. He sniffed the air, then stepped backwards off the log, into the clearing. He sat where we had, in the flattened circle of grass. But he sat with his back to us, and would not look round.

'Leave him,' said Fioluana. 'He wants to be left alone. He still worships the mountain. Every day he climbs up here. You won't tell Herod, will you?' Fioluana's eyes were mournful, pleading. 'Don't tell him about any of this.'

The rain was beginning again. The jungle dropped into an oily darkness; in the dim light all definition disappeared and I lurched forward on the path, over dips and rises I could no longer see. On the roof of the jungle, two hundred feet up, the first of the rain crackled like a far-off forest fire.

We hurried back towards the village. Through the rain came the muffled sound of a dog barking. As we climbed down, manoeuvring over huge, tangled roots, I heard an excited whooping. Round the corner five men stood on the path, pointing into the branches of a tall tree. A boy stood beside one of the men, holding his hand. The dog scratched at the base of the tree, whining and panting. As we stumbled down, one man turned and held out his hand, motioning us to stop.

High up, where the branches were leafy, an animal was hunkered in. It was a tiny *cuscus* with chestnut fur, currant eyes and a pouch for its young, wedged between the trunk and a thick branch, immovable. One of the men stepped back, treading round for a better view. He had an arrow half cocked in his bow. The *cuscus* was fifty feet up. The man lifted his bow and drew in his breath. He pulled the arrow back. Its tip nudged his knuckles. The arrow struck the *cuscus* through the chest and its head flew back, then dropped forwards. It slumped to one side, then toppled, impaled on the arrow shaft. It bundled down the jungleside and the dog, tripping over its legs, yipped after it.

By the time we fell out of the jungle into the village the rain was drilling straight down from a low, black sky. The valleys that had earlier been so clear in the sunshine had now disappeared under grey haze. The roofs of the houses shone with wet; it felt like the last place on earth.

Crouching under the banana trees at the top of the village, I thanked Fioluana. I complimented him on his shorts – he was the only man I'd seen who didn't wear leaves. Yasaro gave them to him, he said, grinning his peculiar lopsided grin. He'd not taken them off for a year.

Water was slicing off the banana leaves. We shook hands quickly. His felt beaten, like elephant's hide, yet it was slender and bony, too, and the knuckles cracked when I took it. He watched us as we ran across the mud to Herod's house, staring at us till we were out of sight.

Herod wanted to know where we had been. Dunstan, who knew, was saying nothing.

Titus lay his long body down on the floor to rest. But Herod would not let him be. He was rolling a cigarette, trying to look relaxed, but his voice, reedy and insistent, gave him away. Titus explained that we'd been for a walk. Where? Herod pressed. 'Longwe liklik, long bus – into the forest,' Titus said. He closed his eyes and folded his arms behind his head. Herod pulled feverishly on his cigarette and turned to me. I repeated Titus's words. 'Mi no save. Long bus. Long wokabaut.'

Herod spat in the fire. 'I know where you go. And I tell you, everything you hear is lies. Things have changed. They don't talk to the mountain, not any more.'

Chapter 13

Herod began to watch me more closely after this. Living in his house, I came under constant surveillance. I could not even go to the lavatory without his tailing me across the village. Even when I explained that I wanted nothing more sinister than to squat in private, he would still linger nearby until I had finished.

The lavatory was his pride and joy. Grudgingly, he had pointed it out to us, indicating that we, unlike the Liawep, had his permission to use it. It was the size of a telephone box, with a sloping roof of saksak leaves and a sleeve through which one passed to enter. He had shown a febrile pride. 'Very clean,' he boasted, waving away flies as he pointed out the drop.

I emerged from the lavatory the next morning to find Herod waiting for me outside his house. After another night of rain, the air felt rinsed, cool. It was bright, but there was no sun. Pale cloud hung solidly over the mountains, with only the occasional crack of dark green showing the deep wet jungle underneath.

I walked over the bare expanse of the helipad, across the slick mud, down towards Herod. He looked solemn, concerned. He was wearing only tanket leaves and there were goose bumps up his arms. I asked him what the trouble was.

'Fioluana's here,' he mumbled. '*Insait long haus* – inside the house. He wants to see you.'

Fioluana was crouched by the fire talking to Titus. He jumped up when he saw me, wringing his hands anxiously. We shook hands; Herod stood just behind me, watching and listening. Smoke from the fire, stirring in the rafters, made Fioluana blink continually. He wanted me to accompany him to the big house at the top of the village. There were people there. He would make the introductions: I should not worry.

Herod stepped forward and snapped out something in Liawep. Fioluana looked at the ground, his enthusiasm crushed. Titus, listening nearby, intervened.

'Herod, why don't you come, too?' Titus was taller than Herod and spoke kindly, like a father.

Herod looked from me to Fioluana. He knew we would go, whatever he said. He forced a smile. 'Wait a minute. I will get my Bible.'

So the five of us – Herod, Titus, Fioluana, Dunstan and I – walked up the village together. Fioluana's helpfulness bewildered me. It was so at odds with the others' timidity. Why was he different? I edged up to ask him, couching it as thanks, but he grinned shyly, drew up his shoulders and said, 'Later, later. I tell you later.'

I owed him more than he knew. Because of him I was witnessing more than just the sanitized, Herod-approved version of Liawep life. Fioluana had saved the journey from farce.

Rainwater was sheening across the mud, like tiny broken mirrors in the early morning light, filling our footprints as we walked. The night before had been one long storm, the endless grind of thunder, the static hiss of rain. The drainage ditch round the church had overflowed and the church floor was underwater. There had not been this much rain before: the downpour was building; every day the rivers would be filling. I worried for the bridge – it had been shaky enough on the way over. How long would it last with the river rising? Herod paused at the door of the church. He shook his head sorrowfully, as if lamenting some malicious act of vandalism.

The big house was another thirty yards on, up a path that weaved between gawky tobacco plants, their thick stalks and leathery dark green leaves dulled with wet, their bases spotted with mud where feet had splattered them.

The house, like Herod's, was built precariously, on the very edge of the clearing. As we neared I heard the low hum of voices. Underneath the house, on sheltered dusty earth, a pig was tethered. A woman was seated near it, cleaning mud from a pile of newly dug kaukau.

I called out a greeting. She turned and gaped. She looked struck dumb, as if in a horror movie, seeing a raised dagger over another's shoulder. Panicking, she jumped up, only to hit her head on a beam. Fioluana laughed, half shocked, and she glared back accusingly. She wore one of Yasaro's T-shirts over a rumpled grass skirt, torn open over one breast and so soiled and stretched that it ended below her knees. When I moved forward, in a gesture of friendship, she dropped the kaukau and, ducking low, scurried away.

'That woman', Fioluana sniffed, composing himself, 'is the mother of my wife.'

'Your wife? You never said you had a wife.'

'She stays in my house and cooks and makes the garden. That is what women do.'

A rickety ladder led from the ground to a narrow veranda which skirted the uphill side of the house. No one, it seemed, fancied themselves as handymen. Planks had rotted or fallen through and not been replaced, and we had to pick our way along to the door, from one strut to the next.

The planks were spongy from the rain, and squeaked alarmingly. Our clumsy approach had silenced the voices inside. I put my hand on the wall, listening for noise, but heard nothing. Smoke whispered out where I pressed, seeping through my fingers.

Fioluana explained that the house had two doors. This meant enemies could not surprise those inside; you would hear them walking along the sleeve, the darkened buffer between the first and second doors, and – 'Bang!' Fioluana yelped, cracking his knuckles – you would be waiting for them. I examined Fioluana, this slight, stooped, ageless man, but could not imagine him as the warrior he believed himself to be. So far, indeed, bar the hunting the day before, I had witnessed nothing that substantiated the fears of those we'd met along the way, who had warned us, quaking, of the Liawep's thirst for blood and their valour in battle.

I followed Fioluana, fumbling past dark shapes in the corridor, groping after him towards the second door and a smudge of dim orange light. Behind me, Dunstan tripped. There was a wooden clatter. He cursed, shuffling the obstruction to one side.

Inside, the house seemed at least twice as big as Herod's,

with a steep roof and a tiny window cut high into one wall, through which light beamed narrowly, like torchlight, into curling smoke and dust. There were people in the room, but with the light in my eyes I saw them only as dark shapes at the shadowed edges of the room.

When we moved further in, away from the window, the room seemed lost in an eternal twilight. The air was soupy with smoke from four fires, one set near each corner. We sat in the middle of the room, surrounded.

Fioluana spoke; as my eyes grew used to the light I noticed string bags hung from the walls at shoulder height, bulging with everything they owned — taro, kaukau, hornbill beaks, bunches of emu feathers. One corner was the armoury, five sets of bows and arrows stacked together, the arrows twine-whipped into bunches.

I counted the people. There were eight of them and, strikingly, all men. So far I'd encountered only two women and one little girl; it was as if women did not exist, or at least existed in some place to which I was not allowed access.

I recognized five of the men: they were the hunters we'd run across the day before. They looked no different: bare-chested, their leaves tucked under them, slim bodies but hefty, callused hands and scarred, splayed feet. I noticed their nipples, too — as dark and protuberant as India rubber. They listened to Fioluana in silence, turning at points to take me in. One of them began to sharpen an arrow tip with persistent, deliberate strokes.

Three others sat apart. Two were young, barely out of their teens, with hazy moustache hair and twitching hands. They wore high, narrow turbans, which sloped wildly backwards.

The last man was much older. Like the others, he had dark eyes, set wide apart, sunken cheeks and a high, regal forehead. But he was marked out by his colouring: his face and body were painted entirely in yellow clay. He looked dazed by life and sat on his haunches, his back against the wall, knees pulled up. He stared at me, unblinking. Every inch of him was yellowed, mustard-ghostly and otherworldly. Even his hair was stained a dusty straw.

I had a handful of cigarette lighters, bought as presents. I asked Fioluana to hand them round. Herod, suddenly suspicious, leaned forward greedily.

'Givim.' He grabbed one from my cupped palms. 'You give me one.' He wrapped a tobacco leaf round it and tucked it in his Bible. He could not look me in the eye.

Fioluana distributed the rest. The old man reached towards me and held out his hand in thanks, offering the tips of his yellowed fingers. They felt cool and powdery. He sat back against the wall again. He had a way of staring, with round, bulging eyes, that seemed a parody of puzzlement.

His willingness to shake hands did not surprise me. I'd seen Yasaro's photographs and so expected this greeting, oddly formal and western though it was. Yet no one could tell me when it had begun. Anthropologists believed the white men introduced it to the highlands sixty years ago. The Liawep, I supposed, having had no contact with whites, would have learned it from their contact with traders from the coast.

I explained through Titus that I'd seen the mountain, had visited the clearing where they offered up prayers. They nodded silently, coolly. The man sharpening the arrow laid it on the floor and picked up another. He worked his thick forearms with tiny, precise movements, like a body builder knitting a tea cosy.

'Do you still go there to pray?'

Beside me Herod banged his foot on the floor. I laughed, astonished by the violence of the act, and span round to face

Fioluana, suddenly and painfully aware I'd broken my bond: in front of Herod I'd spoken of our trip to the mountain. But Fioluana was laughing, any disappointment with me seemingly overcome by his shock at Herod's violence. I looked at the priest, expecting further reaction, but he lacked the courage, faced with so many, to sustain his fury openly. Instead he rolled a cigarette, his head bent away from me. He flaked the tobacco on to his Bible, crushing it angrily to powder.

I repeated the question, careless of Herod's discomfort. The yellow man's attention began to waver. In the pale light his face was the dusty dry of old ladies' compacts. His large dog eyes swam around the room.

Two men answered at once. One clenched his fist, then suddenly opened his hand, as if releasing a butterfly he had caught. He shook his head at me. I began to worry. Everything about these men – the way they were lined up against me, backs to the wall, the heaped weapons – made them feel threatening, unpredictable. But their answer, spoken softly, surprised me.

'We go to the mountain when we fight. But we have not fought for a long time – two years perhaps.' Two years ago Jack had walked to Oksapmin. Was it this – their first contact with the outside world – that had put a stop to their fighting?

No one answered. Eventually, when none of the men came forward, Fioluana spoke. 'Since Herod comes, we know we can be locked in prison for fighting.'

Slowly, we warmed into the conversation. It had not started well, but talk of war stirred the men to garrulous babble. Two of them curled their arms round each other's shoulders. They had never been beaten in battle, they bragged. Their traditional enemies were a tribe which used to live on the other side of the river. These were the bogeymen, and any excuse was good enough to start a fight with them. Every few months the Liawep would send a message that the other tribe were 'not fit to fight', that they hadn't the stomach for it. Pride ensured this challenge was not ignored. The Liawep would invite their opponents to a ceremonial feast and ambush them on the way over.

There were other, less gratuitous catalysts to war. It was not uncommon for a dying man to blame another's evil hand for his demise. This might have been one of many comments uttered delirious or close to death, unreasoning, but when he was buried the tribe would gather and pick over his words. It was part of the healing process of grief, I supposed, to pick on a tribe from the other side of the Lagaip, arm and set off for blood.

They became animated when they talked, goaded to manly laughter by the remembrance of spilled blood. And, as they became more passionate, so Herod shrank into himself, muttering miserable, inaudible curses that left no doubt as to the force of his disapproval.

When they finished talking, I scanned their faces, trying to gauge how much was bluff and how much real. Why should I believe that they no longer fought, when they spoke of it with such relish? Their promise that they had renounced it may have been just a nod to Herod's authority, no more than an empty gesture.

The man who had been sharpening the arrows took one and, as if to test the point, pressed it into the hard muscle of his calf until a bead of black blood swelled out. He dipped his finger in the blood and touched it on his tongue.

'No one lives on the other side of the river any more. The jungle is empty.' His laugh was innocent, almost girlish. 'Where are they now? I tell you – we kill them all.'

I was losing control of this encounter, I could feel it. They swaggered unprompted, each one's boasts needling the next into greater extravagance. In my mind they became one, a small army, all muscle and sweat and cold eyes, whose laughter might easily turn cruel. So I asked them about the women, in the hope of dissipating their aggression. Where were they? Why had I seen only two since arriving?

When the question was translated the two young men with turbans turned to each other and giggled. One of the warriors, throwing them a dark look, answered elliptically. He indicated the doors: the one by which we had entered, then the two other, small openings. The last two were for women. The four fires in the room were for four families. Men and women lived together in this house, he said, stroking his chest as if to indicate intimacy. Husbands, wives, sons and daughters sat round their fire together. This was different to the houses we'd passed along the way, in which men and women had been strictly segregated, with separate doors and separate sides of the house. Odd, in the jungle, where there was space for unlimited privacy, to choose such proximity, but perhaps that was just the point. Where all else was wild and unknown, comfort lay in contact.

'And the women?' I repeated. 'Where are they?'

The hunters looked at me suspiciously. Eventually, the old, yellowed man answered. He shifted, revealing a plucked-chicken scrotum, also daubed a morbid yellow. His eyes bulged.

'Perhaps they are in the jungle, perhaps they are in the gardens, perhaps they look after the children.'

'And you? What do the men do?'

He paused, then looked to the others for support. 'We,' he stuttered, 'we hunt.'

His timidity irritated me unaccountably. Why was he so fearful, and the others so bullish? I prodded him cruelly. When the women returned from the gardens to their houses, and they wanted to lie down with their husbands, where did they go? Did they do it in front of everybody else?

He gawped, horrified. His eyes seemed to fill with tears. Repentant, I reached out my hand, but he backed off, into the corner. I turned to Fioluana, guiltily.

Fioluana whispered, 'His wife died. That's why he has painted himself. That is why he does not like to talk about the other women.'

I opened my mouth to apologize but one of the hunters interrupted. He had a scar across his chest which, unstitched, had healed bulbous, shiny and pale.

'We do it outside.' He was looking at the other hunters, grinning.

'In the jungle, you mean?'

'No, in the gardens, when no one else can see, under the banana tree.' He laughed, a burble of catarrh.

Herod nudged me hard. 'Yumi go. We go now.' He dropped his cigarette, spit-soaked and dead, into the nearest fire, and prodded me with his Bible. I wanted to stay, but Herod was determined. He stood and walked to the door, waiting for us to follow.

I did not move. Titus, Dunstan and Fioluana waited for instruction. Herod was hunched over, one foot across the threshold. He addressed Dunstan. 'You come. These are not good men. It is not good to stay here.'

'I'm staying,' I broke in. 'Let Herod go.' I tried to catch his eye, to show my resolution, but he looked at his foot, scratching the floor. When I turned away I sensed him look up.

I had lost my train of thought. There was so much else I wanted to know from these men, but Herod's petulance was distracting. I pressed on, Herod still watching me, and mentioned the weather, all the rain, my worries for our return journey, to which one of the hunters offered, unsmiling, 'If the bridge has gone, you stay here.' I asked about the mountain. Why, every night when the storm came, did it seem to attract lightning? 'That', another hunter sneered, 'is the mountain's anger.'

This proved too much for Herod. He grunted heavily and stormed out down the dark passageway. His footsteps were heavy and deliberate. When he hit the ground outside the pig screeched, terrified, and banged at its leash. Herod snapped at it and, as he kicked off down the village, I heard the sticky slap of his feet stamping through the mud.

I expected Herod's departure to relax everyone, but they had become edgy and confused, like lawless schoolchildren deprived of a teacher against whom to rebel. I thanked them for talking to me, explaining why I had come. They had expressed no curiosity about me, but I wanted to offer them something about myself, something for them to discuss and think over. I did not attempt an explanation of the mechanics of news production, or how a story that broke in a Papua New Guinean newspaper could be read over a suburban breakfast in London two days later, just that, where I came from, people told stories of how the Liawep had just been discovered – that, until Peter Yasaro came, no one knew of their existence. The Liawep, I suggested tentatively, were a 'lost' tribe.

Far from offending them, the idea fed into their notion of themselves as the conquerors of the jungle, the ruling warlords of the forest. They nodded vigorously and answered one another, rather than me. Their voices mixed and tumbled, competing to be heard. 'It's true . . . We are the lost tribe . . . We are way out in the bush. We haven't got lots of friends. Everywhere is very far. We can't say we are related to any

people living round here, in fact we don't know who our
ancestors are. We have no brothers nearby. We are the lost
tribe.'

This was so unexpected I sat and stared. Although, despite
Jack's journey, they clearly knew very little of the outside
world, I had been wary suggesting they were lost. It seemed
indelicate, like calling a backwoodsman primitive. I had
expected a denial, or at worst a stonewalling, but here they
were agreeing with me. I wished Carol Jenkins had been there.
She would have reached for her Benson & Hedges, spat, cursed
goddamn, poked her aviators back on to the bridge of her nose
and accused me of asking loaded questions. But there it was,
all the same.

My astonishment must have been obvious. One of the
hunters tapped my knee with an arrow. Before he spoke he
signalled for Titus' attention, emphasizing the weight of the
,words to come. Titus's interpretation, he seemed to be
indicating, would be crucial.

'The reason we are the lost tribe is because we killed
everyone else. And then we live here on our own, a long way
from anywhere. That is why people are frightened and why
you hear stories along the way. We are the people who fight
and kill a lot of people.'

'And you? All of you have killed people?'

'Yes.' His smile fell away. It was a pose, this, melodramatic,
but I was caught up nonetheless, swept along in awe. 'But
Uana, the old man, he has eaten men. We, who are younger,
have only killed.'

I looked at Uana, saffron-gilled. He seemed an unlikely
cannibal, so shy and bewildered, unable even to cope with the
novelty of myself sitting asking questions. I tried to imagine
him as a young man, taut and hungry like these hunters, but

could see only his morose, aged self, lost in his own grief and self-pity.

One of the hunters leaned over to him. As he spoke, a smile spread over Uana's face: his few remaining teeth were chipped and blackened. I could hear his breath, heavy through his nose. The hunter seemed to be goading him, his voice tipping upwards encouragingly. Eventually Uana spoke.

'It's like pork.' The hunters clutched their sides and rocked with laughter. It seemed rehearsed, this scenario, a party piece that had been played before, Uana shocking the impressionable by describing the taste of human flesh. He looked at my neck while he spoke, adding something about its sweet taste, but I took no more in. I was picturing veal, or sweet and sour chicken, the meat soft and melting in the mouth, and Uana's old face bent over, skin slack and sallow, drooling blindly, working the loose meat with toothless grey gums.

They were still laughing when we left. I felt glad to be off; they were anarchic, their humour a lawless weapon directed as much at myself as at Herod or Uana. And this was their good side – I did not want to encounter them out for blood, worked up into a lather of revenge.

Outside, the sun was trying to break through: the pattern for midmorning. Mud was drying into crusts, still slippery underneath. We looked into the church, halfway down the spur. The flood had already drained away, and the water was now confined to the surrounding ditch.

I walked in silence, confused about the Liawep hierarchy. Officially, Jack was the leader, but these men, insolent though they may be, seemed far stronger. And what of the chief? Where did he fit in? I asked Fioluana if he could arrange a meeting.

He promised to try. But it would not be easy. 'He lives alone now. He does not speak to anyone.' This was Yasaro's doing. By appointing Jack as *luluai*, or leader, he had undermined the chief. Now he lived alone with his son, in a house isolated in a new clearing, away from the village. Perhaps, Fioluana suggested, he might speak to me. Perhaps not. He would ask.

We disbanded: Fioluana to his wife and children, Dunstan and Titus back to Herod's house. I circled the village, walking along its perimeter, along bare earth and round the houses, always with the drop-off into jungle just one step away. Cloud was clearing from the big mountain, creaking slowly upwards like a giant safety curtain.

As I passed the church I saw movement in the tobacco plants. I walked closer. It was the little girl with the flowery dress who had been so sick in church. She seemed better now, covering her face with a leaf in the hope that this would somehow conjure her disappearance. I moved on, not wishing to frighten her, but she must have wanted me to see her – she flapped the leaf to attract my attention. I swung round, expecting to see her smiling or waving, but she crouched down, holding her breath, her eyes screwed up tight.

Chapter 14

Slowly, I recovered from the journey. Although, having finished our food, we were reduced to the Liawep starch-only diet, I was feeling stronger and sleeping more deeply. The days were gentle: endless conversation with Fioluana, children and the occasional adult circling timidly; weather like a speeded-up film, the panicked tumbling and darkening of clouds, rain, lightning closing, then, come morning, sunshine again, hot and clear.

Herod grew to enjoy our company. Although he distrusted me, and resented Titus interpreting, he was starved enough of company to recognize a chance to offload his frustrations and anger. Besides, three of the carriers – Andrew, Dison and Miniza – came from Wanakipa, Herod's home. They gossiped late into the night.

Darkness fell around seven; at night the house was full. The floor trembled as Herod trod carefully round the fire, preparing his family for sleep, and the carriers shifted on the floorboards, trying to get comfortable. Dunstan and I had been given special treatment — a room, just wide enough to lie side by side and long enough, if I angled my feet out of the door, to stretch full-length. The door at our feet gave on to the fire; the side wall, a papery partition of bark and banana leaves, separated us from the veranda, which skirted the front of the house. Before Herod lay down he would drop one last log on the fire. As the flames leapt upwards, they threw drunken shadows across the roof: Herod's tobacco; my socks hung to dry; the close-weaved leaves sloping upwards. By ten everyone would be asleep.

At five thirty every morning — well before dawn — we were awoken violently. It began as a dry, scratching sound on the veranda, just a few inches from my ear. Then a sniffling and snorting, the unmistakable ruderies of early-morning pigs, hungry and impatient. When Herod and breakfast showed no signs of appearing, the pigs started squawking, first one, then the others chorusing behind. It started like whispers, mild complaints, almost mouse-like, and degenerated into the sound of chickens being strangled by thick-fingered farmers. Through the house I could hear people turning, waking, twisting away from the screeching in the hope that it would quieten and dissolve. It was like ten pairs of long-nailed hands scratched down a brand new blackboard. Herod woke within seconds, stumbling over the bodies round the cold morning fire and struggling with the beaten-out plank that rested against the doorway. He lifted and moved it sideways and, in his rush, banged it too hard on the floor. He spat out an invective and kicked on to the veranda. The pigs scuttled round his feet, yapping like hungry terriers. Dunstan pretended to sleep through, as if he could wish it away. His eyes were closed, but his arms were folded over his chest and his fists were clenched.

Herod shooed the piglets off the veranda and threw them half-eaten *kaukau*. The potatoes thumped into the mudbank. The pigs snuffled and gargled with pleasure.

It took a few days, but gradually my presence seemed to frighten the Liawep less. They certainly avoided me less; even the women, who at first had fled, now continued with their work when I passed. I imagined this to be Fioluana's doing: he must have explained who I was.

The village was a quiet place. Little happened each day. Sometimes I saw boys playing a bastard soccer with an inflated pig's bladder, belting it around the flat earth of the helipad, scrabbling for possession with their elbows and fists. Near the end of the day women built fires outside their houses, burning the logs down and heaping the ash to make *mumus* to bake kaukau and taro. The fires glowed like beacons up the village as darkness fell. Then they died, and the rain came.

Fioluana opened up slowly. It took him four days to tell me that he had not only a wife, whose mother we'd seen under the big house that second day, but two daughters. This, it emerged, was the key to his helpfulness: he wanted his daughters to be educated; Herod and Jack had told him about schools. He saw me as a go-between. He reminded me his family had been in church, all but the baby. The woman who'd looked so exhausted, and the girl in the flowery dress who'd toyed with me, hiding in the tobacco bush, they were his wife and daughter. He promised to introduce me later.

The longer I stayed, the more I witnessed the Liawep's strength and independence. They believed, and bragged as much whenever I was near, that they were the 'last people' because they had killed most of their neighbours; in recent years, no one had dared approach. This seemed to explain Herod's difficulties: if the Liawep had managed to remain undiscovered until 1993, they could surely keep a single priest at bay. Even the handful who had consented to baptism, such as Fioluana and his family, seemed to be in it largely for the novelty, for something to tell the others.

Like other Liawep, Fioluana exercised a quiet defiance. He admitted to me that he still had tokens – shells, good-luck plants – that Herod had banned. But more than this, he had the forest, in which his and all the Liawep's real imaginative life found expression, and which Herod could never touch.

For me, the jungle was the dark unknown, a place without markers, with no beginning and no end. For the Liawep, it was home. But more than this, it had become the landscape of their mind. The jungle floor was littered with meaning. The gurgle of a brook across a plate of pebbles was a child spirit's laughter; the papery crumple of leaves was another spirit's skin, shed in a hurry; birdsong was the calling of the other world. The Liawep, ever wary of my curiosity, dropped this much inadvertently.

Only once, climbing up through the jungle to the village, did I see one of these objects with my own eyes. It happened by accident: I sat on it.

'Get up! Get up!' Fioluana was hopping from foot to foot, anxious tanket leaves flapping up and down. Titus and Dunstan were behind him, gesturing furiously.

'Wh . . . what?'

'That rock,' Fioluana pointed, elbowing past me.

I had sat on a holy rock, he stuttered. Its peculiar shape – smooth and round, with two soft dips, half filled with rainwater – held meaning. '*Long taim bifo*', when the world was beginning, a man lived down here, on the lower slopes of the big mountain. One day out hunting he spotted a wild woman, the first he'd ever seen. He chased her across the jungle, across gullies and over boulders until, exhausted, she collapsed on this rock. The shallows in the rock were the imprints left by her breasts. Fioluana made me promise to keep the story to myself. 'Yu tokim i no gat man. Tell no one, especially Herod.'

I kept my promise, but Herod, fighting a hundred battles at once, had stopped asking me where I'd been or who I'd talked to. For days, a rebellion had been building, and he was summoning his strength to fight it.

A woman was dying. Herod had forbidden ancestral remedies, exhorting her family to turn to God for help. He had expressly banned the killing of a pig, traditionally the most reliable sacrifice. They defied him three hours later.

I was sitting with Dunstan on the lip of the helipad, gazing out over the jungle. He was smoking uncured bush tobacco, a habit he'd begun since the start of the journey and which increased as the storms built and his nerves frayed. Behind us, near the top of the village, came a terrible scream, more animal than human, ripped-out and hoarse.

A crowd had gathered near the church. In the centre, men were bent over, shouting. They were hurling spears, in turn, into the centre of a circle. I realized these were the hunters we'd met earlier. The helpless beast at their feet, stuck with a bristle of spears, was a pig.

Two of them stood aside to let us watch. The pig was tied to a stake by its neck, its eyes rolling, hosing blood, stuck like an exhausted bull at the mercy of the matador. One spear had pinned it to the ground through its neck. When it screeched and tried to lift its head, the shaft tore further into its windpipe. Purple blood darkened the earth and seeped downhill. The men screamed and stamped their feet; blood splashed up their legs.

Herod, disgusted, had shut himself in his house. He had

tried to intervene earlier in the day, but the men had nodded silently and gone ahead anyway.

This sacrifice was the core of the healing ritual. The first part, which had been performed that morning, saw crushed bark sprinkled over the sick woman's face. Then the pig had been dragged into the house, its face held up close to her skin. Only when she could stand its smell no more had it been taken outside and speared to death.

In the evening the men built a pyramid of logs seven feet high. They lit it after sunset and the flames flew like crazy tattered flags against the black night. As it burned, so they beat it down. Finally they laid the dead animal in the flames and the flesh spat and cracked and bubbled.

They pulled it from the flames when the skin had charred, and one of the hunters, the squat, determined warrior who had been sharpening his arrows when we'd talked a few days earlier, began tearing skin from the rib cage: great sweaty slabs, pink and bleeding on one side, burnt black on the other.

The men dismembered the animal and carried it past Dunstan and me. One hefted a haunch on to his shoulder, the leg sagging where the bone had been broken. They walked to the bottom end of the village and dropped off into the jungle. Unconcerned by the undersea darkness of the jungle at night, they were on their way to the sick woman's house. She would eat and the sickness, so the belief went, would fall away.

Herod was silent with anger when we returned to his house. That we had dared watch made us accomplices. He would say only one thing that evening, repeating it over and over again. 'She will die.'

In his failure to bring the Liawep to their knees, Herod was atypical. The last century has seen missionaries bulldoze unchallenged through most Papua New Guinean societies. The people, astonishingly, have seemed only too willing to forsake the old for the incomprehensible new, with its shiny emissaries in starched collars, clasping buckskin-bound Bibles.

This had certainly been the case in Tari, eighty miles south from Liawep, where I'd started my journey. In the early 1950s, when the white men moved in, they built everything – churches, mission and government buildings – from hoop pine, little knowing that the trees protected religious sites. And yet the people did not fight it. They bent to the new wind, rather than let it uproot them, mixing even Christ's crucifixion with their own belief, of a boy whose blood had been shed in the cause of social harmony, to create a workable hybrid.

Rare were missionaries who respected indigenous beliefs. A handful, like the pioneering German Lutheran Georg Vicedom, embraced at least the concept. In the late 1930s he railed against Mick Leahy for flying wide-eyed highlanders to the coast: to show such innocents the sea, Vicedom claimed, was to explode their understanding of the universe. 'The natives who travelled with the Europeans have never discovered the spirits abroad which they thought to encounter and particularly did not find the sky legs and the land of the sun and the moon in the east, but the sea. With this, the main support of their beliefs collapsed.' Humbug, of course: among 'his' tribes, Vicedom had been only too quick to replace traditional beliefs with Christianity.

Only in a few cases have missionaries experienced deliberate and sustained resistance. It took Des and Jenny Oatridge, two determined translators from the Summer Institute of Linguistics, most of the 1950s and 1960s to wear down the resistance of the Binumariens, a tight-knit group in the eastern highlands. For almost a decade, the tribe refused to divulge all but their language's most basic building-blocks. When the Oatridges floundered in syntax and vocabulary they did not understand, the Binumariens watched, amused, and did nothing to help.

It was not this bad for Herod; he, at least, had been helped to learn the language. But that seemed to be as far as it went; the rest he was having to fight for. The Liawep, unlike the tribes Mick Leahy or Jack Hides encountered, seemed wary and knowing. This made sense: Herod was not their first experience of the outside world. Jack's stories of Oksapmin, and the arrival of Yasaro's patrol, had prepared them for change. Likewise, when I arrived, they already knew of the existence of white men. They may not have understood who I was or why I was there, but they knew I was not the walking dead.

But, like Leahy and Hides' adventures, mine was still in essence a 'first contact': the first time our two worlds had met. And as with the first explorers, one thing was guaranteed: none of us would be the same again.

Like Leahy and Hides, the responsibility this brought dawned on me only slowly. The mistakes they had made should have alerted me earlier. Those two, caught up in a battle for status, to prove themselves the best, the bravest, the first, were reduced to squabbling infants. In 1935, as he sailed to England for a holiday, Leahy learned with shock that, back in New Guinea, Hides was claiming to have been the first to discover populations Leahy believed were 'his'. Like Speke in his quarrel with Burton over the source of the Nile, Leahy laid his claim before the Royal Geographical Society in London. Urged to be 'frank', Leahy coolly detailed his search for gold over eleven separate journeys, the total of thirty-one dead and an unknown number of wounded. He admitted the murders casually, as if they were an explorer's everyday hazard, like flooded rivers or dysentery.

*

The Liawep surprised me constantly. Even the fact that they were monogamous was unexpected. I'd guessed the old man we met the day before arriving at Liawep would be typical. He had boasted of three wives, even though nominally a Christian.

I fancied the Liawep's monogamy was down to numbers: with twice as many men as women, no man would be allowed more than one wife. It followed, too, that there would be men doomed to bachelorhood. These last wore a distinctive headgear – the back-sloping turban I'd seen earlier.

There were five of these young bachelors, not all oafish adolescents like the ones I'd met in the big house. But they were all young, with bronze unmarked skin and a feline grace which provided the only feminine element in this drab place, where the women were too ground down by working the land and feeding the children to give much thought to vanity.

They walked about together. They lived, it was said, in a big house an hour down the mountain, looking west up the river towards Oksapmin. They appeared only occasionally, walking very close together, sometimes holding hands.

They looked like brothers, and dressed identically. Each wore a tapering turban, two feet high, cocked back on the head. So crazy was the angle that only the tightness of the forehead binding kept it from toppling. The turbans were made of a dark, oily weave, into which scarlet flowers were threaded. This was their sole sartorial extravagance – their tanket leaves were tidy but undecorated, and they were otherwise naked.

They were shy with me, which was hardly unexpected. But the more I saw of them, and observed their effeminacy, the more I suspected that 'unmarried' might be a polite Liawep euphemism. I put this to Fioluana. He spluttered in astonishment. He placed his hand on my knee, anxiously. 'They are friends. They are waiting for women, that's all.' Yet there were no eligible Liawep women. Perhaps these men had simply given up waiting and turned to each other for intimacy.

They took a superficial interest in me – who I was, what I was doing, why I was staying with Herod. But when I explained, they only nodded blankly. In return I asked them if they wanted to marry. They nodded in unison, smiling blandly back. I noticed their nails – trimmed and clean of dirt, a degree of purity that must have taken dedication.

'Your hands,' I remarked. 'Have you never fought?'

The tallest fanned out his fingers and looked across his nails. 'No,' he answered, 'we are too young.'

It made no sense. Herod, when I found him in the church and asked his opinion, made no attempt to hide his loathing. He was brushing the dirt floor with an angry witches' broom, kicking through a dust cloud. He hated the men, their hats, their habits. They lived 'like Sodom', and they would rot in hell.

There was one recent activity, however, in which Herod found succour. There had been a wedding. Better still, Herod's persuasions had prevailed and it had taken place in church. He took this as a sign that things were changing, that his message was getting through, but since the ceremony the couple seemed to have disappeared. They cropped up in conversation, but did not appear. People spoke of them in hushed tones, expectant.

I noticed the bride first, a few days on. She was not living in one of the houses on the spur, but a little way off, in the jungle. She had walked up to the village with an older woman, who watched her fiercely. The older woman wore a skirt of muddied, knotted grass and had a deep-lined, weathered face. She was driving a handaxe into something on the ground. The bride looked on, terrified, clutching vegetables to her chest.

Her crown of flowers, worn fresh on the wedding day, was wilting and crumpled.

The whole custom seemed bizarre. For a week after the wedding, a bride would live with her mother-in-law, who passed on skills and wisdom; during that time, the groom hid out with his friends. I saw him a day later. He was hunting in the forest with the warriors, looking grim and bloody.

Like his bride, he wore his wedding blooms still threaded in his hair, blowsy red petals that had kept their colour. He stood at the head of the hunting party, his body still slippery with pig grease from the wedding ceremony. When he saw Dunstan and me approaching, he stopped and glared. He threw his fist in the air and brandished his bow at me. I stopped. Behind me, Dunstan blasphemed into his beard.

Fioluana stepped forward and mediated. The groom eyed me suspiciously, focusing on my muddied trainers, nodding repeatedly. Eventually he lowered his weapon and led his men past us. Not until they were out of sight did their voices rise again.

He believed, Fioluana explained, that I was some kind of spy. As a newly married man, he had to be especially wary — any strangers encountered during that first week were believed to be hostile, a bad omen for the success of the marriage, for his potency and his wife's fertility.

Two days later, I saw the couple together. After the separation they seemed distant and cautious. When she looked into his face, he looked away irritably. When she stretched up her hand as if to stroke his head, he swatted it away.

His payment for her hand had been two pigs. One was a sow, with swollen teats, the other a runt with a backbone ridged like knuckles. This humble offering was his 'bride price', a pattern common throughout Papua New Guinea. The only difference between the Liawep and moneyed, Land-cruiser-driving highland businessmen was the size of the gift. Among the latter it might be a car or a house; in Liawep it was a couple of pigs, some shells, or bows and arrows. The pigs scuffed in the dust and strained at their leashes. The small one would be eaten; the sow kept for breeding.

From then on I saw the couple separately. There was a reason for this – he was hacking a clearing from the jungle in which to build a house and plant a garden, an activity from which she was excluded. The other men helped him, and at the end of each day they all climbed back up to the village, laid down their axes in a heap and waited for their women to feed them. Months later, the garden would yield its first harvest. If it bore heavy, fleshy fruit and firm *kaukau*, the couple would give thanks by throwing a party for the woman's family, as if it were she who had sprinkled magic dust on the ground.

I began to wonder how much longer we should stay. The carriers were becoming bored and impatient and I was feeling a creeping sense of unease, dreaming lurid, melodramatic nightmares in which I would be abandoned by them, left to the warriors' mercy. To begin with, I had been tolerated as a curiosity; now I felt a growing irritation at my endless questioning. Only Fioluana, whose helpfulness I did not yet understand, stuck by me.

The weather was worsening, too. The first two or three days in the village did not seem like the wet season. The sky had been clear and the clouds pale, broken, unthreatening. Increasingly, as the days passed, the rain came down. It approached slowly, visible a long way off, sweeping in across three valleys. It beat on the roofs of the houses, turning the leaves soggy and dripping down pillars and the inside of walls; it pummelled little craters into the mud and filled the streams and the rivers.

The amount that fell had a direct impact on the safety of our return and the noise of the storm breaking made me sick inside. I thought of the last bridge we had crossed, which sagged so precariously over the Lagaip, dragging in the river. By now, I felt sure, it would have broken away in the high floodwater.

Like sailors in a small boat on a high sea counting their flares and checking their life vests, we talked of little else but the rain. If the bridge was washed away, what would we do? I was in favour of building a raft which, if strong enough, would rush us downriver to Wanakipa in six hours rather than six days. Dunstan played along, but was unconvinced. We'll see, he kept saying.

One evening a boy we'd met in the jungle arrived in the village. We were sitting round Herod's fire and the house was soupy with blue tobacco smoke. Everyone smoked turnip-shaped cigarettes, with fat cigar-ends and tapering waists. The boy walked with a stoop, as if embarrassed by his height. He wore sideburns, an unusual affectation, and walked with his bottom out, as if perpetually climbing through sodden jungle. His skin was very black and he wore a fuzz of moustache and chin hair. He talked with eyes bulging and restless, crouching with his knees against his chest, his tanket leaves brushed under him. He had come from the bridge that day and said it was still intact. He'd crossed, but in the middle, he said, pointing to just below his knees, the bridge was well underwater. There were few ropes remaining and he didn't think it would last much longer. How long? I said. He didn't know: 'One day if it carries on raining. Two weeks if it doesn't.' He was distracted by grief. He'd been hunting and had tried to carry both his dogs across the river. In the middle, where he could no longer see his feet, he'd missed his footing and one dog had slipped from under his arm into the warm opaque water. He'd grabbed the handrail as he went down, watching the dog's head turn in the current, nose raised for air, then disappear in the enfolding water.

The storms came in the evening and gathered force as they neared. If the Liawep had had any notion of the mechanics of lightning, or if any of the houses had boasted lightning conductors, I would have slept easy. For houses built further down the jungleside, this was not a problem – the canopy would draw the lightning first. But the houses on the spur were exposed. Herod's church was the highest, and if lightning struck anywhere I hoped it would be the church, during the night, when people were safe in their houses. I had yet to see any way Herod's God had improved the Liawep's lives. All I saw was their puzzled faces and their lives brought to heel. I would have enjoyed the dismay on Herod's face and the Liawep's suppressed excitement when they looked on the smoking ash in the morning.

One evening I watched a storm come in. It started raining long before the lightning came. The sky turned black and, as darkness fell, the clouds sank over the mountain, obliterating everything. There was no one about. In Liawep cosmology, I'd learned, lightning was just another sign of divine displeasure. They cowered in their houses, crouched about their fires, smoking incessantly. Before the storm hit the mountain there was a stillness and the rain beat straight down. It was utterly dark. There was only the crack and rumble of cosmic electricity as it approached, and the startling white neon of the lightning, like a striplight poorly connected, jerking into life. In seconds the two synchronized and the village was bright, frozen. I was sitting, foolishly, on the edge of the spur in the half-built house, and looked up towards the church. The lightning forked down into the jungle at the top edge of the village, and everything went dark again, just the shhh of the rain. In the blackness I ran, panicking, falling forwards, backwards, arriving with mud all down my back and up my side, breathless, at Herod's house.

Jack Hides had suffered these feelings, too, not only the terror of the wilderness, but the ache of being deeply and unforgivably foreign, and had attempted to bridge the divide with generosity. To people who had fled their villages in terror, he left beads, bushknives and mirrors. But often he found these returned to him: the people thought he had forgotten them, and would return, vengeful, to collect them. Mick Leahy, a man with a harder heart, was less inclined to fear. He photographed the people rather than attempt dialogue; he had come for gold, not to understand another culture. When he became irritated, or felt himself cornered, he put away his Leica and reached for his rifle.

Chapter 15

I woke continually through the night, jolted upright by thunder. Oblivious, the rain fell with cruel monotony, seeping through the walls, softening the floor. It eased off around five and I lay awake, listening to the forest hiss and began to breathe again. The jungle was like a giant waking animal, its pulse quickening as dawn drew near.

As grey began to filter through the blackness I struggled from my sleeping bag. First light would bring the piglets and I could not bear their desperate snufflings and squeakings. The fleeting charm of novelty had faded days ago.

Swollen from the rain, the floorboards made no sound as I tiptoed towards the door. Only one of the carriers was awake – the curmudgeonly Dison, who looked up blankly as I left the house, his eyes blind from a sleepless night.

I had a loose arrangement with Fioluana. After days of promising, he had agreed to take me to meet the chief in his house deep in the jungle. It was not far, but I would not have been able to find it on my own and, besides, needed Fioluana to make the introductions. He had promised to come to Herod's house early. I walked to the top of the spur, tore a handful of leaves from a tobacco plant, shook them free of water, and lay them over a sodden log. Sitting here, with the village stretched out below, I would see him arrive.

I was the only person about. This was the edge of the day, with no colours yet risen from the mud-grey half-light. It was cold, too, and I longed for the sun to warm my back but, more than this, for something other than *kaukau* or taro to eat. My provisions, carelessly rationed, had run out on our first day in the village, and since then I had been forced to barter our few luxuries. Dunstan's torch, complete with two dying batteries, had bought a mound of *kaukau* so substantial I worried that the Liawep had left none for themselves; the earth, though dark and peaty, seemed to yield little.

Significantly, it had been three women who had come with the food. Catering, gardening and childbirth were women's duties; unlike elsewhere in Papua New Guinea, females were not believed to have special powers and were never segregated, even during menstruation. It could not have been more different for Jack Hides, who was once flashed at by a row of grass-skirted native women, intent on terrifying him off their land. Liawep women, by contrast, seemed put-upon and exhausted.

Power was balanced subtly between the sexes. There was no easy comparison to draw with other highland societies: all were different. To one tribe, women were cannibals who clawed through graveyards, eating putrefying male flesh. To another, they were wide-eyed innocents who had only the most marginal role in the reproductive process; in these societies both sexes agreed that the semen alone created the foetus. The Liawep women certainly enjoyed more equality than this but, in the absence of war, it was only a partial freedom: now the men loitered idly, and the women worked the soil alone.

Gardens were scattered through the nearby jungleside; an overhead photograph would have revealed the central gash of brown – the village – then the spread of dark green jungle, infected with tiny pale green blotches of new-cut undergrowth. Often I tried to find these gardens, but would only stumble into the clearings by mistake, on the way to somewhere else. Once, exploring with Dunstan, we had disturbed two women unearthing *kaukau*. The roots came away with bricks of wet, coffee-coloured earth. The women wore grass skirts and their breasts, as they bent over, stretched almost to the ground. Dunstan snickered; one heard him and turned, clutching at her vegetables as if afraid we had come to take them. The other dug on, unconcerned, her forearms buried in the fleshy soil.

Dawn spilled rather than broke, leaking pale light over the mountains and into the valleys, lifting red mud and bluey-green jungle from the bleak uniform grey. Clouds, broken and insubstantial, clung to the valley walls far below the village.

Light brought Herod's pigs up the mudbank from under his house. I watched them with a malicious pleasure, just glad not to suffer them this morning. Further up the spur behind me, from the big house in which we had first met the hunters, came the stumbling of creaking boards and wet, early morning tobacco coughs. They carried like gunshots in the hazy stillness.

Inside the church, thirty yards down the mud slope, there was movement. I had seen nothing when I passed earlier, but now in the daylight I could see a figure shifting about inside.

From the heavy lumberings, the broad shoulders, it was clearly a man. I slipped from the log and skirted the edge of the clearing, rather than approach the church direct and risk frightening the furtive penitent. The mud was as slick as wet clay and twice I slipped, catching myself on my side. I reached the edge panting, and stopped behind a clutch of tobacco plants, hoary and overgrown. I hid myself, water shedding over my legs.

A man was up at the altar, running his hands along the lip, lovingly or distractedly, it was impossible to tell. I did not recognize him. His head was shaved and every man I had met so far had curly hair: short, but never close-cropped. His skin glowed dully through the stubble.

He began to edge up the aisle towards the door, turning every two or three steps to look at the altar. He stepped into the daylight cautiously and looked about, squinting uphill towards the mountain.

To my shock, I realized it was the chief. It was his silhouette that had confused me: he had had overgrown, wiry hair before. His newly shaved head made him look several stages more decrepit. His back, I noticed when he turned away, was ribbed with glassy scars. His tanket leaves were torn and dusty and gaped open over one buttock. He scanned the tobacco plants where I was hiding, but his face registered nothing. His white wounded eye made him look half blind. Across the bright morning air I heard his breath, hoarse and tight like an old man's. He stood before the cross and stared and stared, as if trying to understand. Growing stiff from crouching, I knelt down, yet despite all the rustling and my own cursing, he did not seem to hear. His whole body seemed slack inside, as if the puppet master had cut his strings. After a while he turned towards the edge of the clearing, where the mud turned to grass and the jungle began again. As he disappeared from sight

I noticed the soles of his feet, printed bright with orangey mud.

I picked myself up from the ground; mud was smeared all down my knees. I walked to the door of the church and looked in, wondering whether the chief had left anything, any clue as to his intentions, but the altar was untouched, the fringe of flowers curled and browning. The aisle was sticky and his footprints were clearly marked: wide soles with splayed toes. I wondered why he had come here. He had acted with a curious respect, quite at odds with the aggressive demeanour I'd encountered before; this seemed a solemn, very personal pilgrimage.

As I was climbing the log barrier in the middle of the village below the church, before returning to Herod's house, I spotted him again. I squatted near the base of the logs. The chief was forty yards off, beyond Herod's house, standing on the distinctive flattened mud circle that passed for the helipad. He must have scouted along the edge of the clearing, rather than drop down into the jungle as I had thought, and crept up again stealthily.

He stood in the middle with his arms outstretched, like a child pretending to be an aeroplane. He turned his face to the sky and, shuffling his feet with tiny birdlike movements, began to turn. He span towards me, and away, and round again towards me. He slowed to a stop with his back to me and lowered his arms to his sides. Before he slouched off, to disappear into the jungle, he stole one last glance at Herod's house. It was the look of a superstitious man, obsessively checking that things were as he had left them, that no one knew his secret.

I mentioned none of this to Herod, or indeed to Dunstan or Titus, though they could be trusted to keep counsel. I barely understood what I had seen myself; there was no simple explanation I could pass on. Instead, when I returned to Herod's house, I said I'd been unable to sleep and had wanted to watch the dawn rise. Dunstan eyed me strangely, but Herod, still bleary from sleep, simply sniffed and continued stoking the fire.

Puzzling over what I had seen, I forgot that I had arranged to meet Fioluana. When Dunstan reminded me, I was already an hour late. I slipped from the house, cursing my forgetfulness, whispering for Titus to follow.

Fioluana seemed unconcerned by the delay. He was standing by the church, whistling to himself. He grinned when he saw us.

'He's been here,' he said, pointing to the chief's footprints round the door.

I nodded. 'I know. I saw him.'

Fioluana hiccuped in surprise, wiping his nose on the back of his hand. 'You?'

'He was in the church. And further downhill, too.'

'You are lucky he does not see you.' The sentence trailed away ominously. He turned. 'Come, we go.'

We steered wide of Herod's house. Even at forty yards, muffled by wood and leaves and firesmoke, his voice grated. At the edge of the clearing I looked back, but no one was around. Pale smoke steamed from the roofs of the five houses on the spur, each set about the perimeter, secure in its own half-acre of mud. The plank was still in place across Herod's doorway, just as I'd left it.

I followed Fioluana and Titus, dropping down the path towards the valley, walking from waist-high grass into the jungle, vast and dark and cool. A cockatoo, brilliant white, sailed over the treetops, far above in breaking sunshine.

The chief's house was an hour down, across overgrown,

tangled paths. The clearing was tiny, the space round the house
barely enough to walk unhindered. No vegetables had been
planted, nor were there any animals. The house was raised
on stilts four feet high, but underneath, in the dry, where
normally there would be heaped *kaukau* or a tethered pig
scratching in the dirt, there was only limp, yellowed grass. The
tree stumps still looked jagged and shiny, as if they had been
cut only days before. The whole place had an air of eerie
impermanence.

I followed Fioluana up the steps, so newly cut they were still
bubbled and gluey with resin. I could hear the hiss and split of
a new fire; smoke, thick like burned dung, roughened the back
of my throat.

'He's here,' Fioluana whispered. 'He waits for us.'

It took my eyes a minute to adjust. I saw first the red of the
embers, then smoke curling in shafts of daylight.

Titus was the first to speak. 'Lukim. In the corner.' He
crouched. From the darkness there was an animal scuffle. Titus
moved forward and pointed. I picked out a shape: a little boy,
no more than five or six, squatting naked, his hands over his
eyes. Titus held out his hand and spoke softly.

This was the chief's son. He did not know where his father
was, but said he had not been gone long. I suggested we wait.
Fioluana disagreed. It was not polite, he said. We must leave.
Unwilling to waste the journey, I suggested we talk to the boy.
Fioluana assented grudgingly, his arms folded, shaking his
head.

The two of them, father and son, lived here alone. Until
Herod came, the chief had lived in the biggest house in the
village, the one in which we had met the hunters. It was the
coming of Herod, and Yasaro's appointment of Jack as the new
luluai, that had undermined him. He moved away, taking his
pain and his little boy with him. I asked the boy how often he

came up to the village now, but he shook his head and tucked his head between his knees.

'He never comes,' Fioluana said, hustling me towards the door.

But the sight of us leaving shook the boy out of his shell. He stood up and waved to gain Fioluana's attention. He pointed to the dark corner behind us, reached into the shadow and pulled out a longbow and a sheaf of arrows with plain, unfeathered shafts. He handed me the bow. It was filmy with dust. These were his father's weapons, he said. The bow string had gone slack and the arrows were blunt.

'He does not hunt any more,' Fioluana prompted. 'Not since Peter made Jack the *luluai*.' Until then, the roles had been clear: the chief had been the chief. Now, all was in flux, and the chief's discarded weapons, his whole beleaguered demeanour, possibly even his newly shaved head, reflected this.

Fioluana took the weapons from me and returned them to the boy. The chief used to be a great fighter, he went on. His strength and leadership were real and impressive, and not just reserved for combat with enemy tribes: he had been a forceful arbitrator in domestic quarrels, too. 'When one man's pig ate another man's *kaukau*, the chief thought that was very serious.' Fioluana spoke soberly, reverently. 'If the man meant his pig to do that, then the chief would kill the pig. But other times he makes peace: if two men are fighting over a pig or a woman, he will stop them. They always obey him.'

'And now?' We were outside in the clearing, the boy watching us from the top of the steps.

'Now?' Fioluana laughed bitterly, the first time I'd seen real anger in his eyes. 'Now we have no leader. Jack is too young. No one follows Herod. And Peter? He will not come back.'

*

We climbed in single file back through the jungle towards the village. I was sure we were being followed. The three of us walked close together, but nearby, whenever I stopped to listen, there seemed something else, a big animal, echoing our footsteps. But I saw nothing: the undergrowth was too dense, and the jungle too dark. Even when it cleared a little and the sun broke through the canopy, there was only silence all around.

As we began the scramble out on to the village plateau, I saw a figure up ahead. It was the chief, sitting on a fallen tree beside the path. His shaven head made him look pitiably naked; whatever status he once had was now fallen from him. He sat with his forehead rested against crouched-up knees, and I remembered his son, an hour earlier, hunched over in the dark house.

Fioluana and he shook hands. I offered mine, but he would not take it.

'Why?' I pleaded.

The chief spoke sullenly, looking at my shoes.

Fioluana turned to me, shaking his head. 'Because you are Herod's friend. That is what he thinks.'

Choking back disbelief, I tried to explain. The chief listened, brushing his tanket skirt absentmindedly with the back of one hand. By his side lay a string bag, collapsed into grimy folds. Fioluana translated Titus' words in a measured, kindly tone. He seemed to be taking great care.

The chief looked me over cautiously. Silently, he touched a finger down his chest. Slashed diagonally across his sternum was a six-inch scar which, left to heal unstitched, had ballooned into a fat, pinky slug. He waited while I took it in, but offered no explanation.

He leaned over and fished open his bag. His skull was nicked with tiny black scabs where he'd shaved too close. He turned back to me with both hands full: two fistfuls of tiny cowrie shells, many half broken, with milky pearl insides. He tipped them back into the bag and took out two bigger, pink-fringed cowries. These were his riches. Just like the highlanders whom Leahy and Hides had encountered sixty years before, the Liawep currency was shell. The chief's, however, were poor specimens; tarnished and chipped. I took one when he insisted; it rattled, as if broken inside. Was this all he had? It seemed a meagre haul for a former *bigman*.

Fioluana shook his head. 'Herod. He took them all.'

I suggested we walk the rest of the way to the village together, but the chief would not move. He patted the earth, indicating we stay with him. I explained that we had been to his house, and were disappointed not to find him in. He smiled quietly, making it clear he not only knew this but had tracked us there and back. Close to, I found him less intimidating. He was well built, certainly, but his eyes would not settle and jerked about erratically. He seemed barely sane, on the verge of a terrible madness no one else could share and he could not explain.

I asked him about the future: what did he want to happen? When I mentioned Jack and Herod, he pouted in disgust. 'Jack is no leader,' he grimaced, displaying a mouth like a cave, with only three or four teeth remaining in pale, diseased gums.

And his hair? Why had he shaved it all off? It had been the custom, he said, before Herod came. When the men went to fight they would razor their heads smooth.

When we stood to climb the last stretch to the ridge I expected him to stay, stubborn and sullen, but he got up, too, and started following us. I asked him why he now wanted to come, but he stared ahead, his pupils pulsing, as if he did not understand the question.

We emerged from the jungle at the bottom of the village, at

the helipad lip. Three small boys were throwing stones at each other, ducking and weaving while the missiles slugged into the earth.

The chief let out a strangled cry and muscled past us. He thundered screaming on to the plateau, pumping his arms above his head like a comic-book farmer chasing trespassers. The boys dropped their stones and kicked away in panic, slipping in the mud.

We followed warily. The chief was muttering, shaking his head. It must be kept clean, he repeated, 'or no one will come'; no helicopter would land. He knelt to pull a weed at his feet, crumpling it in his fist.

We left him like this, lost in his dreams and confusion. Finally he moved away to begin the long walk down through the jungle to his house and his son. As he left, I noticed the boys he'd chased away begin to edge out of their hiding place. They crawled from the short grass at the edge of the clearing, mud streaked up their bellies, huge grins splitting their faces. When the chief dropped out of sight round a corner, and they were sure he would not turn back, they jumped to their feet like monkeys, waving rubbery arms victorious to the sky. One of them, carried away, stuck out his tongue and honked a long, loud raspberry.

Chapter 16

I had begun to notice great birds circling, gathering after the storms had passed. I imagined them to be vultures, but that bird was unknown here. They were huge and black-bellied, with wings like claws; a giant bat's reach. But then I saw one land and settle, smoothing itself, straightening its neck, looking out of the lower branches of a tree. It was just a hornbill. Somehow, up in the sky, it had looked like death approaching. Now it was down I could place it. It fixed me with its tiny oil-black eyes, turned its head slowly, cocked its beak, and took off. The noise of its wings was like beaten leather.

The weather was wilful, erratic. At night the rain wheeled about crazily, coming after dark then in flashes or quiet and steady, like sleep, through the night. Evelyn, Herod's daughter, was weakening and would not take milk. She lay in his lap, or close to his wife's breast, with the blackness outside, and mewled and puked warm, translucent vomit that dripped through the floorboards. Herod believed she had malaria and asked me if I had any medicine. I had quinine and Fansidar, packed in Goroka, but Herod had already dispensed quinine and I hesitated to offer Fansidar, a malaria antidote of such power that, so I'd been told, to take it more than three times would be fatal. Evelyn was not yet one and, although she wouldn't eat, her eyes were still bright and her forehead felt peach-warm, not fevered. So I did not mention my Fansidar. Instead I gave her two chunks of my last chocolate bar, in goodwill, as she would be sure to reject it.

Herod's concern for Evelyn had overtaken his antipathy towards me. He wanted to take her to the doctor at Wanakipa and, desiring us as travelling companions, pressed us to start back, too. Despite all he had done to stand in my way, I began to warm to him again. My feelings for him had oscillated as violently as his moods – from belligerence to a kind of warped affection. He was no longer the obstructive priest, but the worried parent. He stared at the fire, twisting his beard in his fingers. It was a long way, he said, and with rains like these he did not want to walk it alone. Elisa would stay at Liawep and keep the fire burning.

The carriers made no secret of their boredom. While I scuttled around gathering information, they sat and smoked in Herod's house. They had no interest in the Liawep, only a morbid fascination in their history of brutality. Once or twice one had expressed an opinion, but these were couched as complaints. Why were we staying so long? Didn't I know the Liawep were dangerous? What did I expect them to do all day long?

Dunstan, taking my side, became less and less genial. 'Look, you guys,' he spat, after a week of such lethargy, 'what are you doing sitting around?' No one stirred. Someone coughed, irritable. Since waking, none had moved more than a few feet. 'Hey, come on! Why don't you go and make a garden for Herod? Why don't you go and hunt wild pig?' There was a dusty shuffle as they tailed out of the door.

Later I saw them sitting on a tree stump by the church. Only two – James, the boy, and Miniza, the oldest, with his goatee and easy giggle – had done as Dunstan said. They had taken a bushknife and were somewhere down the jungleside, slashing away at the undergrowth, clearing ground for a garden.

When we approached the others by the church, Dunstan said, 'You're still here, you guys. What did I say?'

Only Dison, who had grumbled all the way from Wanakipa and was sure to grumble all the way back, spoke. 'I washed *masta*'s trousers this morning,' he said, rolling a cigarette. I was *masta*: Dison was old enough to regard the old colonial form of address as appropriate; all the others called me by my name. I had not asked him to wash my trousers. Dunstan had suggested it, anything to alleviate Dison's lethargy. Now he was holding it against us. He coughed out *masta*, like something stuck in his throat.

The tension eased after my food was finished; the carriers eyed me less resentfully. I had bought for three, and we were eight, so naturally I had rationed them more than I had Dunstan or myself. Dunstan had fewer qualms about this than I. He told me not to worry. 'Before, *kiaps* ate their own food also. Only they lazy guys. Don't worry, we eat the rice and noodles.'

Nonetheless, when we made tea, we'd pour the water into the three cups, squeeze out the tea bags, sprinkle on the powdered milk and pass them round. The same with the white plastic salt grenade. Each of them would pour out a tiny pyramid into the middle of their dark palms and lick it off in one lisp.

Since learning we were planning to leave, Fioluana's interest in me had become insistent, as if he was worried I'd escape without knowing the rest, everything he'd held out this long to tell me. He eyed me desperately. I was prepared to do whatever he wanted; I owed him that much.

He arrived at Herod's house early one afternoon. The day was hot and close, with a naked, eye-frying sun and a hot wind stirring, a sure sign of wild storms to come. I was sitting on Herod's veranda with Dunstan and Titus, enjoying the shade. Fioluana propped one leg on the veranda, attempting a macho carelessness, and screwed his mouth into a pained grin.

'You will come?'

This was my part of the bargain. He wanted me to see his house and discuss his future. His eyes were set on the far horizon, on the promised land described by Jack and Yasaro. I nodded, and followed him away, taking Titus as translator. Dunstan, who had begun slipping into lengthy homesick reveries, waved us away, his mind on his wife and sons and the baby that was due any day now.

Fioluana moved fast. The climb to his house, round the shoulder of the mountain, cut through untrod jungle. Without a path, I slipped constantly, flailing out for creepers to stop the slide. Fioluana beat ahead with a bushknife. I had to run to keep up. Twice, breathless, I skidded across the mud on plate-leaf. Further in, where the jungle was deepest and coolest, we came to a fallen trunk that crossed a gully. The memory of my previous falls came sweeping back. I rested while Fioluana went ahead, steeling myself.

Halfway across the trunk, Fioluana turned and swung me a vine. I caught it and pulled down; it stretched elastic from some treetop far above. I held it tight and walked fast along the trunk, determined not to fall too far behind. I scuffled along as Fioluana had done and jumped down the other side, congratulating myself at having escaped an indignity I had thought inevitable. My complacence came too early. I landed on sugary topsoil, both feet kicked from under me, my bottom hit the mud and I began to slide. Panicking, I flailed my arms furiously. A vine caught my elbow. Laughter bubbled from above.

By the time I had struggled to my feet and climbed to where I'd fallen, Titus and Fioluana had composed themselves, their mouths set politely straight but their amusement visible in their bright, vivid eyes.

'It's not far now,' Fioluana reassured me, checking the skid marks up my side. 'We will go slow.'

Ten minutes later we broke into a sunny clearing. There were two houses in the centre, one broken-backed, with only rafters and torn-out walls remaining and half the steps to the veranda missing. The other was newer, but by no means immaculate. One corner of the roof, an overhang, had been blown through, as if hit by lightning. Leaves drooped in a tattered fringe. A woman was sitting in the crippled house, her legs hanging through smashed floorboards. She hauled herself upright as we approached.

This was Fioluana's wife, the woman who'd been in church; her skittish tattoos, etched inky blue over each temple, marked her out. She watched us with narrowed pillbox eyes and greeted Fioluana timidly. She wore just a grass skirt, newly made, with the grasses still pale green. She crawled out from under the ruined house and led us across towards the other.

Fioluana became suddenly, nervously voluble. They were both his houses, he babbled, the old one and the new one. Abused by rain, which soaked and swelled, and by sun, which dried and cracked, bush houses did not last long. The older of the two was only five years old.

The newer, barely a year old, creaked and groaned as we climbed the steps. There was a tidemark, charred firesmoke, where the roof met the wall. The door was tiny, and I had to crouch to pass through. In the buffer corridor lay an old dog, greying round the chops. It growled as I approached, but its heart was not in it and, by the time I stepped over its back, it managed only a benign sniffle.

Inside, the house was as dark as every other house I'd visited; faces blushed and bloated by the light of the fire, giant shadows loomed across the walls. Fioluana's wife was kneeling the other side of the fire, her face turned away from the heat.

Fioluana rubbed his hands together: the novice lecturer on the first day of term. His daughters, he said, were the problem. They were sick. All the rain had brought fever. It made the air heavy and diseased. He spoke with conviction, forbidding dissent. He wanted to know what I would do.

I stepped round the fire to where his wife was hunched over. The younger girl cannot have been more than one; the other, still wearing the flowery dress she'd worn that first day in church, was older, perhaps four or five. They lay at their mother's feet, asleep. She lifted their heads gently, as if they were fragile china. They slept on, their woody skin pale and buffed with feverish sweat.

Their mother nodded at me, expectant. I touched their foreheads with my fingertips. I sensed the heat, busy and troubled, before my fingers reached the skin. I made reassuring noises; it would pass, I told her. Fioluana would not accept this: he knew I had medicine. I hedged. I had already decided against handing over anti-malarial drugs to Herod's daughter, fearing she would not be strong enough to take the dose. The same applied here.

'Well, then, you must take them with you when you go back to the village. Tonight there will be a storm and they must not stay here.' He stood very close, searching my face. 'I am going hunting. You must watch over them until I return.'

He took my elbow and guided me towards the door. The sunshine bleached the grass and the ruined house, throwing black shadows with straight-ruled edges. It was already well into afternoon, and the sky was clear. Storm? Today seemed the gentlest of all the days so far, the least likely to spoil thunderous.

He climbed down the steps. When I reached the ground he waved an arm under the house, indicating I should take a look. I kneeled. The earth was damp and fresh-turned. At the far side, half out of the shade, was a tobacco plant, the hairs on its leaves turned to gold scratches by the afternoon sun.

'What . . .' I half turned, unclear what I was supposed to notice, but Fioluana was already pressing in beside me, his hand gripping my shoulder. I could hear the soft rush of Titus breathing, as he crouched behind.

Fioluana dug his hand into the earth, squeezing the clod until it backed out through his fingers. This was Herod's doing, this piece of inexpert weeding. There had been plants here, ancestral tokens which brought luck in hunting. Herod had uprooted them all.

'And you let him?' I stared at him, astonished. Why not simply refuse? Herod could not have forced the issue; he would have been outnumbered.

'Because of my daughters.' Fioluana shrugged helplessly. 'Herod says if we go to church he will take them to Wanakipa when they are older. There is a school there. I want them to go to school.'

I wondered if the handful of others who had appeared in church that first morning had been subject to similar bribery.

With his methods exposed, Herod seemed a pitiful character, weak and corrupt. I worried over the violence of his coercion, the bold uprooting of all that held meaning. Had he left anything?

Fioluana pulled back and stood up in the sunshine, rubbing his knee like an old man soothing arthritis. He smiled bitterly. 'We have thrown our things away.' He made it sound as if houses had been stacked with charms, objects to stroke for luck, everyday totems. There was one for each activity – pigs, health, children, hunting.

'Everything? You haven't kept anything?'

Fioluana held up his hand, silencing me. He led me round the other side of the house, to where the tobacco plant was stretching for the sun. He reached down and parted the leaves. Round its base was a dusting of tiny seedlings, as timid and fragile as day-old cress. These were from the plants Herod had ripped up; Fioluana had salvaged some seeds. When they were stronger he would replant them at the edge of the clearing. They would grow into a broad-leafed grass, with a gnarled ginger root. They smelled strong, he added, sniffing his fingers, chef-like.

'I will not tell Herod they are there,' he said, nodding grimly, as if already imagining the scene, Herod's frantic searching. 'He will never find them.'

Above us in the house I could hear Fioluana's wife moving about, collecting food for the night, wrapping her daughters for the journey. Fioluana stood up. There was one more thing he wanted to ask.

He delivered a speech so long, so punctuated by deliberate hand movements, that I imagined he had rehearsed it many times before. In his willingness to speak to me, to deal with my inquiries direct, he was, I reflected, unique among the

Liawep. I remembered two men I'd met in the church a few days earlier: their reticence had been typical.

Nervous, they had wrapped their tobacco in leaves that were still too green and fizzed and spluttered near the burning tip. I had wanted to question them – these two were a father and son, and I hoped they would draw a picture of manhood and family life and the passing-on of knowledge, but all that came through was their fear of me. They had sat side by side, heads inclined identically, like two drab parrots.

The father looked the same age as the son, the only mark of his seniority a small bald patch, a sanded-away disc at his crown. His eyes were blunted: it was as if he had been looking at my eyebrows or my nose, afraid to fix me in the eye. He gulped air noisily as he spoke.

'A lot of people' – gulp – 'are hiding from you, because you are a white man. White men' – gulp – 'never come here.' He had not understood why I was there; he thought I planned to 'break up the mountain'; worse, that I had come to put them in jail. He covered his eyes with his fingers, like a child who believes no one can see him.

Fioluana was knowing, sophisticated, almost cynical by comparison. 'We want modern things,' he was saying, 'things like you have, and like Peter. We would like a hospital, more bushknives and an airstrip.' This, finally, was the real legacy of Yasaro's patrol: a want like the pain of hunger for the 'better' life Yasaro had promised. Fioluana spoke greedily, his lips wet and full.

I stopped him: there was no room for an airstrip. But he had it all worked out. Had I not noticed that the houses were all built around the edge of the spur, that there were none in the middle, that the spur was fifty foot wide? Planes could land there.

He was overlooking the small matter of the church, however, that stood plumb in the middle of the clearing. I could not see Herod tolerating its demolition, and even then, even if he were persuaded, the strip would rate as an uncompromising test of a pilot's nerve, only navigable on the clearest, stillest days.

But to Fioluana these concerns seemed like excuses not to fulfil his wishes. With my white clout, I should effect change. 'If we build an airstrip, we can move the church further up the mountain. No problem. You will tell the government these things?' Was this not Peter Yasaro's responsibility, rather than mine? But he said Yasaro had been away a year now and would not return. They'd built a helipad and still no one had landed. Besides, Yasaro wanted them to move, and they would not leave their houses and their gardens. So, under duress, I promised, because he wanted me to, and felt immediately hollow, knowing my word would carry no weight and that his hopes would go unrealized.

We were pitched against each other. The more I equivocated, the surlier he became. He clapped his hands and shouted up at the house. It was clear, after all the help he had given me, that he hoped for more than thin excuses.

His wife appeared on the veranda, the elder girl cradled close to her neck, arms pinned in, limp by her side. She trod gingerly down the narrow boards to the steps, hunkered forward protectively. She had slung a deep net bag over her shoulder and it hung heavy over the small of her back, weighted pregnant with the sleeping baby. She looked us over, then craned her head towards the sky above. The wind was picking up. She trod uncertainly on to the first step, muttering something over and over.

Titus bent towards me. 'She says the storm is coming. She can feel it.'

Fioluana stood at the bottom of the steps and lifted his

sleeping daughter off his wife's shoulder on to his own. He held the back of her head and she slept through. He consulted intently with his wife. She nodded soberly, turning occasionally to us.

Fioluana walked over. 'Titus,' he said, 'you will look after my daughters?' He did not look at me. Titus nodded dumbly, his mouth ajar. I wanted to ask Fioluana more – where did he plan to leave us? What should we do for his family? – but he was already striding towards the edge of the clearing, slashing ahead with the bushknife, scything impatiently with his free hand. His wife trod blindly after, following his tracks out of the clearing into the jungle.

We seemed to be returning a different way; although I was incapable of telling two stretches of jungle growth apart, we were definitely losing height now. On the way over we had kept high, dropping into Fioluana's clearing only near the end. So now we should have been climbing. I worried silently. Every ten minutes there would be a long arcing cry, the animal call of Fioluana far ahead, spurring us on.

Through breaks in the jungle canopy I saw clear blue sky being slowly tarnished by advancing storm clouds. It had looked so settled all day; now black was nosing in steadily from the north. Slowly, the forest was darkening, shadows and colours merging into a rotten mud-green.

Ahead there was a clearing; a bright patch a hundred yards on. There was rising smoke and voices. As we neared it seemed there were a hundred of them, all male, barracking and clamouring to be heard. Fioluana was standing silhouetted at the edge of the clearing, striking his bushknife into a tree trunk.

'This', he said when we reached him, 'is where I stay. You go back to the village.'

His wife reached up to him to take the girl, but she had already woken, her eyes wide and surprised. In the clearing there were fifteen, perhaps twenty men, some the hunters I'd met the first day, others I did not recognize. They were building a fire, milling around, turning towards us, laughing and jabbing their fingers in our direction. These were the men Fioluana was to join hunting. They would not return to the village for a day, perhaps longer, depending on their success. They were men together – hard-hearted, competitive, edgy.

I walked towards them, stepping clear of the deep grass, to say goodbye to Fioluana. This would be the last time I'd see him; we would likely leave the next day to begin the long journey back. I reached out to embrace him, but he recoiled and looked around anxiously. Confused, I offered my hand instead. He squeezed it once, then slipped free.

'You go now.' He looked into the sky. 'The storm is coming. Take my family to the village.' He turned, paddling his hand in the air, dismissing me.

I watched him leave. He stopped by two men who were bent over the carcass of a pig, a rope round its neck and its face swollen tight with blood. They looked like cheesemongers with their long bushknives, heads down, bottoms in the air, tanket leaves in a spray like the tail feathers of ducks disappearing underwater.

Titus fussed with my sleeve, anxious to be off. But I wanted to watch for a bit longer, observe these preparations for the chase. Through this break in the jungle the view stretched for miles, down towards the valley which curled away with the river, a snake groove through the jungle. Again I noticed the sartorial debris of Peter Yasaro's patrol. He must have distributed clothes with abandon. There was one man, his face tarred with charcoal, under whose uniform profusion of tanket leaves, a pair of ladies' knickers, frilly-bordered, sagged over his muscled buttocks and bunched round his genitals.

Two men tore the carcass open, breaking its back, forcing

the legs outwards till the long rib fingers looked like the bones of a wrecked galleon. Another man was building a fire, making a firebox with rocks round a circle of cold ash. At his feet lay the squirreled body of a *cuscus*; half the arrow, torn off, was still bolted in its side. It had round, trusting eyes popping in surprise, and soft, expensive-looking fur, demerara-coloured.

Their behaviour puzzled me. Would they take this meat with them, or was it just for tonight, a kind of celebratory supper? I picked out two of the hunters I'd met before and approached to ask, but Titus would not follow. He folded his arms and ground his heel obstinately in the dirt.

The hunters were all watching me; they had stopped laughing now and were waiting to see what would happen. I smiled falsely, and began to back away, but my foot caught against a log. One of the butchers pulled his knife from where he'd wedged it in the earth, cut off a strip of pork and held it out towards me. Someone else laughed, a poisoned rattle. Everything moved very slowly, as if this had all happened before; far off, torn pennants of rain were sweeping across the mountains. I took the meat, inclining my head in gratitude. It smelled of death. The men stared at it with hungry dogs' eyes.

The smell clogged my nostrils. I passed it on to Titus, who took it greedily, forgetting for that instant the compulsion to leave. He stripped it with his teeth and ran his tongue over his lips. A crumb of fat lodged in his beard.

Fioluana stood up from the fire, a butchered joint, the skin burnt and peeling like a tyre frazzled on scalding blacktop, gripped club-like in his hand. He trod towards me. I looked round for Titus, but he was leading Fioluana's wife to the edge of the clearing, the elder girl cradled against his shoulder. I began to retreat, fearing this unaccountable change in Fioluana was something to do with these men all around. It was his bald, macho edge, reserved for posturing in front of his fellows. It scared me.

He swept his hand across the sky, across the great sagging canopy of rain, plump and low, which was already spotting the dust at our feet. He grunted a gravelly order, and pointed towards Titus. I understood nothing of what he said, but the meaning was clear. I turned away.

Titus was waiting for me at the edge of the clearing, sheltering behind a wall-smooth tree-trunk. He walked on when I reached him, throwing short-tempered explanations over his shoulder.

'*Em laik yumi go. Family bilong em sik. Ren i kamdaun.*'

But this was only the half of it. There was more here neither of us understood. Why had Fioluana turned so cold, so suddenly? Was it an anger born solely of disappointment? And the others — why had they acted as if they had never met me? It was as if I was a complete stranger once more. I might as well — for all they seemed to have absorbed — have been a miner out to exploit them or a government officer tracking down inmates to fill his jail cells. I had expected the stereotypical remote tribe, children touching my white skin, old women perplexed by my blue eyes, but the Liawep had confounded me. They feared me because they did not understand me; I feared them for the same reason. They believed I was there to break their mountain. I'd now heard that several times, from different sources. In deference, to counter this fear, I had treated the mountain as they did. I nodded to it as I walked up the village: the priest to his crucifix. And in truth it frightened me.

When I looked back one last time, Fioluana had turned to rejoin the butchers. Desperate now for an amicable resolution, I waved, trying to transmit a relaxed chumminess. Two of the men noticed me and alerted the others. They swung round and stared. I tried again. Fioluana lifted the haunch to his face and sank his teeth into the bubbled skin, tearing out pink, half-cooked flesh. He sucked it from the knuckle in oily swabs. I waved again, trembling now, but this time they mimicked me, giving precious, girlish waves. I felt beaten, overwhelmed, sick and frightened.

I had arrived prepared to feel pity for them, to examine the changes being wrought on their lives, but they were stronger than me, more insolent and proud. They were too much for the neighbours they'd coolly massacred; they were too much for Herod, who struggled to make them believe; and they were certainly too much for me. Cast out, I felt an unexpected brotherhood with the priest. It was not what I'd expected to feel, but it was real enough. It gave me comfort that I was not the only outsider.

Now they were driving me out, laughing cruelly, drunkenly. 'Bye! Bye! Bye!' they parroted. As we climbed into the jungle and I looked back one last time, one of the butchers stood up. He was shouting something, I couldn't hear what. In his left hand he flashed the bushknife. In his right he held the haunch, a hefty triangle of meat. His hand was dark with blood, running in oily tracks down his arm.

I ran into the jungle, after Titus, tripping in my panic to get away. Heaving asthmatically, I fell in behind Fioluana's wife climbing slowly on Titus's heels. We were heading straight up now and I'd lost my bearings. I had no idea where the village was, the river or the mountain. Underfoot the ground crumbled wet and sugary, overlaid with leafmould and rotting pulp, the smell so strong and sweet it was like these were bones we were walking on, mashed to fertilize a vegetation already grown monstrous. I wanted to be free of it, to walk in a field of grass, but all around there was jungle, endlessly deep, endlessly high, closing in and cutting out the light. The sky was now as dark as overripe fruit, but still, somehow, the rain was holding off. Titus kept turning to soothe us. 'Not far. *Longwe liklik.*'

We rested only once. Titus, ever the peacemaker, tried to engage Fioluana's wife in conversation, but she was too absorbed in her children, rocking the elder girl in her arms, her dress rucked up round mud-crusted knees, to respond. Empty eyed, he turned to me.

'I'm sorry. *Mi no save.*' He reached for my hand. 'When I was a boy and the first white man came to my village, my father ran off to hide in the bushes. He covered himself in mud and stayed in the bushes until the white man had gone. It is the same here, with you. *Wankain long* Liawep. White men are different from black men.'

It was dusk when we reached the village, the mountain buried under cloud, the jungle all around a deep black-green. Up the river valley there were brushes of rain, spilling from low, torn clouds. I prayed we might be spared the worst – it had held off this long.

Titus, convinced the storm was about to break, hustled Fioluana's wife and her children to the nearest house, fifty yards across from Herod's, near the bottom of the spur. I followed, eager to help, but felt already redundant. The woman opened her bag as she stumbled forward, lifting her naked baby clear. Titus set the other girl down at the base of the house's steps. She stood unsteadily, gazing with eyes gone smoky with fever. I remembered how bright she had been before, how she had flirted with such charm, as light as the breeze; now there was shadow round her eyes and her skin was dully bruised. I would bring her painkillers later, I decided. It was all I had that I was sure would not cause her greater harm.

As we lifted them on to the veranda, Titus stroked the back

of her head. Her mother pushed past, steering her towards the door, clutching her baby underneath its bottom. At the door a face appeared – the old yellowed man, his skin still jaundiced with saffron mud, the colour now dissolving in streaks down his cheeks. He looked from me to Titus, his eyes goggling enormous. As the woman approached, he retracted his tortoise neck and disappeared into the dark.

It was the noise I heard first – the hungry-belly rumble that always presaged the most violent storms. The rain started moments later. We ran for Herod's house too late, and were drenched in seconds.

Outside the house Herod was struggling in the mud. In his rush to get to cover, he'd thrust his Bible in his canvas satchel without buckling the strap and, as he'd swept the bag away, the Bible had fallen out, splayed open, face down in the mud. As we skidded past him he was cursing and groaning.

I stopped on the veranda and watched him peel it open; there were clayey globs stuck to the pages. He smeared it across his T-shirt, where it left a mud-red skid. We watched him, shocked.

'Go on, go inside,' he muttered, angry at his clumsiness. Rain was spotting his shirt, flattening his hair, running down his forehead and into his eyes like sweat. He shook his head bitterly and followed us.

Chapter 17

It was a dreadful night, which Herod spent in flight, running between his house and the other, fifty yards across the spur, where Fioluana's wife and his sick children lay coughing in the dark, round the fire. He began to turn delirious himself, repeating over and over that they had malaria. 'Malaria, malaria, all of them malaria.' Each time he returned to us, squeezed together, close to his fire, his eyes seemed madder, his face more drawn. His legs ran with mud and rain and his feet slopped dark wet footprints across the floor. He washed his hands obsessively, frantically scrubbing them under the curtain of water that poured from the roof.

We spoke very little. Elisa, Herod's wife, was waiting for

two boys to return from hunting. She became increasingly fretful. 'They're young boys,' she kept repeating. 'Where are they?' Herod soothed her, saying they were not so young and they knew the jungle and had often hunted alone. 'But what if they get caught?' she butted in. 'Or what if the bridge falls in? What then?' She seemed constantly close to tears.

I worried about the river filling with rain, turning wild. The niggardly Dison, the most cautious of the carriers, wanted to know what we'd do if the bridge was down. So far none of us had dared bring this up, as there was no answer. If the bridge had collapsed we could not cross the river; it would only take us under. I felt too weak to swim floodwater.

'We could build a raft,' Dunstan suggested. This had become a refrain. He pushed his baseball cap back on his head, the peak cocked skyward. Fear made him look like a young boy. It was comforting to discuss this, something real. All else fogged and dissolved under scrutiny. I tore a piece of paper from my notebook and dug around for a pen and drew the kind of raft in which I wanted to cross the Lagaip. It looked more like a jetty, adrift from its moorings. At the front, two tiny stick figures prodded the water optimistically with long poles. The sides were tree trunks, bound one on top of the other. The middle was a vast expanse of planking, the size of a small dance floor. It looked unlikely to capsize.

Dunstan squinted at the picture and half shook his head, half nodded. 'We'll see. Tomorrow we see.' He returned to his cigarette, which had cooled. He had not smoked when we set off. His wife hated it. Now he was smoking as much as the carriers, but his lungs were unused to the uncured roughness of bush tobacco and he coughed windily.

'I'm not going on your raft,' Dison said abruptly. He was sitting back from the fire, his face in shadow. 'Dangerous.' He almost whispered.

'And what will you do, then, when the bridge is down and we cross on a raft?'

'Mi *no save*. I can't swim.'

I kept looking at my watch, obsessively, unnecessarily. It was eight thirty-four. Lightning was somewhere close; the gap between light and sound was narrowing. It had been far off for some time; now it was closing in on us. The rain was hissing and boiling on the roof and drilling wormholes in the mud.

I stood up and walked to the door. It was utterly black outside. Fifty yards across the square I could see the rain-blurred outline of the other house, where Herod was praying for the sick children. I squinted into the gloom, but could only see what was near, the ditch round Herod's house stirred up and flowing, thick like gravy.

Then, from clouds so low they seemed to squat on us, lightning spat out. It was close, just up the jungleside, on the edge of the mountain. The thunder broke slowly; I could feel the shape of it, edgy and precipitous, like crumbling rock face. It shook the house and I felt it in my chest, tight like a drumskin. The lightning tore the sky and I could see every house, the church's roof flattened, running with water, streaming off the fringes, and Herod, caught in the strobe, electric white, mid-stride, running back across the mud, crouched over, his Bible crooked under his shirt. Then it went black again and there was only the slap of Herod's feet in the mud and he appeared, suddenly, in the firelight. He jumped on to his veranda beside me, shaking himself like a dog, water spraying off his hair, pouring down his face. 'My God' he said, heaving. 'What a night.'

I followed Herod inside. No one spoke; they were staring into the fire. Only Dunstan looked up. 'What do we do?' he said.

'I don't know. Pray?' It was only half a joke. I had prayed ever since we'd entered the jungle. I would twist my wedding ring and pray that I would see my wife again; I prayed that we would bring good, not evil; I prayed we would all get out alive.

Following the etiquette, Dunstan prayed first for the sick children, that they would sleep through this night and wake to sunshine in the morning. He prayed for Herod's baby, Evelyn. He thanked God for our food and for enabling us to meet the Liawep. Then he prayed for us, for our safe return home, for our deliverance.

Outside, the sky moaned and heaved and split open and the lightning carved through the night. It was closer. Elisa covered her baby's ears too late and Evelyn started wailing. Titus had his fingers in his ears and was shaking his head. Herod stood up again, unable to relax.

'I'm going over to the other house,' he said, the Bible in his fist. 'If I don't go and pray, they will die.'

Herod had complained about this house before; the family that lived there was 'like stone' to his message, and had never been to church. Cynically, it looked as if he was using Fioluana's daughters' illness as an opportunity to take the others his God, with the drama of the wild storm as backdrop. This time Titus and Dison ran across with him. They had sat too long and Titus, I fancied, had become rather fond of Yawali, Fioluana's elder, flirtatious daughter, whom he had carried through the jungle earlier. He wanted to hold her hand and nurse her.

The lightning was becoming more frequent. It seemed to centre on the mountain, building with intent. It never seemed possible it would just blow over; there was something evil in it which silenced us all and was turning Herod into a madman, King Lear in the mud outside, railing against it. Dunstan, with superb irrelevance and a gravity that embarrassed me, was telling Andrew that I no longer wished to be called *masta*. I had told Dunstan this two days earlier. It was too late to change anything; I was simply sharing my feelings. I did not feel like a *masta*, that was all. I never wanted him to turn it into a command.

Dunstan had nodded and said he understood. 'Yes, it means rich foreigner, and you are not rich foreigner.' Now I could hear him say the same to Andrew. 'You must not call Edward *masta*. It is for patrol officer or rich foreigner.' Ironically, the more I had shied from the role, the more Dunstan had assumed it. The less I exercised my will, the more he cracked the whip. He had become quite a bully. 'Why haven't you made a fire?' he would spit, or, 'Cook now. We want to eat.' This time Andrew puzzled over his words. His cigarette tailed a thin blue line to the ceiling. 'Yes,' he repeated, 'not *masta*.' He looked over Dunstan's shoulder and saw me watching him. He spoke more softly and his words sank in the storm.

It was nine thirty. My watch was steel, with a link strap, and I wondered vaguely whether it would attract lightning. I unclipped it and laid it on the floor. I wanted the night to be over, but it had only just begun. If I went to sleep, perhaps I would wake when it had passed. It seemed a good idea. I left Dunstan and stepped into our room, untied my shoes and slipped, fully dressed, into my sleeping bag. I lay on my back, with my head on my clothes, packed into a roll, socks grey and gritty with mud, trousers and T-shirts with the fug of the jungle on them, the clog of warm compost and decay.

I lay there, thinking about the smoke Herod had seen curling from the top of the mountain. Perhaps the mountain was volcanic. I'd once seen pictures of Mount Sakura-jima in Japan, with a thorny crown of broken-veined lightning, a mad

Einstein head of hair. The swirling ash, I remembered, generates its own electricity. Perhaps that was happening here.

Over our heads the clouds heaved open again. Lightning bullwhipped. Please, into the jungle, I prayed. Save us. Beside the fire Dunstan and the others were silent again, waiting, while the night spewed and foamed.

I tried to remember what I knew about lightning. There was some comfort in facts. It loves golfers, I knew, especially the way they stand alone on the fairway, raising steel clubs to the sky, or huddle under trees when the rain comes down. It looks out for swimmers, too, in open-air pools. Lifeguards watch the storm approach and clear the pool when it's a mile off. Each flash crackles with hundreds of millions of volts. Planes usually escape, singed a little at wingtip or on the ends of their noses; the current passes through them to ground.

Ball lightning is more of a mystery. At the Royal Astronomical Society in London on 25 January 1952, members held what they billed as a 'geophysical discussion devoted to the subject of thunderbolts'. It was an excitable meeting. One speaker stood up and described a plane trip he had made in the late summer of 1938. He had been flying over the Toulouse Gap in a BOAC flying boat, on the way to Iraq, when a fireball flashed in through the cockpit window, burned off the pilot's eyebrows, burst through the forward passenger cabin and exploded in the rear cabin, just beside his seat. At the same time, the hotel in Marseilles where the passengers were to spend the night was hit by lightning and burned to the ground.

I lay inside the mosquito net. It seemed safer, somehow, sagging over my middle, almost touching my face; like being in a coffin. I think I slept, despite the fury outside. It was like trying to sleep backstage at a heavy-metal concert or, worse, lying down on stage, in front of the drum kit, and wondering why sleep didn't come as the guitarists axed out colossal earthquake chords. The thin bamboo wall behind my head was soaked. Water was coming in everywhere. The floor, too, was damp, but it was hard to see whether it had leaked from above or been sucked up from below. Herod's house was hammered into the side of the mountain, just off the edge of the spur, and with each thunderclap it seemed to slide further downhill, towards the edge of the jungle. I slipped into half-sleep, dreaming of the bridge, of finding a lifeboat by the river with four scrubbed lifeguards who would guide us up the gangplank to safety.

I woke to a thunderbolt so violent I thought lightning had torn into Herod's house. I sprang from my bed and became entangled in mosquito net, tearing it away from me, off my face, only to find it manacled round my feet when I tried to stand. Across the square, through the fuzz of the rain, there was a single, demented scream. Dunstan and the carriers stood up from the fire, chattering in panic. As I struggled with my shoes I could hear them clatter to the door, trying to work out what had happened. Someone was out in the rain, running our way, screaming as loud as the thunder. He stamped on to the balcony and I could hear it was Herod, shouting as if he was in a hurricane and we were offshore: he shouted like a deaf man would shout, unable to hear himself. Still half drugged with sleep, it made no sense. Was he berating the carriers for having soaked up his hospitality but given nothing in return? And if so, why would he choose now, late at night, as we were being tossed about by the storm? His screaming sparked hysteria. Dunstan and Titus tried to shout above him, to make themselves heard, and I could hear Elisa moaning, 'God, oh God.' Then, as the thunder broke again, they ran out into the storm, shaking the house as they jumped, leaving only Elisa's pained thin cry and me, struggling to free myself from yards of cream muslin.

Moments later Dunstan was back alone. He bent down in the doorway to our room, blocking out the light from the fire. He was in silhouette. His beard was dark, oiled, tight; I could see every hair. 'Edward, Edward.' His voice was high-pitched, unbroken. He spoke in a halfway whisper, insistent. 'There's been lightning and it struck the other house, the one with the sick children.' He caught his breath, sucking in air in great gulps, wheezing with the smoke.

'The children?'

'Fioluana's wife, his daughter, three more pikininis. All dead.'

'Fioluana's family?' This was not happening.

'I'm frightened,' he said. He took off his baseball cap. I touched the back of his hand. It was cool.

He stared at the floor, pulled at his beard. 'You, you stay asleep,' he said. I was fully dressed, but he couldn't register this: his mind was scorched by what he had seen.

The noise seemed to have abated a little. It was still raining, but quieter and steadier. There was still lightning but the thunder jumbled like loose machinery and felt more like background, less like artillery, less like looking down the barrel. Herod came smashing back into the house as I stood up. He slipped on a wad of mud and hit the doorpost. He was still shouting, pointing to his ears this time, shaking his head.

'Come on!' He waved his arms wildly. His tongue was pink and glistening. He spat as he shouted. He was uncontrollable. 'They need help, come on!' And he turned and swung on the doorpost and ran out into the storm again. Dunstan followed him and I followed Dunstan and suddenly we were out there, in complete darkness, racing across the mud towards the other house, flogged by the monsoon-warm rain. I brought my torch and the white spot made everything around it blacker. I trained it on Dunstan, on his frantic pedalling heels, and ran.

Inside the house there was no fire. Herod was shouting and pointing. I handed him the torch. He aimed it at the roof. It veered around crazily, like an anti-aircraft spotlight.

'There!' he yelled. 'It come in there!' For a second he held the torch still. There was a tear in the roof, like a rock had fallen through, but singed and tasselled like burnt straw at the edges. He swung the torch down to the fire. 'BOOM!' He raised both arms to describe the explosion. The torchlight skidded across the roof.

I made Herod shine the torch at the floor; I'd seen something. He pointed it and its beam picked out two small bodies, on their backs, their hands half raised to their faces, frozen in death like bodies at Hiroshima. Behind them, against the wall, was the old man, his head sunk in yellowed hands and his back curled forward, the back of his neck visible, the skin pulled tight and onion-shiny over his spine, rocking himself slowly. 'I'm sorry. I'm so sorry,' Dunstan mumbled. He stood behind me, rubbing his forehead. 'I'm so sorry for what has happened.'

Closer to us, almost at our feet, was the body of a woman. For a second I failed to recognize her. She, too, was on her back, legs apart, feet near the fire. My foot was near her head. I stepped back. Herod shone the torch in her face. Her eyes stared. Blown petals of white ash covered her skin and the floor. Beside her lay the naked bodies of two little boys, three or four years old, clutching each other. The woman wore only a grass skirt; her breasts were full and nipples rude and pronounced as if she had been breastfeeding. Then I noticed the starfish tattoos on her temples: Fioluana's wife. Her mouth, which earlier had been pursed with the worry of the coming storm and her shivering, fevered daughters, now hung wide open, white ash icing her lips and tongue. I looked around for her children, but was distracted by the sight of another woman, crouched against a far wall, rocking a tiny baby I guessed was Fioluana's youngest. The woman rolled her head, mumbling incoherently. Herod bent down to talk to her. She did not look at us. She wore a T-shirt that looked burnt, but it could have been dirt. Five people dead. Only three survivors.

'I was there,' Herod said. He had calmed down and was no longer screaming. 'There, in the door. I pray for the sick children. Then BOOM! BOOM! This light comes through the roof like a waterfall. BOOM!' His Bible was on the floor where he had dropped it. Through the hole in the roof rain fell like sequins in the torchlight, spangled, sprinkling the ash, spitting on the last hot logs. One of the little boys, who lay with his arm over the other's waist, had broken his nose. It was crooked, squashed sideways, a teardrop of black blood in the nostril.

I grabbed the torch back, desperately hoping that Dunstan had been mistaken and that Fioluana's elder daughter had survived, but I was unable to fix on anything; faces loomed at me, puffy-lipped and blue-veined, like drowned men dragged to the surface. I felt Dunstan's hand on my shoulder; I must have been swaying, about to fall. Then, as I turned, I saw her, half underneath another girl, on the far side of the exploded fire. It was as if they'd been thrown into each other's arms. Her dress was askew, crumpled like burnt paper, torn half off her neck; the soles of her feet were flayed and bleeding.

Minutes passed. Herod ran the torch around, like a circus compère at his chamber-of-horrors sideshow. No one spoke and no one moved and there was something reverent about that, although I knew I was intruding, and I grieved for Fioluana – both his pretty ones, only the baby saved. Our thoughts went no further than the house; we stood silent, remembering. Then the storm came back. Lightning lit the house through the hole in the roof, then thunder, like the start of a rock slide, shook us to action. 'We can't stay here.' Dunstan turned for the door. 'Not in this house.'

Herod held out his hand to the woman by the wall, but she looked at where the fire had been, and where the rain fell softly, and did not respond. Her hands were held round the baby's chest, circling it with no break. The baby's eyes were open and staring at somewhere above her head. Herod reached down and took her hand. He slipped his fingers between hers and the baby's belly and lifted her hand away. 'You must get up,' he coaxed softly. 'It is not safe here.' She shook her head but Herod persisted. He reached down and took the baby and her hands reached up with it, even though it was not hers. Herod lifted it away, above her head, and gave it to Dunstan. Then he reached for her hands again. There was dust in her hair, as if she'd been near a falling building. She let Herod lift her and, when she was standing, fell back against the wall again. There was no urgency: she moved slowly, as if half frozen. She had calmed Herod. We were in the centre of the storm, still. Destruction had brought an uncertain quiet.

'You come, too,' Herod said to the old, yellowed man, who was coiled up into himself against the far wall. Herod had the torchlight in a pool at his feet and he walked through the white confetti ash. The man was the grandfather of Kesime, the other girl who lay dead at his feet. He looked as if his world had been destroyed, that nothing remained. Herod cupped his hand round the back of his neck and I saw for the first time his tenderness. 'Come, come, you come,' he repeated, urging him to his feet by placing one hand under his armpit. The man responded as if to his mother's touch and rose weightlessly.

I stood and watched like a useless voyeur at an accident. Herod handed me the torch and told me to go first. I stepped out across the pale dusted boards on to the dark veranda. The rain had brought cold and I shivered. Herod ushered the broken people with him, the man and woman who had still not straightened, who bowed their heads against the storm. Dunstan followed with the tiny baby cradled into his shoulder, its face bright and pale. For seconds we stood together under the veranda as rain spewed off the roof's grass fringe, inches from our faces. Lightning barked out again to our left, halfway up the mountain. It lit the church and the mudbath across which we'd have to run to reach Herod's house. Everything was glossy with rain.

I expected Herod to run, but he walked slowly, holding the two survivors on either side, cupping their elbows. I wanted to run back, but Herod asked me to walk ahead with the torch. Dunstan alone scurried, bent over, his head and hands covering the baby from rain. I heard a clank and creaking of floorboards as he reached Herod's house. The droplets of rain fell fat and heavy on my head as we walked. We were soaked within seconds. I looked back once but Herod swept me on with his hand. I kicked out at every step to test the way, treading tentatively, but kept skidding sideways, the torchbeam arching overhead and dissolving in the grey underbelly of the clouds, low over us like a marquee filled and sagging with rain.

Dunstan was handing the baby to Elisa as I entered and switched off the torch. The carriers looked up at us for explanation. Then Herod walked in, followed by the two survivors. The woman looked up at the fire and collapsed on to her knees, then her side. She lay with her face against the floor, close to the fire, lips pursed fatly. In the light of the fire her face seemed blackened by smoke, as if she'd rubbed herself in charcoal. One breast hung low from her T-shirt, thin stretch lines in suspension. Her moans sounded as though her insides were creaking, straining to keep whole. Titus reached his long, thin arm out across the fire to touch her, but she drew her shoulders up and pulled her arms into her body.

The man wouldn't move from the doorway, even when Herod beckoned him over to the fire. When at last he did, I could see that his back had been torn by the lightning. The skin hung away from the flesh like a strip of leather, exposing a wound as big as an outstretched hand in the small of his back, just above the tanket belt. It sweated like meat on a butcher's slab. He clutched one of the fire's corner posts as he lowered onto a tucked-under leg, keeping his hand on the post and laying his forehead on the back of his hand. He moved very slowly. He sat there, his eyes filmed over, unseeing, all vision inside, burnt tracks in his memory. The rain had made his chalked face run, like mascara tears. His granddaughter lay covered in white ash in the house on the other side of the village, her eyes still open and her arms raised to cover her face.

Out of respect for their loss, no one spoke. The carriers' fear seemed to be that the lightning would now hit Herod's house. They'd absorbed his description of the explosion, the way the thunderbolt smashed through the roof and detonated in the fire, and now they were scared.

Against the fuzz of rain and the split and rumble of thunder the only sound was the pale whine of Fioluana's tiny naked baby, held close by Elisa who had passed Evelyn, miraculously asleep, into Titus' big hands. She was too young to register what had happened: she just knew that her mother was not with her. No matter how she was rocked and soothed, she mewled like a lost kitten.

I was aching to obliterate this night. It was now well past midnight and I wanted to sleep, to wake up the next morning and leave. But it seemed too selfish at such a time, and instead I dug in my rucksack for my painkillers, the yellow prescription-only torpedo lozenges I'd been promised would dull even a broken leg, and handed them round. 'Good medicine,' Herod said, leaning over the woman on the floor. She did not move and he placed the pill between her lips and raised her head off the floor and waited for her to swallow, stroking her throat and speaking softly.

I gave one to the old man in front of me and he rolled it in the bowl of his palm, then pressed his hand to his face and leaned back against the pillar. 'What about his back?' Dunstan asked.

What did I have to treat a back flayed by lightning? Clearly some kind of measure was required. I unzipped my First Aid kit and rummaged inside. It had been designed for day trips to the Lake District, for grazed knees and thistle-pricked fingers: I had not envisaged disaster. There were two long bandages, rolled tightly, secured with a square of plaster; a jangle of safety pins; a tube of Savlon; three plasters; and there, at the bottom, a surgical dressing. It was wrapped in greaseproof paper, which gave it a 1960s feel, and was greyed and frayed at the edges. I cut it in half with nail scissors, the edge jagging into tiny crescents, and stretched it for size over the wound. I cannibalized the plasters, cutting away the adhesive ends and throwing the spongy, honeycomb middles into the fire where they bubbled. I squeezed pure white coils of Savlon on to the wound and gently spread it over, covering the pink rawness. Dunstan sat beside me. Unusually, no one else showed interest. I found it therapeutic. I did not know why the carriers were so quiet or why they would not look at me, but feared they linked me in some way with the lightning. I busily played the doctor, trying to banish these thoughts. I tacked the dressing in place with the plaster corners and it billowed outwards, sagging away from the skin. It was a hopeless job.

Behind the house, not far down the jungleside, there was a crack and roar of a tall tree tumbling on to the canopy, taking others with it. It was not accompanied by lightning. I did not understand this storm. I did not understand why, when there were higher points, the lightning had hit the house. There were trees nearby that were higher; most exposed was the church. Even Herod's house was isolated. I moved closer to the fire. Herod and Elisa looked across the logs at me. 'The other house,' I said. 'Why did lightning hit the other house?'

'Because', Herod replied, like one who has always known the answer, 'they didn't believe in God.'

'I'm sorry? You were in there praying, Herod, when the lightning struck. Your God was in there, too, surely?'

'I hadn't started when the sky came down.'

'But still, you were there. You're God's man, Herod.'

'I hadn't started to pray.'

'But the people. You're saying it was their fault?'

'They do not believe in God. Yes, it is their fault. For months their hearts are like stone. The people in that house still follow the old ways.'

'So He fries them. Some fucking God you have, Herod.'

'What you say?' I'd spoken in English. His lips were wet and his eyes were burning. He was snorting through his nose. He understood the thrust, if not the words.

'I'm going to bed.' I stepped back into our room, lay down on the mat and listened to the storm. The lightning had moved on. I could hear it crackling in another valley. Would it come back? Wasn't five dead enough for one night? I had closed off my capacity for horror to such an extent that the most real threat to us had not yet crossed my mind. Until Dunstan voiced it. From the anxious pitch of his voice it had been brewing for some time.

'Edward.' He kneeled in the doorway. 'I'm frightened.' Until now, I'd unburdened my fears on him three times a day. This was the first time he'd expressed his. I sat up and looked at him, but the fire was behind him and his features were in darkness. He placed one hand on the floor to steady himself.

'The dead mama and the dead pikininis. The Liawep will blame it on us.' He was whispering, trying to sound relaxed, but his voice quavered. 'We come here, and this happens. I'm frightened they will come for us.'

This made perfect sense. I'd blocked out the thought with the immediacy of the survivors' needs, but there was an awful logic to it. It would compound Fioluana's distrust of me; I was thankful, cowardly, that I would not have to face him. Against him and the hunters we would have had no chance. I tasted sourness at the back of my throat. Instinctively I put my hand to my mouth.

Dunstan reached out for me. 'I shouldn't have said anything, but we people say what we think.' He paused, and added ludicrously, 'But don't worry. You go to sleep.'

He apologized again, but the thought was out and free and could not be locked away. It was his country, he had grown up with revenge and death and I'd grown up with democracy and dialogue. My instinct counted for nothing. I suddenly saw our time here for what it was. The Liawep had not wanted me to come; they had not wanted to answer my questions; they did not regret my departure. And now this. Everything happens for a reason, they believe. This had happened because we were here. That was what they would believe and now I, too, feared it was true. At home I would have dismissed these thoughts as foolish superstition, but such scepticism now seemed empty and irrelevant. Nothing was the same here. I lay back on top of the mosquito net and it tore away from the wall and flattened under me. The storm had stilled. In the quietness I could hear the carriers talking.

'Now He's killed them, He's stopped,' Dunstan said, getting off his knees.

The carriers' voices were rumbles too low for me to understand. Only later, when we were safe, did Dunstan tell me of their discussion. Andrew and Titus were both set on going, disappearing into the jungle right then, five hours before dawn. They were convinced that, when dawn came and the news of the deaths ran round the village, the warriors would come for us. Dunstan defied them to leave. 'We're men, too,' he had said. 'If they come we can look after ourselves. If they want to throw a bushknife at us, we can throw one at them, too.' He had persuaded them that the warriors would not hear of the deaths until they returned from hunting. That gave us a day's start. I lay down knowing nothing of this. To me the whisper of their voices was soothing, but I wished they were lying near me. Only the smell and warmth of other human beings would keep off the fear of death. I was convinced, as my brain turned in on itself and every thought curdled, that I would not live, that I would be carved up. What would I do if they burst in now? I knew I would not fight. For the first time I wished they were model Christians, with love and forgiveness tattooed across their knuckles, stamped on their foreheads. In that shameful moment I wished that Herod had had more success.

I slept for minutes, perhaps half an hour. I woke violently from a ghoulish dream, feeling my face. Dunstan was bending over me. 'Shhh, shhh, you were shouting out.' I struggled to sit up and found I had dribbled down my chin. I looked up at him. He reached out his hand. 'We leave today before light, yes?' he said.

'That's not right. If we run it's like we know it's our fault.' Already I was feeling like a fugitive.

Dunstan disagreed. 'If we stay it's the same. Why would we stay and say sorry if it wasn't our fault?'

'But they'll catch us. There's no way we can outrun them in the jungle. It's their jungle, not ours.'

He snorted. 'It's our jungle, not yours. We are men, too. We can run.'

This was the result of a compromise hammered out with the carriers. We would all leave together, but not until dawn. If we went when it was dark, Dunstan had told them, we'd easily get lost. They had agreed, but throughout the night they had pestered to be off.

Herod was elsewhere. In the stillness after the storm he sat in the other house, conducting a sleepless vigil with the bodies, praying for their souls. He did not move them or close their eyes. He left them where they were. He knew that, in the morning, the house would be full of people crying and staring and that, for a week, the dead would not be touched.

We all prayed that night. The hypocrisy no longer bothered me. While Herod's wife prayed for the life of the tiny baby she held and Herod prayed that his sinners would be spared damnation, I prayed for our safe return. No one slept; for almost five hours we sat round the fire, blindly feeding it logs, uttering banalities. Near the tail end of the night we had a visitor. The beaten-out bark that served as a door shifted and grated on the floor and I saw hands at the top, fingers folded over, lifting it up and across.

It was the chief. He came into the room and looked across our faces; he was the sheriff, his cell full of cattle rustlers. But his face was set and I could not see whether he felt grief or anger, whether he sympathized or held us to blame. I became suddenly edgy he'd brought the hunters, back early from the hunt, and that our time had come, but he was alone. He stood and watched us, then stepped behind us, round the wall, to Herod's bedroom. He bent over and his tanket leaves shuffled.

There was a clink as he picked up Herod's kerosene lamp, its glass fogged and oil-speckled. He held it up and the metal tinked as he turned and left the house with it.

A long while later he returned it, stepping in, just round the corner of the door, not looking at anyone. The lamp glowed faintly and there was a thin splish of kerosene as he put it down, lowering the handle slowly, careful it did not rap the metal base. He left it glowing and, as he turned, his shadow lurched across the ceiling.

At five, my brain fogged with a night of adrenalin and guilt and fear, Dunstan announced our departure. There was no sign of dawn; light would not start leaking into the night until six. Dunstan, calm until now, became frantic, bundling his clothes, my clothes, anything he could see, into his rucksack. The sudden panic made no sense.

'We go now. Now, before it is light.' He was trying to force one foot into a still-laced baseball boot. He was ramming it in, over the tongue. He gave up furiously, throwing it to the bottom of his rucksack.

The carriers saw us move and were up and ready. They had nothing to pack – no changes of clothes, no sleeping bags, no soap powder. Their supplies of tobacco and newsprint were close to exhausted and would be stuffed into a pocket, or under a belt. Titus had a string bag, bulbous with sweet potato, hoarded hopefully.

Herod shuffled back in. He sat down next to the fire, took a stick and pushed around in the ashes, but the glow had gone and he turned up only light puffs of cool ash. He looked drained and broken. Through these days I'd felt everything for him – most often hatred and contempt – and now my sympathy surprised me. Though I despised his primitive evangelism, I could see he was suffering.

'Herod,' Dunstan said. He broke off his desperate packing and leaned over. 'We're going now, brother.'

Herod grunted. He was drawing a circle in the ash, round and round, the same groove. He'd dropped his plan to come with us: he'd stay until the dead were buried.

'We think that if we stay they will come for us,' Dunstan said.

'True,' Herod said. He did not look up.

Dunstan led the way almost at a run, quitting the house while I was still fighting with my rucksack, forcing the drawstring tight over a tangle of clothes and debris it was too dark to identify. I thrust the bag, straps flapping, at Andrew, and he bent down and reversed his arms through it. I followed him out, the last one to leave. Dunstan was already out of sight.

It was dark, but morning was coming. It was the torpid half-light of dusk, only colder and more lifeless. A grey light was leaking upwards in the east, into clouds which sat low over the mountains. Behind us as we fled was Mount Woraitan, hidden in heavy cloud. Everything hung low, the colour of old meat.

I broke into a run, struggling in the darkness and mud. As the ground dropped away into the jungle I looked back one last time. I could see the roof of the house, its wound like a soldier's chest shot open. Herod stood alone in the middle of the helipad, watching us go. His arms hung by his side; his face was undertaker-grim, camouflaged with mudsmears. I looked for grief, anger, even relief at our departure, but he was beyond emotion. I raised my hand to wave, but he seemed not to see me.

We ran and ran and ran. For an hour or more it was dark in the jungle, until the morning warmed slowly through. We struggled to see in the half-light and the mud was thick and cold and cloying. On the way to the Liawep we had stopped to point out flowers, or birds, or stamped-in pits where wild pigs had rolled, but now we moved silent and grim. Ahead I could see the carriers twisting down the mountain, their backs issuing steam, breath hissing and heaving, a mule train on a cold, high morning. Dunstan was far down, out of sight, speechless and determined. We stopped for the first time two hours later, at the bottom of the mountain, down by the river that fed the Lagaip. I felt ludicrously awake, my ears like antennae. I kept hearing whispers in the jungle about us, or the shuffle of wet leaves, and jerked about, expecting to see warriors charge out of the bush.

Dunstan looked over my shoulder, hunted. Above, the sky was lightening. 'We have to keep moving.'

'Do you think they're after us?'

'Not yet, but soon.' I did not like to see him like this. I missed his jokey carelessness.

The first day of flight was the worst. Along the river, down to the Lagaip, the banks had crumbled and what had been dry land was now part of the river, split into grass islands and trees, water swirling a foot up their flanks. I waded after the others, emerging on to land again with my shoes splodged with leech blood and leeches hanging like deflating balloons from my ankles. By early afternoon we reached the Lagaip and passed the camp where we'd built a shelter on our last night in the bush.

The bridge, incredibly, was still there. It had slipped perceptibly and hung, dishevelled, in the water, probably a foot under in the middle. It did not look safe, but it was there. Dunstan and the carriers were grinning madly.

We sat and rested. I handed round my glucose sweets. The

carriers thanked me but waited for me to go first. The sweets dissolved tastelessly and fizzed like sherbet. They swallowed theirs hurriedly, wiping their mouths on the backs of their hands.

Dunstan rolled himself a cigarette. 'I thought they might try to cut us off, up there.' He looked past me, up the mountain. 'Now we are at the river they can't cut us off. They have to catch us.'

I took off my shoes to cross the bridge and laced them round my neck. In the middle, the water came up to my knees. When I lifted one foot to step forward it was knocked sideways by the current. The bamboo underfoot was slimy and almost free of support. The vines that lashed it to the handrails had mostly swollen and split away. Standing on the far pylon, I looked at the joints. The criss-cross of vine ropings were all coming loose. The bridge was unravelling itself. When the others crossed it floundered and creaked. It was a sinking ship, half down, the deck swimming.

We climbed and fell and talked little. I followed closely behind Andrew, or Dunstan, or whoever was leading. At one point we were joined by a hunter, who carried his arrows in one hand and a small, glass-eyed pig in the other. He climbed with his toes deep in the mud and I walked right on his heels. He smelled of firesmoke and week-old sweat.

Through the jungle I saw shadows, like deer moving through twilight woodland, only half there. I shouted ahead, for the carriers to stop, but when they turned, the shapes stilled. At the front of the line, Dunstan was growing impatient. '*Hariap. Yumi go.*' He levelled his bushknife through a tangle of creepers and stamped on.

I peered again through the gloom, convinced I'd seen the

Liawep, that they'd finally caught us up. Fifty yards off, through hanging vines and mushrooming vegetation, I saw movement again. I ran after Dunstan and pulled him to a stop.

'They're here,' I heaved. 'Look.'

He turned. The shapes were clearly men – fifteen, perhaps twenty – coming straight at us.

'Oh God.' Dunstan scratched his head frantically.

'Quiet,' Titus broke in, crouching down. 'No ken mekim nois. It's the hunters.'

There was no use running, as they were twenty yards off and closing. I was convinced they had come for us, and yet their voices were raised, almost jubilant.

Fioluana was at the head, yelling my name. He disappeared into a gully and clambered out towards me, flashing a spear above his head. He was distinguished by his mud-discoloured shorts; the hunters who followed him all wore tanket leaves. As he closed, I noticed the slaughter hauled by the others: bony black-skinned pigs, koala-cuddly tree kangaroos, cockatoos and parrots in bright bunches, like prize vegetables. The hunters gathered round us.

Fioluana looked us over, muddied and exhausted, and grinned. Dunstan and Titus grimaced nervously back. Fioluana stabbed his spear in the ground and approached Titus. He stretched out his arms and embraced him. I saw Titus' eyes: wide and alert, scanning the warriors, while Fioluana's closed in ecstasy.

Fioluana moved towards Dunstan and me, and shook our hands warmly, with respect. He was pleased to see us, he explained. The hunt had been a fierce success – he gestured round the warriors, laying the spoil at their feet – and now they were returning to the village. Had we left this morning? I nodded.

'You walk fast. You must leave very early.' He grinned

uncertainly, unsure why we had not greeted him more ful-
somely. 'Why did you leave so early?'

I looked at Titus. How to answer? With the truth — that the
storm had killed his wife and elder daughter, and we were on
the run, fearful the Liawep would hold us responsible? Titus
returned my gaze, his eyes dark, regretful pools.

Dunstan stepped forward. 'We wanted to get back, to start
early. *Meri bilong mi wetim pikinini.* My wife's expecting a baby.'
He patted his stomach, rolled his eyes. Fioluana spluttered out
laughing. Not for the first time, I was struck by Dunstan's
unnerving plausibility. Lies came easy, despite his gentle, pious
demeanour.

The hunters watched in silence. When we had left Fioluana
with them the day before they had been roused and belligerent.
Now they took us in soberly, their heads erect, as if they knew
our secret. One of them, I noticed, had been wounded, a
machete-slash across his thigh. The skin had torn open, and the
wound looked wet and taut. He saw me looking at it and glared
back: a challenge, insolent and proud.

Fioluana was rubbing goose bumps off his forearms; it was
still early morning and the jungle was cold and wet. His initial
cheeriness had hardened. He could sense our reticence and did
not trust it.

'We are going to the village now.'

We nodded in unison.

'My family? You took them to the house?'

'Yes, yes,' Dunstan put in. 'We're just tired. It's a long way.
Longwe tru.'

Fioluana laughed, relieved. He turned and walked towards
one of the hunters, who gripped a piglet by its hind legs. He
took the animal and handed it to me. It had stiffened; its hair
was sparse and wiry. It would help us get to Wanakipa; we

looked thin and hungry. He sucked his cheeks. One of the hunters laughed harshly.

We watched them off, the hunters lumbering big-boned after the sylphic Fioluana. When the jungle had swallowed them again, and their voices were tiny and far off, Titus turned to me, his hand over his mouth.

'Oh my God,' he breathed. 'Mi *sori*. What have we done?' I shook my head in reply, despairing of our cowardice, yet no longer surprised by it.

'It's OK, Titus,' Dunstan soothed, misunderstanding Titus' disquiet. 'We're on our way home. They'll never catch us now.'

His assurances came too easy, and he knew it. They could reach the village in six hours, gather the rest of the men, and return for us. They moved twice as fast through the forest; they could, if they wanted, cut us off long before we reached the safety of Wanakipa.

The afternoon became evening and the sky cleared and gathered again. Fear kept our pace from slackening. We came out of the canopy, briefly, on to a ridge where we could see back across the Lagaip to Liawep. The sky hung too grey to see the village. Over the mountain blackish cloud billowed and rose. While we watched, lightning exploded somewhere inside.

What was it about that mountain? In my search for an explanation for the disaster I returned again and again to the mountain. I had feared it from the first. It had seemed a calculated presence and I had never felt easy with it. Dunstan believed it was a volcano; Herod had seen it cough forth smoke.

Something came back. One day, Dunstan and I, feeling the dirt behind our ears, ingrained up our legs and backs, had walked up the mountain to wash. We'd not gone far, just to

the nearest stream, but as soon as we'd undressed, rain came
spattering down through the trees. I scrabbled with the soap
and pulled my clothes back on, half-soaked. Dunstan had pulled
his shirt on with soap still frothing in his armpits, in bubbles
on his chest. Now, long after, he admitted he'd been afraid the
volcano would split open. 'Volcano or landslide,' he said. 'One
or the other.'

His fears were more grounded than mine. In my mind, the
mountain had become a malevolent beast. It had drawn the
storm not because of its size but because it was evil. I had come
to fear it because the Liawep feared it. I remembered Peter
Yasaro's comment, filed to his superiors, that they should stop
the Liawep worshipping the mountain. These deaths, then,
were the mountain's response: cavalier, disregarding of the
sanctities. If I lived there, I would surely have worshipped it. It
was real and magnificent and, unlike Herod's God, did not
have to be conjured to life on bended knees. More than this,
though, it moved. Later, I discovered it sat on a fault line
between two tectonic plates. It shifted, it issued smoke, it spat
tongues of fire.

We reached two houses on a crest, built recently in new
gardens. We had stopped here on the way; it was here we'd
met the Liawep boy and marvelled at the bananas, great fat
sausages they'd insisted on baking green. This time there were
thirty people sitting round a fire as darkness fell. They'd just
eaten, and scattered, astonished to see us.

I took off my shoes and a crowd of children gathered round.
We had climbed up and down, immune to hunger, for fourteen
hours.

Behind me, coming into the clearing, were Titus and Miniza.
They knew some of these people − the old man with a
downturned pig's tusk through his nose, the man with the steel

axe – and had gossiped with them on the way over. Now, disaster survivors making the most of the drama, they stumbled into the clearing, groaning, knees buckling. The crowd was hushed to silence.

Titus performed first. He rubbed his left eye and limped heavily, wincing every time he trod. He struggled to the nearest log and lowered himself, the old soldier, the suffering visible in his eyes. A little boy started to giggle, but was silenced by two adults. Miniza staggered up afterwards, leaning on his hip, his face twisted with pain. He sank to the ground at Titus' feet and buried his face in his hands. It was an astonishing change from the morning, when they'd been almost jaunty. When we'd crossed the river they'd run, jumped, even joked.

The end of the day was a reddish rim over the far mountains and the sky rose overhead through deepest blue to tar black. With Titus and Miniza groaning, insensible, it was left to Dison to tell the story. A space cleared round him and he swung from Titus and Miniza – his props, proof of the catastrophe – to the mountain, across the deep valley. He pointed to it, squaring his body, facing it. When he shook his fist in the air and raged, the audience stared mutely. When he screamed out the sound of the thunder, they turned as one to the mountain, struggling to understand. Dison spoke in Hewa and, although I spoke not one word, I could understand everything. It was a morality play in another tongue; it followed a scheme we all understood. When he finished he sat beside Dunstan and put his head in his hands. No one spoke for a very long time.

Chapter 18

Four days later we arrived back at
Wanakipa. We walked uphill to the village and the long grass,
as we left the river for the last time, was hot as an oven. The
carriers were jubilant. Back on home turf, they no longer feared
ambush.

I remained uneasy. That we were now among friends only
increased my guilt at having fled so quickly. Before, I had
focused on escape; now I had time to fret over what had
happened. Deep inside I felt that I, the intruder, had brought
ill luck. More immediately, I was sure the Liawep warriors
were only hours behind us. I wanted to be out of the jungle.

The jungle had affected me as it had Jack Hides and Mick
Leahy, sixty years earlier. They, like me, felt shame for what
they had left behind. Hides omitted many of his killings from

Papuan Wonderland; Leahy similarly censored *The Land That Time Forgot*. The outside world, however, overlooked these excesses. Hides was compared to Scott of the Antarctic, Lawrence of Arabia, Stanley of Africa. Leahy, who had thought nothing of murdering ten or twenty 'loud-mouthed bastards' to 'teach them a lesson', became the hero of countless books and documentaries.

As we crested the hill and saw Wanakipa's scattered houses again, I picked out an aeroplane at the top of the airstrip. People were climbing the aluminium stepladder; others watched from a distance. Dunstan turned to me and we broke into a run, up the hill, past the church, across a bright cool stream with cracked turtle-back rocks, up a bank where clothes were stretched to dry, scattering chickens as we vaulted the wire fence on to the airstrip.

The pilot's door was open. He was half turned, wiping his sunglasses with a pinch of shirt. He spoke without looking up. He was flying to Kopiago, halfway to Tari. He had two seats left. This was perfect. If we made the connection, we could be in Tari tonight. Dunstan could see his new baby. I could be on my way home.

Dunstan, however, wanted to stay. What was he thinking? Why had he flogged up the hill if not to catch the plane? I raised my voice, suddenly exasperated. The pilot watched us, rolled his eyes and kicked the right propeller into life.

Dunstan had his arm round Andrew's shoulder. He was telling him how much he'd miss him. I fronted them and Andrew looked at the ground, pinching grass between his toes. I told Dunstan we were leaving.

'It's better to stay here,' he said, gazing into Andrew's eyes. 'We know people here. If we stay three days in Kopiago we don't know anyone.' I disagreed. We had to get on. I would only feel safe in Tari, perhaps not even then. But Dunstan insisted. 'They won't come. This is too far. We are safe here.'

I gave in and waved the pilot away. He trod on to the wing and jumped down to the grass. He heaved shut the fuselage door, climbed back into the cockpit and strapped himself in. When the engines reached a high whine he released the brakes. The plane bumped off downhill, the sound fading as it pulled away from the ground. It banked, rose, and flew over our heads. People waved, hands like corn in the breeze.

That afternoon, while Dunstan played volleyball with Andrew and his friends, I tried to persuade John, one of the pastors, to switch on the radio. If we contacted MAF we could book seats on the next flight to come past. I felt ashamed at my desperation to leave, yet to stay any longer might mean having to confront the Liawep.

The radio stood on a low table in a cupboard tacked on to the guest house. John sat on a three-legged stool, designed for very small children, and his knees looked huge. He switched on the radio but it made no sound, not even the obstinate rush of static. 'We wait for it to warm up,' he said. We waited for a minute, then two. Still nothing. The red 'on' light was dark: the battery was flat. It was solar-powered and would recharge but, in the wet season with intermittent sun, this could take two days or more.

As the afternoon wore on, I worried less about the arrival of the vengeful Liawep. I sat in the two-roomed guest house, Wanakipa's only iron-roofed building, from where Father Frank had waved us off a month before, and rested. By way of diversion I read the visitors' guest book. There were aid workers setting up vaccination clinics, whose frustrations spilled out. One moaned, typically, 'Although we vaccinated four hundred children, many more didn't turn up.' There was one tourist, a lone Englishman, and the inevitable family of American SIL volunteers, who had coldly reduced the experience to its linguistic interest. It had been a 'valuable opportunity to interact with people of this western dialect'.

Dunstan did not return from his volleyball until dusk was falling. When he did he was running, short of breath. I heard his footsteps banging up the veranda. I was lying on the bench, dozing. He kicked the door open.

'They're here,' he said, looking round for me. 'They've come for us.' His voice was gravelly. 'What do we do?'

I pulled myself up by the table edge.

'Jack and Fioluana and two others. They're here.'

Chapter 19

Now, looking back, I always knew it would end this way. I knew I would have to pay, I just didn't know what form it would take. I would, somehow and somewhere, be faced with the consequences of what had happened. I had tried to slough off guilt, to rationalize it away, and yet because the Liawep held me to blame, I felt responsible. I came from a country of rational explanations, where lightning was seen as an act of nature rather than God or man, and felt I could escape guilt as I'd escaped the village. But it didn't work that way. They believed I had wronged them and now they were here, calling me to account.

I sat up, rubbing sleep dust out of my eyes. Dunstan moved back outside. There were voices. A man, high-pitched, was shouting in nervy, broken pidgin. He stopped talking and I could hear Dunstan's hollow cough.

I stepped barefoot through the door. There were forty people watching, standing up close, leaning over the balcony. At the foot of the steps, ahead of me, stood Jack and Fioluana and two of the Liawep hunters. I looked at Jack and he lunged forward on to the first step. Four men barred his way, almost as if they were my bodyguards, yet I'd never seen them before.

Jack retreated on to the grass. He was wearing the same clothes he'd been in when we first saw him. The men on the steps unbunched, loosened. Jack had a canvas bag, with jungle twine handles roped and knotted. It sagged open, broken. Inside was the long, curved horn of an axe handle, dark and polished with use.

Jack started shouting. His voice cracked; his face gleamed with old sweat. As he spoke he wiped his hands down his shorts. I looked at him and tried to speak, but he spoke over me, and would not look at me.

Behind him, Fioluana staggered on to his knees. His eyes were hollow and sunken. He collapsed at the base of a tree, pulling his knees to his chest. He closed his eyes and shook his head, over and over, obsessively. When Jack paused I could hear Fioluana's mumbling, an incessant moan, like the crying of his baby the night of the storm.

Jack addressed the crowd. He said he'd returned to Liawep the day we'd left. He had met Fioluana and the hunters, and found his people vengeful and confused. They'd shown him the bodies. No one had ever died in this way, Jack said, not like that, covered in white, and they'd left the bodies as they'd found them. Then they sent Jack after us. Fioluana had insisted on joining them.

He pointed at me. 'What were you doing in my village?' This was the second time he'd asked this question. When we'd first met him in the jungle, I'd asked him about Liawep life and his own discovery of the modern world. I'd explained, simply enough, why I wanted to go and had thought he'd given his blessing. But now, after the tragedy, the reasons I had given him made no sense.

What should I say? I felt sick with remorse, yet knew that to admit it would encourage Jack to assume my guilt. I did not know what he wanted, or why he had chased us all this way. He stared at me, with mourning in his eyes. I took a step towards him and said what I'd said before, that I'd heard the Liawep were a lost tribe; I had simply wanted to meet them and hear their stories. I was so sorry – mi *sori* tru, the last word dragged out, dying – for what had happened.

Jack shook his head. 'Now it is different. People have died; Fioluana's family is dead.' He pointed to Fioluana, who covered his ears with his hands and mumbled louder. 'What will you do about that? You saw him the day after the storm. Why did you not tell him? You must pay us for the deaths. I know you white men have money.' It had been figured out. He wanted what I was to pay the carriers, the total. It was a sum he knew I'd have.

I looked at Fioluana, hoping he might turn towards me, reassure me that he would survive, that there was still hope, but he had been crippled by grief and would not raise his head. This was not the man I'd known before, the man who'd become my friend. And now Jack wanted compensation: he, alone among the Liawep, understood money. But I had no money – it had all gone to pay the carriers – and anyway I knew it would not have been helpful. I knew what the Liawep wanted; I'd heard it before so many times. They wanted to be taken from their muddy mountainside and led down into the world they dreamed of, where illness was curable and food plentiful. But how could I, an illegal alien, facilitate that?

Jack stopped. He knelt down and dug in his bag, underneath the axe. He pulled out a tobacco leaf, limp like dried skin. 'You were looking at the mountain through your camera. Does the camera have special powers? Could you see through the mountain?'

Again this gulf of experience. Here, though, I could help explain. I stepped back into the guest house and found my camera, almost as old as me, a 1960s single-lens reflex, hardly the latest thing. I remembered the photographs I had taken. I'd thought I was being discreet, but my interest in the mountain must have been obvious enough. I had become obsessed by it, half wondering whether the shots would come out black or clouded over. The camera was on the table with my notebooks, its leather case cornered with dried mud where I'd fallen on it. I took it down the steps and handed it to Jack.

He held the lens up to his eye, the wrong way round. 'The other way,' John, the pastor, prompted, but Jack, confused, put the camera on the ground. He rubbed his eyes with the heel of his hand. He leaned down again and picked up the camera and handed it back. He held it by the snub lens, warily.

I had an idea. I asked John if he had any photographs – anything, it didn't matter. From a drawer under the table he found me a photograph album with a buff plastic cover and raised gold lettering. Inside were fading colour photographs, four to a page, showing the airstrip being built, five years earlier. The Lutheran church had paid for the strip and the photographs showed pasty white men in towelling sunhats, posing by caterpillar earthmovers.

John handed the album to Jack. Jack looked less angry, more lost. To his four there were forty of us. There was nowhere for his anger to go. He was confronted by logic and reason, by people who believed in God and wore as a medal their freedom from the 'old ways'. John was proud of his photographs. They showed his village as part of the modern world. Jack looked at one page. He shook his head and passed the album back.

'Mr Edward', John said, 'took ordinary photographs, just like these ones.' A little boy pulled at his sleeve. He cradled a colour magazine – an old copy of *Paradise*, inflight reading on Air Niugini. Inside were pale-skinned women and apartment blocks and smiling couples diving off multicoloured coral reefs. John took it reverently. The cover had come loose from the binding and he held it open for Jack. 'Just like these photographs,' he said. 'Taking photographs is a good thing. It helps you remember.'

Jack looked at the photographs. His eyes darted over the images. He'd smoked his cigarette to the butt. He pinched it in his fingertips and pulled on it until his fingers burned, then dropped it. He looked at me, hard.

'Did you bring poison with you?' he said.

He believed and trusted nothing. A river flowed between us, and although we could yell across the roar in pidgin, we could never cross. Poisons? Why would I have brought poisons? No, I said, feeling the pain of extreme tiredness, the tragedy of the insoluble, build behind my eyes, I carried medicines. After the lightning, I had looked after the injured.

But he did not hear me. 'Someone else brought poison.' He looked around for the carriers.

'I will ask,' I said. All this was patching-up: too little, too late. There were only three now – Andrew, Dison and Miniza – the three with whom we'd begun the journey. A little boy stood beside Andrew's leg. Andrew held his head. Deliberately, for Jack to see, I asked each in turn, had they brought poison? Miniza's nose curled up. Each shook his head, gravely.

The guest-house veranda was solid with people. Others

spilled on to the grass. An old woman with cobbled potato feet stepped up close to Jack, and looked into his bag. Children wedged their faces through the banisters.

Fioluana leaned his head against the tree. We were speaking in pidgin and he understood nothing. He opened his eyes, but would not look around. A man crossed his gaze but he did not follow him with his eyes, only stared through him, at a point far beyond.

Jack moved back a step. 'If you'd stayed,' he said, arching his back stiffly, 'they would have killed you. You came, and five people died. They think you killed those people. Why did you leave so early?'

Again, I hedged guiltily, explaining that we were always going to leave that morning. This was true – we just hadn't planned to leave quite that early. John, who did not suffer my anxieties, leaned towards me impatiently and whispered in my ear, 'We must tell them how we do things.' His breath was hot and ticklish. 'Not all Papua New Guineans are primitive like the Liawep.'

I would have preferred tact and gentleness, but John was already off, swinging a hand round the crowd. 'There are places round here,' he said, pausing for effect, 'that people say are evil. They say that if you go to these places you will be killed and the people will eat your flesh, that you will never have children and your line will die out. Those are the old ways, and the people who believe in those things live in the old times. I am a Christian. I have been to the places people say are evil and I have never been harmed. Look at me.' He thumped his chest and it was muffled, like a drum filled with old clothes. 'We are Christian now and we do not believe in fighting, fighting all the time. We believe in love and forgiveness. Love thy neighbour.'

Jack puckered his mouth as if he'd eaten something tart.

John continued, pushing through the crowd, down a step, pointing his finger at Jack, 'And this thing, how your people died. It happens. It has happened before. Andrew, you know about it.'

Andrew looked to me, as if for permission. He'd told this story before, the night after we'd fled from the village. He raised his eyebrows. I shrugged at him. He rubbed his hand over his head. 'Yes,' he said, finally, turning sincerely to Jack. 'I have seen it. I was living in Kopiago. Three people were killed. A man and his brother and a young girl. They were broken inside.' He pointed to his chest.

Jack did not hear. He looked up at me. 'Did you see the bodies?' he said.

'Yes.' I was following him now, willing to agree to anything.

'They were white all over. What are they? Why did my people die? We have never before seen this. The people are saying the white man brought the white flakes and shook them on the people and that's why they died.'

Dunstan stepped forward. 'Mr Edward was asleep when it happened.'

Jack turned towards Fioluana and laid a hand on his forehead. He looked up and spoke quietly. 'They will kill me if I go back with nothing. They will not bury the bodies until I get back. They are waiting until I can give them news.'

He did not know what he wanted. He had been charged to exact a revenge but was exhausted, outargued and outnumbered. Worse, Fioluana, the one most in need of reassurance, was there to witness his failure. Yet he wanted something, some assurance. Dunstan suggested we try and help, promise action which Jack, in turn, could promise the Liawep. But what could we do? To pledge anything, as much as I wanted to, seemed shamefully empty. I dithered; Dunstan prodded me forward.

'When we return to Tari,' I offered, reluctantly, 'we will go to the district manager's office and tell him about your people.'

'We need a hospital,' Jack said, echoing Fioluana's earlier words to me, 'and an airstrip. We need these things. If the district manager comes, I will be happy. If not, I will be upset.' He knew he was powerless. He stroked his leader's badge, pinned to his T-shirt.

His voice rose. 'And if the district manager will not come, will you ask the company men to look at the mountain?' He was covering every angle. 'There is gold in the mountain, I know there is. We can live better lives if they find gold.'

I promised this, too, although I knew I would never file an official report. People began to drift off into the dark. I arranged for Jack and Fioluana and the two others to stay with Andrew. I tried to approach Fioluana, to attempt a reconciliation, but he twisted away when I came near. Andrew took his hand and guided him downhill, over the stream, towards his house. Jack followed them away, shuffling in the dust, his shoulders humped and rounded, his bag dragging.

Epilogue

The creeping sickness of guilt stayed with me, unbidden, for long afterwards. Two weeks later, I saw Carol Jenkins again. She was amused by my story, nothing more. She was in a hurry, stuffing notepads and loose sheets of typescript into a briefcase. She was due at a conference somewhere and I followed her erratic path to her Landcruiser. She pulled on her jacket, portable computer pillowed under one arm, its plugwire trailing. The engine clattered into life. The window squeaked as she wound it down and leaned out. 'One last thing,' she shouted. 'Don't call them lost. No one's lost any more.' The car fell into a pothole as she moved away. She hammered the accelerator and the wheels spun, kicking up dirt. I covered my mouth. My shoes were covered in red dust.

*

For months, lightning tailed me like a conscience, reminding me for ever of the bodies in that house and of the Liawep, who held me to blame. The reappearance of the familiar world did little to settle my head.

It haunted me long after I returned home. My friends said I was being self-indulgent. One accused me of harming the Liawep far more than the missionaries or the government. This was unfair, but my protests sounded thin, even to me. Although I had gone as an impartial, liberal observer, I knew the Liawep had seen me as something quite different, and on their territory their beliefs counted more than mine. With no recourse to science they believed that everything happened for a reason, that disasters were brought about by evil forces. Death, they believed, happened for a reason. When five people died in the storm they searched for a cause, and the finger pointed at me.

Somewhere inside me I knew there was a truth in this. Despite the protests of my rational mind, I felt culpable. From every act, however insignificant it may seem, ripples spread outwards.

I thought I had learned from the examples of Mick Leahy and Jack Hides, yet, in the end, I had brought an equal destruction. Before setting off into the jungle I had scorched their stories on my brain. They had progressed, careless and murderous. In one day alone, Leahy had 'bagged' twenty warriors; Hides, despite being the gentler and more open-minded of the two, killed a total of fifty-four Papuans. Both men were exonerated by the government. They were typical. The white legacy in Papua New Guinea has been one long avalanche of murder.

And I was another white man, only more guilt-ridden. I believed the lightning and the deaths held a message to me and those like me: do not meddle in what does not concern you. The Liawep made me feel I had no business interfering with their lives, nosing around asking difficult questions. And the lightning confirmed their worst fears of me.

After the storm I did not know what to think. Had the disaster not happened, the story would have been straight-forward. I had gone because I wanted to find out how quickly, and how radically, contact with the outside world would alter the Liawep's lives. I found a lunatic priest, jungle deeper than I had ever imagined and a tribe too proud to give much away. I wanted to be the observer, watching coolly from the side. But I had been dragged unwillingly on stage.

When Ignatius Litiki refused me permission to visit the Liawep, he gave a reason I thought extremely feeble. They might be dangerous, he said. Equally, I might harm them. I dismissed it as an off-the-cuff remark designed to shut me up. With hindsight it seemed prophetic. It was true, I had brought them harm. Just as Leahy had wanted his gold, Hides his pioneer's glory and Father William Ross his souls, I, too, had an agenda – curiosity. So I was a taker, too, and the pattern of exploitation the same. I wanted so badly to draw a line between myself and the pioneers, to label them bad and ignorant and myself good and enlightened, but the distinction was blurred. Definitions, too, had turned on me – 'lost' applied far more to my escapade than it ever had to the Liawep.

When I returned to Britain I wrote to Peter Yasaro. I did not admit to my own, illegal journey, rather expressed a detached interest. Had he returned to Liawep? Had he started their relocation? To my surprise, he replied. Plans for a second patrol were already well advanced; he had collected pots, pans and more clothes. The Oksapmin Seventh Day Adventist pastor was to accompany the patrol, stay at Liawep and build a rival church. Yes, he still planned to move the tribe, but was prepared for it to take time.

I wrote, too, to the gold consortium, requesting information on their mining plans. I received a Xeroxed press statement. Their application to excavate had been approved; no 'start date' had yet been fixed. I felt sure it would not be long; things had been set in motion that would never be halted. Certainly it would not have taken long for Herod to have organized a Christian burial for the bodies and explained away the disaster.

I see Herod now, sitting across the fire that night, mud and wet streaming down his face, half-crazed with shock, saying that the women and the babies had died because they did not believe in God. He had spoken with absolute certainty. It was the one thing he knew for sure.

Acknowledgements

I would like to thank the Authors' Foundation for a grant which bought me time to write. In Papua New Guinea I was variously advised, dissuaded, egged on, tolerated and accommodated by the following: Tim Bainbridge, Brian Brunton, Chris Bullen, David Dewa, Sean Dorney, Norm Draper, Jan Dyke, Tom Feldpausch, Peter Gay, Brian Glassock, David Hand, Carol and Travis Jenkins, Dunstan Kapu, Dipop Kimonhan, Joe Mangi, Charlie Marriott, Duncan Overfield, Megan Passey, Wamu Walu, Brian and Royale White, Peter Yasaro and Jeff the vet.

At home, my thanks for the help and support of my mother and father, Jane Bradish-Ellames, Alexa de Ferranti, Matthew Hamilton, Rachel Heath, Kate Hubbard, Richard and Florence Ingleby, Chris Paling, Jeremy Seal and Peter Straus. But most of all to Milla, to whom both I and this book owe more than I would like to admit.

Bibliography

Anderson, R. and Connolly, B. *First Contact: New Guinea's Highlanders Encounter the Outside World*, Viking, New York, 1987

Brown, P. *Highland Peoples of New Guinea*, Cambridge University Press, 1978

Bushell, K. *Papuan Epic*, Seeley, Service & Co, London, 1936

Chalmers, J. *Pioneering in New Guinea*, Religious Tract Society, London, 1885

D'Albertis, L. M. *New Guinea: What I Did and What I Saw*, Sampson Low, London, 1880

Dorney, S. *Papua New Guinea: People, Politics and History Since 1975*, Random House, Sydney, 1990 (republished 1991 and 1993)

Downs, I. *The Australian Trusteeship: Papua New Guinea 1945–75*, Australian Government Publishing Service, Canberra, 1980

Feil, D. K. *The Evolution of Highland Papua New Guinean Societies*, Cambridge University Press, 1987

Flynn, E. *My Wicked, Wicked Ways*, William Heinemann, London, 1960

Frankel, S. *The Huli Response to Illness*, Cambridge University Press, 1986

Griffin, J. and Nelson, H. *Papua New Guinea: A Political History*, Heinemann Educational Australia, Melbourne, 1979

Griffin, J. (ed.) *Papua New Guinea Portraits: The Expatriate Experience*, Australian National University Press, Canberra, 1978

Hides, J. G. *Papuan Wonderworld*, Blackie & Sons, Glasgow, 1936

Hurley, Captain F. *Pearls and Savages*, G. P. Putnam's Sons, New York, 1924

Kelly, R. *Etoro Social Structure: A Study in Structural Contradiction*, University of Michigan Press, 1977

Kilage, I. *My Mother Calls Me Yaltep*, Institute of Papua New Guinea Studies, Port Moresby, 1981

Lawson, Captain J. A. *Wanderings in the Interior of New Guinea*, Chapman & Hall, London, 1875

Leahy, M. The central highlands of New Guinea, *Journal of the Royal Geographical Society*, vol. 87, pp. 229–62, London, 1936

Diaries 1930–1934 (unpublished), National Library of Australia, Canberra

Leahy, M. and Crain, M. *The Land That Time Forgot*, Hurst & Blackett, London, 1937

Lett, L. *Knights Errant of Papua*, Blackwood, Edinburgh, 1935

Matthieson, P. *Under the Mountain Wall*, Viking, New York, 1962

McCarthy, J. K. *Patrol into Yesterday*, Cheshire Publishing, Melbourne, 1963

McFarlane, S. *Among the Cannibals of New Guinea: Being the Story of the New Guinea Mission of the London Missionary Society*, London Missionary Society, London, 1888

Monckton, C. A. W. *Some Experiences of a New Guinea Magistrate*, John Lane, The Bodley Head, London, 1921

Moresby, J. *Discoveries and Surveys in New Guinea and the d'Entrecasteaux Islands: A Cruise of H.M.S. Basilisk*, John Murray, London, 1876

Nelson, H. *Black, White and Gold: Goldmining in Papua New Guinea 1878–1930*, Australian National University Press, Canberra, 1976

Taim Bilong Masta: *The Australian Involvement with Papua New Guinea*, Australian Broadcasting Corporation, Sydney, 1982

Oates, L. *Hidden People: How a remote New Guinea culture was brought back from the brink of extinction*, Albatross Books, Sydney, 1992

O'Hanlon, M. *Paradise: Portraying the New Guinea Highlands*, British Museum Press, London, 1993

Radford, R. *Highlanders and Foreigners in the Upper Ramu: The Kainantu Area 1919–1942*, Melbourne University Press, 1987

Missionaries, miners and administrators in the eastern highlands, *Journal of the Papua and New Guinea Society* 6, no. 2, 1972

Read, K. *The High Valley*, George Allen & Unwin, London, 1965

Reiner, R. and Wagner, H. (eds) *The Lutheran Church in Papua New Guinea 1886–1986: The First Hundred Years*, Lutheran Publishing House, Adelaide, 1986

Sartre, J. P. *Being and Nothingness: A Phenomenological Essay on Ontology*. Translated by Hazel F. Barnes, Washington Square Press, New York, 1966

Schieffelin, E. L. *The Sorrow of the Lonely and the Burning of the Dancers*, St Martin's Press, New York, 1976

Schieffelin, E. L. and Crittenden, R. *Like People You See in a Dream*, Stanford University Press, Stanford, California, 1991

Simpson, C. *Plumes and Arrows*, Angus & Robertson, Sydney, 1962

Sinclair, J. *Wings of Gold*, Pacific Publications, Sydney, 1978

Sinclair, J. P. *Behind the Ranges: Patrolling in New Guinea*, Melbourne University Press, 1966

Souter, G. *New Guinea: The Last Unknown*, Angus & Robertson, Sydney, 1963

Trégance, L. *Adventures in New Guinea: The Narrative of Louis Trégance, a French Sailor: Nine Years in Captivity among the Orangwoks, a Tribe in the Interior of New Guinea*, Sampson Low, London, 1876

Von Ehlers, O. *Samoa die Perle der Sudsee (Samoa Pearl of the South Seas)*, Paetel, Berlin, 1869

Wallace, A. R. *The Malay Archipelago*, Macmillan, London, 1869

Wetherell, D. *Reluctant Mission: The Anglican Church in Papua New Guinea 1891–1942*, University of Queensland Press, 1977

Willis, I. Who was first? The first white man into the New Guinea highlands, *Journal of the Papua and New Guinea Society*, vol. 3, no. 1, 1969